1990

THE
THIRD
AMERICA

Michael O'Neill

THE
THIRD
AMERICA

The Emergence of
the Nonprofit Sector
in the United States

 Jossey-Bass Publishers

San Francisco • London • 1989

THE THIRD AMERICA
The Emergence of the Nonprofit Sector in the United States
by Michael O'Neill

Copyright © 1989 by: Jossey-Bass Inc., Publishers
350 Sansome Street
San Francisco, California 94104
&
Jossey-Bass Limited
28 Banner Street
London EC1Y 8QE

Library of Congress Cataloging-in-Publication Data

O'Neill, Michael.
    The third America : the emergence of the nonprofit sector in the
United States / Michael O'Neill.—1st ed.
       p.   cm.—(The Jossey-Bass nonprofit sector series)
    Bibliography: p.
    Includes index.
    ISBN 1-55542-165-2 (alk. paper)
    1. Corporations, Nonprofit—United States. I. Title.
II. Series.
HD2785.054   1989
338.7'4—dc20   89-33760
                                               CIP

Manufactured in the United States of America

JACKET DESIGN BY WILLI BAUM

FIRST EDITION

Code 8939

**The
Jossey-Bass
Nonprofit
Sector
Series**

☆★★ Contents

Preface   xi

The Author   xvii

1. The Nonprofit World: Its Scope and Significance   1

2. Religion: Godmother of the Nonprofit Sector   20

3. Private Education and Research: Quest for Ideas and Ideals   43

4. Health Care: The Sector's Quiet Giant   67

5. Arts and Culture: Supporting the Survival of Creativity   81

6. Social Services: A Nation of Helpers   94

7. Advocacy and Legal Services: Conscience of a Nation   109

8. International Assistance: The World Role of America's Nonprofits   123

9.   Foundations and Corporate Funders: The Money Trees   137

10.   Mutual Benefit Organizations: A Nation of Joiners   156

11.   Prospects for America's Nonprofit Sector:
      An Agenda   169

      References   183

      Index   197

 **Preface**

The Third America is about the idea and reality of the private nonprofit sector in the United States. The reality of the sector has permeated American society for nearly four centuries, through the activities of churches, private schools and colleges, arts organizations, social service agencies, mutual aid associations, and countless volunteers and donors. The idea of the nonprofit sector, on the other hand, is just beginning to assert itself. Throughout the colonial period and well into the nineteenth century, the distinction between public and private institutions often had little practical significance. In the latter part of the nineteenth century, for reasons to be explained in the following chapters, the concept of a separate part of American organizational life that was neither profit-oriented nor governmental began to take clear shape. When Congress, at the turn of the century, created federal corporate income tax, it exempted charitable corporations, thereby bestowing on them both a tax break and the public attention that inevitably followed. During the twentieth century, nonprofits periodically came under public scrutiny: once when it was suspected that John D. Rockefeller, who seemed to own everything else, was trying to take over the nation's charities through his new foundation; once when nonprofit New York University started running a macaroni company and was promptly attacked by for-profit macaroni producers; and periodically when various Elmer Gantrys and flim-flam men tried to use churches and other nonprofit agencies for their personal gain.

It was not until the last twenty years that the sector began to be discussed seriously by scholars and policymakers, as a result of such efforts as the seven-volume report of the Commission on Private Philanthropy and Public Needs (often referred to as the Filer Commission report), the extensive research conducted by Yale University's Program on Non-Profit Organizations, and the consciousness-raising work of Independent Sector, a national coalition of nonprofit groups. The immense size and impact of the sector is only starting to be recognized, and serious theorizing about the dynamics of the sector has only just begun.

The Third America presents a comprehensive overview of the American nonprofit sector. A good deal of the best nonprofit sector literature that has emerged in the last twenty years is of a fairly technical nature and is not easily accessible to the general reader. The few overviews of the nonprofit sector that are in print are outdated or partial treatments, or both. Even recent discussions have generally omitted any serious reference to such important parts of the sector as religion, international philanthropy, and mutual assistance.

Audience

This book is intended for students, nonprofit staff and volunteers, and general readers, as well as for scholars interested in a broader framework within which to view nonprofit activity. The book borrows from a variety of disciplines: history, sociology, anthropology, demography, economics, political science, policy analysis, and, to a very limited extent, law. Such a quest for synthesis is obviously fraught with danger. The problem of such a book is not to write it but to stop writing it, since virtually every sentence could be qualified, footnoted, and developed in a dozen ways. I have attempted to limit references to important data sources and works on relatively specialized issues that some readers might want to pursue in greater depth.

Analysis of the nonprofit sector is so recent that one is still somewhat free to divide up the sector at will. The nine subsectors I have chosen—religion, private education and research, health care, arts and culture, social services, advocacy and legal services, international assistance, foundations and corporate funders, and mutual benefit organizations—generally parallel major categories of nonprofit activity delineated by researchers and government agencies. While this classification, I believe, works reasonably well, it is important to note that nonprofits have a way of escaping neat categorization and even of transforming themselves from one type of nonprofit to another as you watch.

Overview of the Contents

Chapter One sketches the size and impact of the nonprofit sector as a whole and analyzes the roles that it plays in American society. I hope that the reader will not find the chapter's statistics too cumbersome: they shed light on just how large and important the sector is. As I suggest in the theoretical overview, the nature and workings of the sector are by no means as self-evident as we tend to assume. In spite of Tocqueville's comment 150 years ago that few things about America are so intriguing as its "intellectual and moral associations," only recently have a few theorists become sufficiently intrigued to attempt a serious explanation of them.

Not at all accidentally, the first subsector discussed is religion. One of the most remarkable aspects of the nonprofit literature is its almost complete neglect of this subsector, in spite of the major role that religion has played and continues to play in the nonprofit sector and in American society. Chapter Two is an effort to help restore religion to its rightful place in the study of nonprofit activity.

There is, by contrast, no particular reason for the order of the other eight subsector chapters. The early development of private education is intimately connected with American religious history, but the same could be said for the early development of social welfare, health care, and other components of the nonprofit sector. After reading Chapters One and Two, the reader may prefer to skip from one chapter to another.

Private education and research may well constitute the most influential part of the nonprofit sector, yet their activities are often underestimated and stereotyped as the work of a few religious schools and a handful of elite colleges and think tanks. In Chapter

Three I describe the size, complexity, and long history of the private education-research enterprise and seek to explain why this large and powerful part of the nonprofit sector faces a very troubled future even as its importance to the society grows.

Nonprofit health care has been so successful that some want to make it for-profit. Chapter Four traces the rise of modern health care in the United States and documents the dominant role that nonprofits have in this industry. Nowhere is the strength of the nonprofit sector clearer; yet paradoxically this form of health care faces serious challenges, the greatest being the possible loss of its nonprofit identity.

At first, art and culture seem totally a product of the nonprofit sector, but a closer look shows that many important artistic relationships exist between the nonprofit and for-profit worlds—not the least of which is the patronage of art by corporations and wealthy individuals. In Chapter Five I describe the unique and sometimes precarious role that nonprofit cultural organizations play in supporting artistic creativity in the United States.

Social welfare agencies—such as soup kitchens, shelters for the homeless, and counseling centers—are what most people refer to when they talk about the nonprofit sector. These agencies are indeed the heart and soul of nonprofit effort. Yet they are also heavily funded by government, and their increasing reliance on government aid has become an urgent public policy issue, highlighted by but by no means confined to the Reagan cutbacks in social programs. In Chapter Six I examine the important work of nonprofit social agencies and their complex relationships with government.

Advocacy and legal service organizations are considered by some to be the purest example of nonprofit activity, in that they are completely separate from government and business and use sparse resources to benefit others, with very little expectation of personal or institutional gain. The classic example is still that of the abolitionists, mostly Northern whites who labored for decades to free Southern blacks. Modern advocacy organizations, such as the environmental and peace movements, have somewhat similar characteristics but face the challenges of a much more sophisticated society and entrenched institutions opposing change. I describe in

Chapter Seven how advocacy and legal service agencies have responded to these challenges over the years.

Few Americans realize what a prominent role their nonprofits play in alleviating human problems in other nations. American military and economic activity abroad is well publicized, American philanthropic activity abroad much less so. Chapter Eight analyzes the extent and importance of this international effort.

Foundations and corporations account for a relatively tiny portion of nonprofit revenue but have a large role in setting priorities and highlighting issues. Both are largely middle-of-the-road institutions supporting mainline causes such as orchestras, hospitals, and universities, but in some cases their grants have brought about dramatic new developments in American society and throughout the world. In Chapter Nine I examine the role foundations and corporate giving programs play in the nonprofit sector and in society.

Mutual benefit organizations are the least understood and, with the possible exception of religious organizations, the most ignored part of the nonprofit sector. Some would argue that they should not even be included in the sector, since they are "selfish," whereas the nonprofit sector is "altruistic." I argue in Chapter Ten that in practice this distinction is often difficult to maintain and that mutual benefit organizations have in fact often created or grown out of philanthropic, charitable efforts.

A word on the structure of the nine subsector chapters: the first section of each chapter, on scope and impact, presents the most useful data I could find on the size of the subsector, with particular attention to statistics on organizations, members, staff, volunteers, revenue and expenses, assets, and other such information. This section also delineates how and to what extent the subsector relates to and influences the rest of the nonprofit sector and the society as a whole. The second section describes the historical development of the subsector in question. More prudent authors might avoid such a task; I feel that it is impossible to understand the American nonprofit sector without having some sense of the history of its component parts. The third section of each chapter raises a few selected policy issues about the subsector, both societal policy questions and nonprofit sector policy issues relevant to the particular subsector. Clearly many other policy issues could be raised, and those raised could be discussed in much more detail. I invite and urge readers to use the few issues I have selected as a jumping-off point for their own reflections and discussions.

In the final chapter, I try to suggest what all of this might mean, with particular emphasis on important nonprofit sector trends for the immediate future. Chapter Eleven includes thoughts on both what will happen and what should happen. In general, based on the trends of the last quarter century, my conclusion is that the future of the American nonprofit sector is quite hopeful. The nonprofit reality is closely interwoven with the fabric of American life, and the nonprofit idea continues to grow in clarity and fascination. There are, to be sure, many problems; and there have been prominent prophets of doom in recent years. But I cannot imagine, on the basis of what has happened in the last few decades and in the long historical development of the nonprofit sector, that this third America is about to vanish from the scene or shrink seriously in size or importance. The data, in my opinion, suggest just the opposite conclusion.

Acknowledgments

Finally, I wish to give thanks to and request general absolution from several people who helped me with this project: Jon Van Til, Paul Ylvisaker, and Dennis Young, who read and commented on the entire manuscript; and Mary Anna Colwell, Paul DiMaggio, Donald Erickson, Ralph Kramer, Elissa Matulis Myers, and Bruce Vladeck, who read and commented on particular chapters. Their criticisms and suggestions were insightful and invaluable. To Ruthe Stein, who contributed love, support, and astute editorial remarks, I owe a very special debt.

San Francisco   Michael O'Neill
July 1989

☆ ★ ★ The Author

Michael O'Neill is professor and director of the Institute for Nonprofit Organization Management and director of the Department of Public Management at the University of San Francisco. He received his B.A. degree (1960) from Saint Thomas College in Kenmore, Washington, in philosophy; his M.A. degree (1964) from Catholic University of America in education; and his Ed.D. degree (1967) from Harvard University.

O'Neill has been at the University of San Francisco since 1976, serving as a faculty member, program director, and dean in the School of Education. Since 1983 he has been a faculty member and program director in the College of Professional Studies. He has also taught at the University of Notre Dame, Boston College, and Fort Wright College. Before coming to the University of San Francisco, he was a superintendent of schools for nine years.

O'Neill has written two books and over fifty articles on education and management topics. He is also the coeditor with Dennis R. Young of *Educating Managers of Nonprofit Organizations* (1988). He has served on the editorial board of the *Harvard Educational Review* and currently serves as an associate editor of *Nonprofit Management and Leadership,* a quarterly journal to be launched by Jossey-Bass in 1990. He is a board member of the Association of Voluntary Action Scholars and a member of the Research Committee of Independent Sector.

To my parents,
Mary Lou Maginnis O'Neill
and
John Patrick O'Neill

THE
THIRD
AMERICA

THE NONPROFIT WORLD

Its Scope and Significance

Americans are continually made aware of government and business. We debate politics, cringe at tax time, devour news of secret CIA plots, vote for new public schools and libraries, and create legends of presidents such as Washington, Lincoln, Roosevelt, Kennedy, and Reagan. We ponder stock market reports, shake our heads over signs of Japanese dominance, study the *Wall Street Journal*, follow with fascination such business celebrities as Donald Trump and Lee Iacocca, and remember legendary figures such as John D. Rockefeller, J. P. Morgan, Andrew Carnegie, and Thomas Watson.

We often talk of government and business, the "public" and "private" sectors, as if there were no other. Yet there is a third division of American organizational life, a sector that is huge, complex, important, and barely recognized. Philanthropist John D. Rockefeller III called it "the invisible sector." Former Stanford president and historian Richard Lyman has said, "It is perhaps the biggest unknown success story in American history." This organizational third America is the world of private nonprofit agencies, groups that are neither government entities nor business firms. The nonprofit sector includes churches, schools, colleges and universities, research institutes, hospitals, foundations, social action movements, welfare agencies, arts and cultural organizations, community development groups, mutual benefit societies, and a host of others. Nonprofits employ more civilians than the federal government and the fifty state governments combined. The yearly budget of the American nonprofit sector exceeds the budgets of

1

all but seven nations in the world. Seventy million American adults and teenagers do volunteer work in nonprofit organizations. Seventy percent of American households donate to charity. The pantheon of the third sector includes figures such as civil rights leader Martin Luther King, mental health advocate Dorothea Dix, abolitionist William Lloyd Garrison, suffragette Elizabeth Cady Stanton, preacher Billy Graham, social reformer Jane Addams, community organizer Saul Alinsky, and family planning pioneer Margaret Sanger. The third sector has had a major impact on the history of the nation, continues to shape its social and cultural values, and provides services to millions of its most needy citizens. The third America may be "invisible," but it is hardly insignificant.

What Is a Nonprofit Organization?

The most common definitions of third-sector organizations are negative: a nonprofit organization is one that is not part of government and does not exist to make a profit. The Internal Revenue Code states that an "exempt organization" is, among other things, one in which "no part of the net earnings . . . inures to the benefit of any private shareholder or individual." Yale lawyer-economist Henry Hansmann (1980) argues that this "nondistribution constraint" is the most accurate and efficient way to define the nonprofit sector.

Nonprofits can also be distinguished by their organizational purpose or mission. Whereas businesses exist to make a profit and government exists to provide an essential structure of law and order and "promote the general welfare," nonprofits typically exist to provide some service or advance some cause. The service or cause may be physical or psychological health, historical awareness, religious improvement, protection of minority group rights, development of low-income housing, or the prevention of child abuse. But there is usually some relationship to the good of society, even if the immediate beneficiaries (for instance, developmentally disabled children) are a more narrowly defined group. Thus, nonprofits are often characterized as philanthropic, charitable, or "public benefit" organizations. They are private organizations serving a public purpose.

Some nonprofits, however, are focused primarily not on public service but on the benefit of their members. The twenty-seven types of organizations exempt from federal income tax include credit unions, small mutual insurance companies, pension trusts, country clubs, fraternal organizations, cemetery companies, chambers of commerce, business leagues, trade associations, labor unions, and veterans' organizations. A distinction is often made between these "mutual benefit" organizations and philanthropic nonprofits. The latter account for more than 90 percent of the total employees and revenues of the nonprofit sector. This book will focus principally on philanthropic groups, but one chapter (Chapter Ten) is devoted to the mutual benefit organizations.

Philanthropic nonprofits are officially described in Section 501(c)(3) of the Internal Revenue Code:

> Corporations, and any community chest, fund, or foundation, organized and operated exclusively for religious, charitable, scientific, testing for public safety, literary, or educational purposes, or to foster national or international amateur sports competition (but only if no part of its activities involve the provision of athletic facilities or equipment), or for the prevention of cruelty to children or animals, no part of the net earnings of which inures to the benefit of any private shareholder or individual, no substantial part of the activities of which is carrying on propaganda, or otherwise attempting, to influence legislation . . . , and which does not participate in, or intervene in (including the publishing or distributing of statements), any political campaign on behalf of (or in opposition to) any candidate for public office.

The strangeness of the 501(c)(3) definition illustrates the problem in getting a clear, comprehensive statistical picture of the third sector. The definition does not mention health care, which alone accounts for half the expenditures and employees of the entire nonprofit sector, but does mention such relatively minuscule operations as literary societies, agencies "testing for public safety," organizations promoting national and international sports competition, and groups established to prevent cruelty to animals. Nor is

the problem limited to the IRS. Every five years the U.S. Census
Bureau collects organizational statistics in its Census of Service
Industries. Its 1977 survey provided valuable data on nonprofit as
well as for-profit service industries, but the 1982 survey omitted
hospitals, elementary and secondary schools, labor unions, and
political organizations, on the grounds that there were other data
available; this decision eliminated two-thirds of the employees of
the nonprofit sector (National Center for Charitable Statistics, 1985,
p. vi). And neither the 1977 nor the 1982 survey included religious
institutions, by far the largest group of organizations in the nonprofit sector.

Another distinguishing characteristic of Section 501(c)(3)
organizations and a few other nonprofits is that donations to them
are tax deductible. This is not true of mutual benefit nonprofits,
apparently because their work is viewed as less directly beneficial to
the public good (Weisbrod, 1988, pp. 70–72).

Major Types of Nonprofit Organizations

There is no canonized method of grouping private nonprofit
organizations. The National Center for Charitable Statistics has
proposed a taxonomy with twenty-four categories, summarized in
nine major groupings: arts, culture, and humanities; education;
environment and animals; health; human services; international
programs; public/society benefit programs; religion; and other,
including mutual membership benefit organizations (Sumariwalla,
1987). For the purposes of our discussion, nonprofits will be
organized into the following categories, by principal activity:

> Religion
> Education and research
> Health care
> Arts and culture
> Social services
> Advocacy and legal services
> International assistance
> Grantmaking
> Mutual benefit

The diversity of America's nonprofit sector has often astonished observers. In the 1830s, French commentator Alexis de Tocqueville remarked: "Americans of all ages, all stations in life, and all types of disposition are forever forming associations. There are not only commercial and industrial associations in which all take part, but others of a thousand different types—religious, moral, serious, futile, very general and very limited, immensely large and very minute. Americans combine to give fêtes, found seminaries, build churches, distribute books, and send missionaries to the antipodes. Hospitals, prisons, and schools take shape in that way. Finally, if they want to proclaim a truth or propagate some feeling by the encouragement of a great example, they form an association" (Tocqueville, [1835] 1969, p. 513).

Today, more than 150 years later, Tocqueville would be even more amazed or amused. There are nonprofits whose assets exceed those of several nations, such as the Ford Foundation, Harvard University, and the J. Paul Getty Trust, and there are nonprofits that conduct intense civic campaigns out of someone's kitchen with volunteer labor and never more than $500 in the bank. There are associations dedicated to saving the world from nuclear war and associations dedicated to promoting the values of birdwatching. There are organizations such as the Democratic and Republican parties, which want to get all their candidates elected; and there is Mikes of America, which wants only to get anyone named Mike elected president of the United States. There is Mensa, an association for people with IQs of over 132; and there is Densa, "for all the rest of us." There are 350,000 churches, synagogues, and mosques for the religious; and there is Atheists Anonymous for those of a different persuasion.

How Big Is the Third Sector?

We have more accurate information on soybean production in the United States than on America's third sector. In general, nonprofits must file for exemption and submit yearly reports to the IRS and state agencies; but religious institutions, nonprofits with less than $25,000 in annual revenue, and operating subunits of large national organizations such as the Boy Scouts do not have to file. These exceptions mean that at least 500,000 and possibly a few million nonprofit entities are not regularly counted. Consequently, there are no precise figures on the number of nonprofit organizations in the United States. Drawing on various government and private sources, Independent Sector, a national organization representing nonprofits, estimated that in 1986 there were about 873,000 philanthropic nonprofit organizations and 370,000 other nonprofits, for a total of 1,243,000 (Hodgkinson and Weitzman, 1988a, Table 1 [n.p.]).

There has been significant growth in the number of new nonprofit organizations since the mid 1960s. For ten years prior to 1965, the IRS received five to seven thousand applications a year for tax-exempt status. In 1965 the number jumped to thirteen thousand, and it has continued to climb steadily. The number of completed applications in 1985 was more than forty-five thousand (Weisbrod, 1988, p. 170).

A more precise estimate can be made about the number of Americans who work or volunteer for nonprofit organizations. Nonprofits employed 7.7 million workers in 1986, about seven percent of the total work force (Hodgkinson and Weitzman, 1988a, Table 3 [n.p.]). Nonprofits in 1986 employed more civilians than the federal and the fifty state governments combined (6.8 million). In the same year, nonprofit employment far exceeded that of the construction industry (4.9 million), the electronics industry (2.1 million), the transportation equipment industry (automobiles, planes, ships, trains) (2 million), and the textile and apparel industry (1.8 million) (U.S. Bureau of the Census, 1987, pp. 387–388). Between 1972 and 1982, philanthropic nonprofit employment increased by 43 percent, compared with a 21 percent increase in the for-profit sector, a 19 percent increase in government, and a 22 percent increase in overall employment (Rudney and Weitzman, 1983). While business and government (including local government) each employ far more workers, third-sector employment has grown twice as fast as employment in the other two sectors. The rapid growth rate slowed somewhat between 1982 and 1984, apparently as a result of the Reagan administration's cuts in social service funding (Hodgkinson, 1986), but picked up again after 1984

(Hodgkinson and Weitzman, 1988a, p. 1). The overall growth rate of the sector since the mid 1960s has been striking.

The number of unpaid workers in the nonprofit sector is even more striking than its paid employment figures. Independent Sector commissioned the Gallup Organization in 1981, 1985, and 1988 to determine how many Americans volunteer. These surveys showed that about half of all Americans eighteen years of age and older (52 percent in 1981, 48 percent in 1985, 45 percent in 1988) had volunteered within the previous twelve months and a quarter did volunteer work every week. Independent Sector estimated that nearly eighty million Americans contributed fifteen billion hours of volunteer work in 1987, at an estimated value of $150 billion (Hodgkinson and Weitzman, 1988b, p. 8). These results were corroborated by another national study, which found that 47 percent of Americans eighteen years of age and older gave some volunteer time in 1984, and half the volunteers gave three or more hours per week (Yankelovich, Skelly and White, 1986, pp. 25–27).

The third sector is a major presence in the American economy. Independent Sector estimated that in 1986, philanthropic non-profits had annual funds of $300 billion (Hodgkinson and Weitzman, 1988a, Table 7 [n.p.]). The sector accounts for about 6 percent of the gross national product and 18 percent of the national services economy (Hodgkinson and Weitzman, 1986, p. 22). This figure does not include the revenue of the 370,000 nonphilanthropic nonprofits; other studies have indicated that the latter constitute about 10 percent of all nonprofit financial activity. Yale economist Gabriel Rudney has calculated that American nonprofits in 1980 had expenditures exceeding the budgets of all but seven nations in the world (Rudney, 1981, p. 3). The Urban Institute, which studied nonprofits in sixteen locations throughout the United States in 1982, concluded that nonprofit economic activity is often far greater than that of local government. In the five-county San Francisco Bay Area, for example, the 1982 nonprofit economy was more than twice as large as the billion-dollar budget of the City and County of San Francisco (Harder, Kimmich, and Salamon, 1985, p. xvi); in the Atlanta metropolitan area the same year, the nonprofit budget was five times the budget of the city of Atlanta (Lippert, Gutowski, and

Salamon, 1984, p. xiii). The nonprofit sector's assets equal nearly half the assets of the federal government (Weisbrod, 1988, p. 64).

Nonprofits have a major impact on other parts of the economy. Rudney (1981, pp. 3–4) showed that in 1980, nonprofits paid $75.4 billion to their 5.6 million employees and purchased $42.6 billion of business goods and services, which created 1.4 million jobs in the for-profit world. He also noted that whereas business put $6.0 billion—$2.3 billion in donations, $3.7 billion in purchase of nonprofit services—into the nonprofit sector in 1980, business got back $42.6 billion through the sale of business goods and services to nonprofits. In spite of the cliché newspaper photo of a generous businessman handing a check to a grateful nonprofit recipient, it turns out that business gets far more than it gives.

Economists Richard and Nancy Ruggles (Ruggles and Ruggles, 1980) have estimated that the physical and financial assets of the third sector, excluding private foundations and churches but including nonphilanthropic nonprofits, were $201 billion in 1975. Private foundation assets for 1975 were approximately $30 billion (Foundation Center, 1987a, p. xx). No comprehensive data are available on the 1975 assets of religious institutions, and the difficulties of calculating the value of some of religion's physical assets (for example, cathedrals in central-city areas) are considerable. If one estimated the 1975 physical and financial assets of the nation's more than 300,000 religious organizations to be $50 billion, or about $170,000 per organization (probably a conservative estimate), the total assets of nonprofits in 1975 would have been about $280 billion, compared to the business sector's $3 trillion in assets for that year. Goldsmith (1982, p. 147) estimated nonprofit assets for 1975 as $243 billion. Given the growth of the nonprofit sector since 1975—foundation assets alone, for instance, were $122 billion in 1987 (American Association of Fund-Raising Counsel, 1988, p. 43)—it is likely that nonprofit sector assets in 1987 were well over $500 billion.

Another measure of the relative financial size of the nonprofit sector is its percentage of the gross national product (GNP), the dollar value of all goods and services produced in the United States in a given year. Ruggles and Ruggles (1980) estimated that all nonprofits in 1975 accounted for 3.2 percent of the GNP, up from

2.1 percent in 1960. By contrast, business accounted for 81.6 percent of the GNP in 1975, down from 86.4 percent in 1960, and government accounted for 14.2 percent in 1975, up from 11.3 percent in 1960. In other words, during this fifteen-year period, the nonprofit "market share" of the GNP grew twice as fast as that of government, while the business share declined.

Independent Sector suggests that a more accurate indicator of the nonprofit sector's economic significance is the "national income," which measures labor and property earnings connected with the production of goods and services. In 1986, nonprofit organizations accounted for 7 percent of the national income (Hodgkinson and Weitzman, 1988a, Table 2 [n.p.]). This figure includes assigned values for unpaid workers in all three sectors, including volunteers and family workers.

The independent sector, though one-tenth the size of business and a third the size of government, accounts for a significant and growing part of the nation's economy.

Where Does the Money Come From?

It is commonly believed that private donations fund the third America, but in fact gifts provide only 27 percent of nonprofit revenue, the remainder coming principally from fees and government. Hodgkinson and Weitzman (1988a) present an estimate of 1986 revenue sources for the independent sector, shown in Table 1. The largest source of income for nonprofits is fees for services.

Table 1. Annual Sources of Independent Sector Funds, 1986.

Source	Amount (in Billions of Dollars)
Dues, fees, and charges	$112.5
Contributions	82.2
Government	81.2
Investment income	15.9
Other (net profit from sales and so on)	8.1
TOTAL	300.0 [sic]

Source: Hodgkinson and Weitzman, 1988a, Table 7 [n.p.].

Nowhere is the distinction between for-profits and nonprofits
clearer. Rudney (1981, pp. 6–8) notes that in 1980, nonprofits sold
$129.2 billion worth of services for $61.5 billion in revenue, forty-
eight cents recovered for every dollar spent to produce the services.
Such a cost-revenue ratio in a corporation would cause heads to roll.
While nonprofit leaders like to jest that there are also nonprofit
businesses, such businesses are usually not around long to appreciate the joke.

To a great extent, it is precisely the gap between production
costs and charges that defines the uniqueness of the nonprofit
sector. Certain personal and societal needs, such as counseling for
low-income families and litigation to protect the environment, are
insufficiently lucrative to be provided on a for-profit basis.
Therefore, they must be provided or subsidized by other sources.
Theoretically, government could provide the entire subsidy or the
services themselves, which is essentially the socialist option; but
Americans have chosen to follow a different path, that of a combination of government and nonprofit sectors providing certain
services whose costs exceed their market value. Still, it is worth
noting that the single largest source of nonprofit revenue is pay-
ment for services. The "charitable" sector is far from being
dependent on charity alone.

Private donations account for a little over a quarter of
nonprofit revenue, and fully 90 percent of the gift money comes
from individuals, the great majority of whom are anything but
wealthy. Half of the money from individuals comes from families
with incomes under $30,000. As John Gardner, founder of Common
Cause and cofounder of Independent Sector, has said, "For the most
part private giving in this country is a Mississippi River of small
gifts" (O'Connell, 1983, p. xii). The other 10 percent of private
giving comes from foundations and corporations, some of whose
grants, such as the MacArthur Foundation's "genius awards," are
much more visible than individual gifts.

Private giving to nonprofits has increased substantially in
recent years. The American Association of Fund-Raising Counsel
(AAFRC) Trust for Philanthropy estimated 1987 private giving as
shown in Table 2 (American Association of Fund-Raising Counsel,
1988). In inflation-free dollars, private giving rose nearly 100

Table 2. Sources of Charitable Giving, 1987.

Source	Amount (in Billions of Dollars)	Percentage of Total
Individuals	$76.82	82.0
Bequests	5.98	6.4
Foundations	6.38	6.8
Corporations	4.50	4.8
TOTAL	$93.68	100.0

Source: American Association of Fund-Raising Counsel, 1988, p. 8.

percent between 1955 and 1987. Private giving has shown a relative immunity to fluctuations in the economy. In spite of the stock market crash of October 19, 1987, and the 1986 tax reform act, which removed the charitable deduction for nonitemizing taxpayers, the increase in private giving from 1986 to 1987 (6.45 percent) exceeded the rate of growth in the GNP and personal income and was nearly double the rate of growth in the Consumer Price Index. The AAFRC report also showed the distribution of 1987 gifts, presented in Table 3. The proportions are highly similar to those of earlier years.

The third major source of nonprofit revenue is government. Nonprofit funding patterns have changed greatly because of governmental actions in the last quarter century. The Great Society

Table 3. Recipients of Charitable Giving, 1987.

Recipient	Amount (in Billions of Dollars)	Percentage of Total
Religion	$43.61	46.55
Health	13.65	14.57
Education	10.84	11.57
Human services	9.84	10.50
Arts, culture, humanities	6.41	6.84
Public/society benefit	2.44	2.60
Other	3.89	4.15
Unallocated	3.00	3.20
TOTAL	$93.68	100.00

Source: American Association of Fund-Raising Counsel, 1988, p. 9.

programs of the 1960s and 1970s brought massive new funds into the nonprofit sector through grants, contracts, student aid, and Medicare and Medicaid payments. Inflationary pressures during the Carter years led to an effective decrease in government assistance, and the Reagan administration cut some programs supporting nonprofits. Salamon (1984, p. 20) estimated that federal support for nonprofits other than health care agencies declined by $4.5 billion, after adjusting for inflation, from fiscal year 1980 to fiscal year 1984. Hodgkinson (1986, p. 56) noted that the growth rate of the independent sector declined between 1982 and 1984, the first such decline since the 1970s; she called the decline "a direct result of federal cutbacks."

The Reagan cuts affected various subsectors quite differently. Religion, private elementary and secondary education, advocacy organizations, mutual benefits, and foundations were not directly affected, since they had not been receiving any federal funds. Federal support for the arts decreased somewhat, but the decrease equaled only 1 percent of nonprofit arts revenue. The administration's efforts to slash the budgets of the National Endowment for the Arts and the National Endowment for the Humanities were consistently rejected by Congress. Federal assistance for higher education students, including private college and university students, increased 15.3 percent in inflation-free dollars between 1980–81 and 1985–86 ("Fact-File," 1986, p. 28).

Health care, which alone accounts for half the entire nonprofit-sector budget, received major funding increases during the Reagan years, primarily through Medicare and Medicaid increases. Hardest hit by Reagan era cutbacks were nonprofit social service and community development organizations, federal funds for which were reduced by more than 25 percent during the Reagan era.

A relatively small but growing part of nonprofit revenue comes from affiliated for-profit activities (Skloot, 1987; Weisbrod, 1988). If the 1960s and 1970s were the age of new government funds for nonprofits, the 1980s were the age of nonprofit entrepreneurial efforts. Such activities are not new; the Metropolitan Museum of Art in New York, for instance, started selling etched copies of its masterpieces in 1871. But the Reagan cutbacks and the probusiness atmosphere of the 1980s have made nonprofits much more serious about for-profit enterprises. To the old standbys such as art objects, Christmas cards, and Girl Scout cookies were added health clubs, travel agencies, and car-leasing agencies. The success that nonprofits have had in the business field has opened up an old area of controversy: whether nonprofits, because of their various tax exemptions, compete unfairly with the for-profit sector. An emphatic yes was given by the U.S. Small Business Administration (1983); and in 1987–88, Representative J. J. Pickle (D-Texas), chair of the Subcommittee on Oversight of the House Ways and Means Committee, prepared legislation to restrict the business activities of nonprofits. The debate continues, as do the hundreds of workshops being offered to help nonprofits start for-profit enterprises.

Societal Importance of the Third Sector

In his remarkable *Democracy in America,* Tocqueville ([1835] 1969, p. 517) wrote about the importance of America's voluntary associations:

> Nothing, in my view, more deserves attention than the intellectual and moral associations in America. American political and industrial associations easily catch our eyes, but the others tend not to be noticed. And even if we do notice them, we tend to misunderstand them, hardly ever having seen anything similar before. However, we should recognize that the latter are as necessary as the former to the American people; perhaps more so. In democratic countries knowledge of how to combine is the mother of all other forms of knowledge; on its progress depends that of all the others. Among laws controlling human societies there is one more precise and clearer, it seems to me, than all the others. If men are to remain civilized or to become civilized, the art of association must develop and improve among them at the same speed as equality of condition spreads.

Tocqueville argued that there is a vital connection between the "principle of association" and the skills necessary to make a democracy work. In an aristocracy, he noted, things get done because there are wealthy and powerful people who can command the action of a great many other people. In a democracy, however, there is no such mechanism for ensuring collective action: "But among democratic peoples all the citizens are independent and weak. They can do hardly anything for themselves, and none of them is in a position to force his fellows to help him" (p. 514). Therefore, a democracy's progress is directly related not only to the ability of citizens to vote for representatives but also to their ability to associate voluntarily in order to solve problems and meet needs. Voluntary associations accomplish many things vital to the full functioning of the society, and they teach group action skills that can be transferred to the political and for-profit arenas.

Tocqueville also held that a strong network of voluntary associations would limit the growth and power of government: "The more government takes the place of associations, the more will individuals lose the idea of forming associations and need the government to come to their help. That is a vicious circle of cause and effect" (p. 515). He further noted that just as an energetic business community is necessary to keep government out of commerce, so vigorous "intellectual and moral associations" are necessary to prevent government domination of "opinions and sentiments": "A government, by itself, is equally incapable of refreshing the circulation of feelings and ideas among a great people, as it is of controlling every industrial undertaking. Once it leaves the sphere of politics to launch out on this new track, it will, even without intending this, exercise an intolerable tyranny" (p. 516).

German sociologist Max Weber ([1910] 1972) argued that voluntary associations play an important mediating role between large, bureaucratic institutions and the individual, a point developed in detail by Berger and Neuhaus (1977). Elaborating on these themes, Smith (1988, pp. 2.2-2.10) presented the following functions or roles of the voluntary sector:

1.   provide[s] society with a wide variety of partially tested social innovations, from which business, government,

and other institutions can select and institutionalize those innovations which seem most promising. . . .

2. provides a forum for countervailing definitions of reality and morality—ideologies, perspectives, and world views—that frequently challenge the prevailing assumptions about what exists and what is good and what should be done in society. . . .

3. provides for the recreational, or play, element of society. . . .

4. has a major impact on the level of social integration in society. . . .

5. is active in preserving numerous old ideas. . . .

6. [is characterized by] its embodiment and representation in society of the sense of mystery, wonder, and the sacred. . . .

7. [is characterized by] its ability to liberate the individual and permit the fullest possible measure of expression of personal capacities and potentialities within an otherwise constraining social environment. . . .

8. [is] a source of "negative feedback" for the society as a whole. . . .

9. gives [support] specifically to the economic system of a society, especially in a modern industrial society. . . .

10. plays a major role in providing for the general welfare of society through all manner of social services. . . .

11. constitutes an important *latent resource* for all kinds of goal attainment in the interests of the society as a whole.

Economic theories regarding the sector (Weisbrod, 1975, 1977; Hansmann, 1980; Ben-Ner, 1986) have stressed that nonprofits provide a level of collective and individual goods beyond that which government and business will provide, goods that do not have enough money-making potential to attract business and that have insufficient popular appeal to attract the mass of voters. Such goods might include opera performances, efforts to protect the environment, and many types of scholarly research. These theories also point out that there are certain important services (for instance, heart surgery) that the typical consumer has insufficient expertise to evaluate and might therefore feel more comfortable securing from an agency that is not driven primarily by a profit motive. Another explanation of some nonprofits is that of "patron control": certain groups adopt the nonprofit form to achieve more control over the clientele and activities of the group than would be possible under for-profit or government sponsorship. This occurs with elite social clubs as well as ethnic and religious organizations. Young (1983) has argued that the nonprofit sector provides the society with unique opportunities for social entrepreneurs who are not motivated primarily by personal monetary or political gain.

From a political science perspective, Douglas (1983) suggests that the nonprofit sector complements government by giving scope to the nation's diversity of political opinions and social orientations without having to carry the burden of law making and law enforcement: "the voluntary sector enables us to achieve a sort of diversity that would require the impossible combination of a secular, Catholic, Protestant, Jewish, Moslem, rightist, leftist, and centrist government operating simultaneously in the same jurisdiction!" (Douglas, 1987, p. 47). Salamon (1987), disagreeing with those who hold that nonprofits do what business and government won't do, argues that the voluntary sector is the primary locus and mechanism for the provision of collective goods, that only when and if it cannot provide these adequately does government come into the picture. The entrance of government is thus contingent on "voluntary failure": the inability of the nonprofit sector to provide certain collective goods on the necessary scale and breadth or with the necessary expertise and equity.

Free from the constant demands of profit margins and elections, the independent sector can experiment with new strategies of social action, respond quickly to new social needs, and generally provide "social risk capital." The problem of child abuse has been a dark secret throughout history; recent efforts to do something about it were pioneered by the nonprofit sector. Family planning and population control efforts began in the nonprofit sector when these issues were politically too hot to handle. All the major social movements in the nation's history have started in the nonprofit sector—child labor legislation, abolition, mental health care, women's suffrage, Prohibition, the civil rights movement, consumer protection, environmentalism, the anti-Vietnam War movement, the women's movement, the nuclear arms control movement.

Nonprofits support new social ideas but also play a major role in nourishing the collective memory of the society through historical societies, ethnic groups, churches, and museums. Often the old is a source of the new: the civil rights movement originated in traditional black Christianity, nonprofit arts organizations move from classical to avant-garde productions, and private schools often combine the oldest and newest approaches to education.

The third sector responds to human needs for sociability beyond the family and workplace. Oscar Handlin's (1951) Pulitzer Prize-winning book *The Uprooted* chronicled the traumatic experience of immigrants who came to America; without ethnic and religious organizations, the experience of these millions of people would have been far more disorienting. In today's increasingly complex society, the humanizing effects of nonprofit organizations seem even more necessary.

Voluntary associations play an important role in leadership development for those with limited access to such roles in business and government organizations. Many women and members of minority groups have had opportunities to become leaders only in their own third-sector organizations.

Nonprofits contribute significantly to the strength of both business and government through education, research, and development. The graduates of nonprofit educational institutions and the research produced by these institutions have had a major impact on other sectors of the society.

Nonprofits daily assist millions of people in need through health care, social service, and legal assistance agencies. Nonprofits work with government in a major partnership to meet the needs of the sick, the poor, the aged, the emotionally disturbed, and the physically handicapped. Nonprofits often play a vanguard, pace-setting role in the provision of such services.

Relationship with the Other Two Sectors

It is sometimes suggested that nonprofits and government are completely separate from and fundamentally inimical to each other.

For example, sociologist Robert Nisbet (1962, pp. 98, 109) has written: "The conflict between the central power of the political State and the whole set of functions and authorities contained in church, family, gild, and local community has been, I believe, the main source of those dislocations of social structure and uprootings of status which lie behind the problem of community in our age. . . . The real conflict in modern political history has not been, as is so often stated, between State and individual, but between State and social group." In reality, nearly every part of the nonprofit sector is closely connected to government. In some cases (religion, for example), the historical movement has been toward separation; but in other areas, such as health and social services, there is far more government-nonprofit involvement than was the case fifty or one hundred years ago.

The Urban Institute's Nonprofit Sector Project has demonstrated the extent of government-nonprofit relationships in health care, human services, and education. Federal, state, and local tax dollars flow through a variety of mechanisms to private nonprofit organizations. When government takes some responsibility for a social need, it does not necessarily launch programs to meet that need; more often than not, it gives money to private agencies to take care of the problem. This arrangement is simple, efficient, and politically astute. Private agencies get money rather than competition. Needy people get help. Government increases its role and influence, gets part of the credit when things go right, and can quickly disassociate itself from programs when things go wrong.

This distinction between providing funds and providing services has in fact characterized American governmental response to social needs for centuries. From colonial times to the present, there have been numerous examples of government funds flowing to private agencies to meet public needs in education, health care, social welfare, and arts and culture. Harvard, Yale, Columbia, Massachusetts General Hospital, and the Metropolitan Museum of Art owe their origins and early support partly to government. Private welfare agencies at the end of the nineteenth century received well over half of their operating revenue from government. A similar pattern continues today. The Urban Institute study found that in New York, 43 percent of nonprofit human service revenue came from government (Grossman, Salamon, and Altschuler, 1986, p. 44); in the Twin Cities of Minneapolis and St. Paul, the figure was 37 percent (Luckermann, Kimmich, and Salamon, 1984, p. 31); in Pittsburgh, it was 51 percent (Gutowski, Salamon, and Pittman, 1984, p. 30); and in Chicago, it was 32 percent (Gronbjerg, Kimmich, and Salamon, 1985, p. 41). Government and the third sector, far from being opponents or isolated social actors, have always been close associates.

The relationship between nonprofits and business is equally strong. In 1980 nonprofits purchased nearly $50 billion of business goods and services and created 1.5 million jobs in the business sector (Rudney, 1981). Business, on the other hand, puts more than $6 billion a year into the nonprofit sector through donations and purchase of services. Thousands of businesspeople serve on nonprofit boards or in other ways volunteer their business and financial expertise. Nonprofit education and research organizations provide a major flow of ideas and trained workers into the business sector. The relationship between Stanford University and "Silicon Valley" is a classic example. William Hewlett and David Packard were young engineering students under the wing of Stanford professor Frederick Terman, often viewed as the father of Silicon Valley, when they started "H-P" in a garage. Stanford researchers helped develop sonar in World War II, and two brothers from the research team founded Varian Associates, another high-tech firm. The Stanford–Silicon Valley liaison and the relationship between Harvard, MIT, and the high-tech firms along Boston's beltway, Route 128, are only two examples of the extensive and mutually beneficial interactions between nonprofits and business in American life.

The third America is best seen, however, not through general theories, legal definitions, or national statistics but in the rich detail of its astonishingly diverse activities. The following nine chapters sketch the historical development and present reality of what Tocqueville called the "thousand different types [of associations]—religious, moral, serious, futile, very general and very limited, immensely large and very minute," which make up the American nonprofit sector.

RELIGION

Godmother of
the Nonprofit Sector

From the Spanish friars and the Puritan divines to Jesse Jackson and Jerry Falwell, religion has played a major role in American life. Tocqueville wrote in the 1830s, "The religious atmosphere of the country was the first thing that struck me on arrival in the United States" (Tocqueville, [1835] 1969, p. 295). More than 150 years later, religion in America is still alive, well, and influential. It has fashioned a relatively peaceful coexistence with science and technology, secularism, the sexual revolution, and material wealth undreamed of in earlier centuries. Under the Constitution, the government officially ignores religion; yet religious observance in the United States far exceeds that in many nations where government officially supports religion. Religion is a large and important part of the nonprofit sector and has given birth to many other nonprofit institutions: health, education, social service, international assistance, advocacy, mutual assistance, and even some cultural and grantmaking organizations. Directly and indirectly, religion has been the major formative influence on America's independent sector.

Scope and Impact

Religion is the oldest, largest, and most generously supported component of the third America. Its activities in the New World go back to Columbus's second voyage in 1493, when missionaries came to bring Christianity to the Native Americans. Seventy percent of Americans are members of the nation's 350,000 churches, synagogues, and mosques. Forty percent of Americans say they attend religious services weekly. Over forty million Americans volunteer in religious organizations. In 1987, $44 billion, nearly half of all

20

private funds contributed to charity, was donated to religion. The number of people who donate to religion is more than twice the number who donate to health care, social services, education, or any other charity.

Religion has had a great influence on other parts of the nonprofit sector. Nearly all of private education in the United States is or once was religiously affiliated. Most health care agencies, especially hospitals, trace their origins to religion. Many human and social service organizations, such as the YMCA, Big Brothers and Big Sisters, and the Salvation Army, were religiously inspired. United Way was started by two ministers, a priest, and a rabbi in Denver in the 1870s. The civil rights movement grew out of the black churches and was strongly supported by other religious groups. Several of the large, mainline religions have been in the forefront of the peace movement. Some foundations, such as the Lilly Endowment and the Conrad Hilton Foundation, were set up in good measure to benefit religion. Thousands of ethnic mutual aid societies were started directly or indirectly by a church or synagogue. Most nonprofit international assistance programs are religiously affiliated. A recent national study found that 87 percent of local religious congregations were involved in human service activities, 68 percent in health work, 43 percent in arts and culture activities, 38 percent in education, and 27 percent in environmental efforts (Hodgkinson, Weitzman, and Kirsch, 1988, p. 18).

Religion is also a major economic force in American society. In 1986, local religious congregations in the United States employed over a million people and had revenues and expenditures of $40 billion (Hodgkinson, Weitzman, and Kirsch, 1988). Religion owns many billions of dollars' worth of property, and indirectly has a powerful effect on home prices, zoning practices, and the location of public services. Realtors, city planners, and economists recognize the importance of religious institutions in community stability and property values.

Religion has long had an influence on American civic and political life. Nearly two centuries after the First Amendment to the federal Constitution, codifying the doctrine of church-state separation, was ratified in 1791, religious leaders continue to speak out on political issues, raise money and organize voters for political campaigns, and even run for political office. Two priests and dozens of ministers have served in Congress; and two ministers, one Democrat and one Republican, were candidates for the 1988 presidential nomination. Religion helped elect Ronald Reagan in 1980 and helped defeat Al Smith in 1928. Many lower-level officials in American political history have won or lost as a direct result of organized religion's influence.

For nearly five centuries, religion has been a major social force in America. It has shaped personal, family, and community values, helped and hindered social change, and influenced many important public policy issues. While religions no longer feel obliged to get involved in the minute transactions of the economic and political realms, they energetically involve themselves in broad social issues such as race relations, drug and alcohol abuse, crime, homelessness, immigration, mental health, marriage and divorce, child rearing and education, and medical ethics.

Religion is the most trusted institution in American society. Gallup polls consistently find that Americans place more confidence in organized religion than in the U.S. Supreme Court, Congress, the military, public schools, banks, unions, newspapers, or television. Twice as many Americans express confidence in religion as in television or newspapers.

Religion and government in the United States have closer ties than is commonly thought. The First Amendment, whose primary original purpose was to prevent the establishment of a national church, says nothing about a "wall of separation between church and state," a later metaphor of Thomas Jefferson's. There are many points of contact between government and religion in America: "In God we trust" appears on our currency, "under God" appears in the pledge of allegiance to the flag, prayers open each session of Congress and the Supreme Court, the government pays the salaries of chaplains in the armed services and in penitentiaries, religious organizations are exempt from corporate income tax and property tax, and billions of government dollars annually go to religiously affiliated health, social service, and educational institutions in the form of grants, contracts, scholarships, Medicare and Medicaid payments, and the donation of equipment, materials, and services.

Religion influences millions of Americans through the broadcast and print media. According to an April 1987 Gallup poll, 49 percent of Americans eighteen years of age and older watch some religious television, and 25 percent watch it weekly (U.S. Bureau of the Census, 1987, p. 54). Publishing religious books, pamphlets, magazines, and cassette tapes is a multimillion-dollar enterprise.

Religions preach that it is better to give than to receive, and they themselves give large amounts of money, goods, and services. Independent Sector found that in 1986 local religious congregations expended or donated $19.1 billion to other than religious activities (Hodgkinson, Weitzman, and Kirsch, 1988, p. 4). This finding was consistent with but even more dramatic than similar findings by the Filer Commission (Commission, 1975) and the Council on Foundations. A 1984 study by the Council on Foundations (McDonald, 1985, p. 127) estimated that American churches and synagogues gave more money to charity in 1983 ($7.5 billion) than all American foundations and corporations combined ($6.6 billion). Religious congregations provide members and nonmembers with food, clothing, shelter, transportation, counseling, adult education and tutoring, drug prevention programs, community development programs, day care, social and recreational facilities and services, youth group work, senior citizen programs, information and referral services, disaster relief, programs for the handicapped, refugee aid, job training, and legal assistance. The Council on Foundations' study concluded that the major philanthropic work of religion was in response to "the scriptural precepts to feed the hungry, take in the stranger, shelter the homeless, and find justice for the oppressed," but found that religious philanthropy was far more diverse:

[T]here were groups active with soup kitchens, but also the group that had funded a greenhouse where those enrolled for meals could grow the vegetables for those meals. And there were groups providing emergency aid to refugees, but also the group that decided to lend refugees mortgage money to bring down interest rates within their reach. There were groups that had been making grants and loans to small businesses, but also the group that, finding this to be "ineffectual," was now making alternative investments for long-range social change.

There were groups providing clothing, temporary shelter, and aid in disasters. But there were also organizations funding low-cost housing research; replacing tar-paper shacks with low-cost passive solar homes; providing seed money to train women for the construction industry; installing computers in alternative schools; digging wells; funding backyard rabbit projects; providing free dental care in mobile vans to migrants; funding rape counseling centers; providing bail money; supplying appropriate means of transportation in third-world countries (jeeps, excarts [sic], landrovers, horses); funding neighborhood organizations that successfully negotiate with their cities for improved services; making films to address toxic waste problems; funding legal aid groups that are bringing justice to minorities; sponsoring a "peace intern" for a summer of travel to show and discuss a film on the consequences of nuclear war [McDonald, 1985, pp. 130–131].

Historical Development

It would be highly anachronistic to attribute to colonial times the modern division of organizational life into government, business, and nonprofit. In colonial days, highways and canals were often private businesses, bridges were often philanthropic efforts, churches were often quasi-governmental bodies, and it took Harvard College two hundred years to decide whether it was public or private. The colonists, faced with more pressing issues, paid little attention to the organizational distinctions we now make. Religion was a case in point. The church was not a subdivision of the state or vice versa, but the two were so closely connected as to be sometimes almost indistinguishable. Both church and state were intertwined with business, as is evident in the charters and activities of such joint-stock settlement corporations as the Virginia Company, the Massachusetts Bay Company, and the Dutch East Indies Company. Nevertheless, religion became the earliest example of the sorting-out process that in the nineteenth century would give rise to a separate and distinct third sector. Colonial religious activity was always at least implicitly distinct from government and business activity, and this distinction grew more evident during the seventeenth and eighteenth centuries as the English colonies became more religiously heterogeneous and the French and Spanish colonies declined.

The significance of this development is that, during the colonial period, religion was by far the most important part of what would come to be known as the nonprofit sector. Arts and culture organizations were nonexistent, health care was primitive and family based, formal education was far less extensive than it is now, social services were minimal and somewhat frowned upon, and there was nothing even vaguely resembling grantmaking or international assistance organizations. As far as the incipient nonprofit sector went, religion was virtually the only game in town. What happened in the field of religion during the colonial period had major impact on the later development of other parts of the third sector.

Spanish and French colonization efforts were clearly motivated not only by economic and strategic interests but also by religious zeal. Columbus's proposal to their Most Catholic Majesties Ferdinand and Isabella promised gold, spices, and souls. When Columbus set forth on his second voyage in September 1493, he brought with him five priests to lead the conversion efforts. The Spanish and later Mexican presence in what is now the United States lasted three centuries, ending with the loss of Texas, New Mexico, Arizona, and Upper California in 1848. During these years, Spanish missionary priests and brothers engaged in pastoral and educational work with the Native Americans. Some of the priests also fought against the cruelty with which the Spanish overlords treated the Indians. The enslavement of the Native Americans and the Church's separation from Spanish government and commercial interests on this issue foreshadowed the social policy independence that would begin to define America's nonprofit sector in the mid-nineteenth century and that would center on the same issue of slavery.

French colonization efforts in North America also reflected a strong element of religious interest. For 150 years after the founding of Quebec by Samuel de Champlain in 1608, French missionaries journeyed to Canada and from there to Maine, New York, the Great Lakes region, the Illinois country, and finally Louisiana. The most stable of the American settlements, New Orleans, had a resident priest from its founding in 1699. In 1727, eight Ursuline nuns arrived and opened a school, which within a year had sixteen boarders and twenty-five day students, including seven black girls. The nuns also staffed the only hospital in town, took care of orphans, and taught catechism to Native American and black children. These first nuns in what would become the United States thus set the pattern for the combination of educational, health care, and religious activity that characterizes American Catholicism to this day.

Religion in British North America was far more heterogeneous than that of the Spanish and French colonies. The English colonies were soon filled with diverse and competing religious groups—Anglicans, Baptists, Quakers, German Pietists, Dutch Calvinists, French Huguenots, Catholics, and Puritans. Even Puritanism was far from monolithic: "Puritanism . . . was no unified historical phenomenon, even in its New England form. Up close, it proves to be a range of beliefs, ideas, and attitudes, clustering into shifting and unstable groupings. If there ever was an 'orthodoxy' in colonial New England it was nothing stable and nothing intrinsic to the religion itself but a socio-ecclesiastical program whose promoters gained a precarious ascendancy within a society boiling with 'dissident' beliefs and sects. The 'dissidents,' the 'radicals,' in seventeenth-century New England—separatists, Anabaptists, Quakers, extreme millenarians, spiritists, antinomians, Socinians, Gortonists, and miscellaneous seekers—were no less 'Puritan' than the elder Winthrop and his clerical establishment" (Bailyn, 1986, pp. 48–49).

What started to emerge almost immediately in the English colonies was the notion that allegiance to one country, culture, language, and tradition could coexist with sharp diversity in religious ideas and practices. With a few exceptions, such as the Quakers, the English colonists were no more favorably disposed toward religious freedom than were the Spanish or French. The Puritans, mildly persecuted in England, came to Massachusetts and vigorously persecuted anyone who differed with them. Rhode

Island, often singled out as the forerunner of American religious liberty, refused citizenship to Catholics and Jews. But the English colonists simply had to deal with the fact of religious diversity; the economic, political, social, and military realities of the New World left them no choice. It was principally this variety of religious experience in colonial New England that prepared the way for the idea of religious liberty. That idea and reality, in turn, played a critical role in the development of the American third sector, since organized religion not only was a major part of the sector but also spawned much of the rest. Without religious diversity and state neutrality toward religion, the American nonprofit experience would have been very different.

The English colonists shared with their Spanish and French counterparts a lively interest in converting the heathen and a naive confidence as to the ease of that task. In 1618, the Virginia Company had planned to start an Indian College and University, but none was established. One of the first buildings at Harvard College, founded in 1636, was the "Indian College" of 1655, a two-story brick building with chambers and study rooms for twenty Indian students; after graduating one student in ten years, the Indian College was converted to a printing shop. Reverend Eleazar Wheelock, the founder and first president of Dartmouth, had originally intended that institution to be an Indian school, with a view to uplifting the natives (Cremin, 1970, p. 328). Wheelock said of one of his Native American students at Dartmouth, "I have taken much pains to purge all the Indian out of him, but after all a little of it will sometimes appear" (Rudolf, 1962, p. 104).

Ultimately, evangelizing the Native Americans became impossible because the English settlers kept driving west and south, displacing the Indians from their lands by force or by contract. The racial and cultural gulf between English and Indians, always wide, was dramatically widened by territorial dispossession. The Native Americans largely continued to reject Christianization and Europeanization. The English religious interest in evangelizing Native Americans gave way to economic and military interests in neutralizing or eliminating them.

One of the greatest achievements of English colonial religion was to provide an institutional structure for the continuation and development of religious activity. This was particularly true in Massachusetts. The Puritans were, for their day, an astonishingly well-educated group. By 1640, more than one hundred alumni of Oxford and Cambridge were in New England. Governor John Winthrop of the Massachusetts Bay Colony had spent two years at Trinity College, Cambridge. Harvard College was founded in 1636 by the General Court of Massachusetts, which was headed by twenty-three-year-old Governor Harry Vane, an alumnus of Magdalen Hall, Oxford. Seven others of this forty-three-member General Court were university products. Harvard was founded in no small part to provide ministers for the growing Puritan colony; a mission statement of 1643 speaks of "dreading to leave an illiterate ministry to the churches." Though it was not exclusively a seminary or divinity school, during Harvard's first seventy-five years about half its graduates went into the ministry. The Puritans also began creating an indigenous religious literature, and Cotton Mather alone wrote 437 pamphlets and books, including the giant *Magnalia Christi Americana* and *Bonifacius—Essays to Do Good,* a popular work that had a profound influence on colonial attitudes toward charitable works. The early establishment and development of a network of religious institutions, continually expanding into education, welfare, and occasional health activities, provided an important structural base and organizational model for later development of the nonprofit sector.

The Quaker "holy experiment" in Pennsylvania anticipated many of the major themes in later American social thought and nonprofit work (James, 1963). Quakers welcomed all religious groups, including Catholics and Jews. They were the first to develop humane treatment for the mentally ill. They condemned slavery at their 1758 Philadelphia convention, and in 1775 they formed the first antislavery society in the Western world (Bailyn, 1967, p. 245). No other major religious group in the English colonies took a similar position. Besides being the only church to protest the enslavement of blacks, the Quakers were among the first to support the enfranchisement and education of women. Their pacifist approach to societal and world problems continues to have a significant effect.

With the single exception of the Quakers, no major religious group in the colonial period practiced religious toleration any more than it had to. The Revolutionary War, however, required New Yorkers and Virginians, merchants and farmers, Anglicans and Congregationalists and Catholics and Jews to fight side by side. Also, it was awkward to discriminate against Catholics while Catholic France was supporting the American independence effort. The issue gathered momentum after the war. Like the parent countries in Europe, each of the colonies had its own established church, which was the official religion and which received the legal, moral, and financial support of the government. Clearly, that could not work in the new United States. If the new nation tried to establish a national church of Anglicanism, Congregationalism, or Methodism—to say nothing of Catholicism, Judaism, or Quakerism—the experiment of national unity would blow up. That simple political fact, combined with a growing European-American theory of religious liberty, produced the American doctrine and practice of separation of church and state.

The First Amendment to the federal Constitution, ratified in 1791, states, in part, "Congress shall make no law respecting an establishment of religion or prohibiting the free exercise thereof." What the First Amendment most simply and basically says is that the national government may neither establish a particular religion nor restrict the free exercise of religious choice. It does not say what state governments can do, and in fact some states kept their established churches for several decades, Massachusetts until 1833. The great significance of the First Amendment for not only religion but the entire nonprofit sector lies in the principle that government is inherently different from religion, that religion is not a department of government or vice versa, and that the power of government must never be used to force religion on people or prevent them from exercising their religious faith. The First Amendment excludes from governmental control a large and powerful area of organizational activity because of its intrinsic closeness to the human spirit.

The implications for other value-oriented associations were and are profound. Not only religion but also education, art, scientific research, political advocacy, human and social services, mutual assistance, international assistance, and organized philanthropy all have elements of this closeness to the human spirit, this central concern with values and beliefs. While "intellectual and moral associations" were nowhere mentioned in the Constitution, the *Federalist Papers,* or the debates before and during the constitutional convention, the First Amendment, which deals with freedom of religion, freedom of speech, freedom of assembly, and the right to petition government over grievances, can without exaggeration be seen as the Magna Carta of the nonprofit sector in American life. These First Amendment freedoms guarantee not only to individuals but also to groups the right to assemble, speak out, and proclaim values and beliefs. The independence of the independent sector finds its strongest legal support in the First Amendment, including its religious liberty clause.

Between the 1820s and the 1920s, nearly forty million people came into the United States from dozens of European and other nations. Never before in history had there been such a massive, complex migration in such a short period of time. Into a new nation barely established came a flood of peoples with vastly different cultures, politics, traditions, languages, and religions. Immigration dramatically and permanently changed the religious composition of the United States, grafting onto the English Protestant stock wild new shoots of European Catholicism, Russian and Polish Judaism, German and Scandinavian Lutheranism, Chinese Buddhism, and a host of other beliefs.

Irish, German, Italian, and Polish Catholics swarmed into the immigration ports. At the end of the colonial period, Catholics numbered about 35,000, less than 1 percent of the population of the United States; by the end of the century of immigration, they represented more than 15 percent of the nation's population. The phenomenal growth of the Catholic community, through immigration and large families, understandably threatened a nation that had been colonized in an era of hatred and suspicion between Catholics and Protestants. Frequent outbreaks of anti-Catholic feeling (Billington, 1938; Higham, 1963) led the Catholic immigrants, already somewhat suspicious of the Protestant host culture, to form an imposing network of Catholic institutions, including schools, colleges, seminaries, hospitals, social welfare agencies, and ethnic mutual assistance groups. This network became one of the largest components of the emerging American nonprofit sector.

Jews had been a tiny presence in the American colonies. By the time of the Revolutionary War, the Jewish community in the new nation numbered no more than three thousand, less than one-tenth of 1 percent of the nation's population. But economic and political changes in Europe during the early and mid nineteenth century triggered a large wave of Jewish immigration; a second and much larger wave at the end of the century resulted from pogroms and economic conditions in Russia, Poland, and Eastern Europe. By the 1920s, the Jewish population in the United States stood at more than four million.

Catholics and Jews in the nineteenth and early twentieth centuries, working to help their fellow immigrants become assimilated, added to the array of nonprofit organizations in the United States. They created lodges, fraternal organizations, literary and cultural associations, young people's groups, orphanages, societies to deal with juvenile delinquency and aid prisoners, patriotic societies, historical societies, lending co-ops, job-finding and apartment-finding agencies, homes for the elderly, and burial societies. Although host-culture nonprofit organizations such as the YMCA, the American Red Cross, and Jane Addams's Hull House have received much more attention from historians, it is likely that the immigrant mutual assistance organizations cumulatively played a much more important role in responding to the needs of America's poor during the nineteenth and early twentieth centuries.

During this period, while Catholics and Jews significantly increased their American presence, Protestantism grew with the new nation and became much more internally diverse. By the end of the Revolutionary War, there were still no more than a half dozen major groups: Congregationalists, Episcopalians, Baptists, Methodists, Presbyterians, and Quakers. The nineteenth century, however, saw an explosion of Protestant diversification. By the 1920s, there were 150 Protestant denominations in the United States. The new denominations were a product of several factors: theological differences, the Civil War, new religions arriving through immigration, and occasional new revelations. This diversification and competition had enormous impact on the development of religion and religiously inspired activities in other parts of the emerging third sector.

Nowhere was the energy of American Protestantism more evident than in the developing Midwest and West. Although the Reverend Lyman Beecher, father of Harriet Beecher Stowe, had warned in his *Plea for the West* that if Protestants did not beat Catholics to the West, "all is lost," he could have rested easy; it was no contest. With a few exceptions, Catholics remained in the cities of the East and upper Midwest; Protestants took everything else by default. The West was won for Protestantism not simply by Catholic absence but by the extraordinary zeal of the Protestant clergy. One early example was Methodist bishop Francis Asbury, who traveled 300,000 miles on horseback and almost single-handedly built the Methodist communion in the United States from 5,000 members at the start of the Revolutionary War to 200,000 at the time of his death in 1816. The energetic Methodists fought the devil, demon rum, frontier conditions, and the equally energetic Baptists. Bishop Asbury advised his ministers not to spend too much time at conferences, because the Baptists would be out stealing their converts. But the Baptists' main triumph came in the Deep South.

The more establishment Presbyterians moved west slowly but did well as the West matured. In 1847, their cause was nurtured by the blood of martyrs when Presbyterian missionaries Marcus Whitman, his wife Narcissa, and twelve others were killed by Native Americans in Walla Walla in the Pacific Northwest. Narcissa Whitman and a missionary companion, Eliza Spalding, had been the first white women to cross the American continent.

To the mainline Protestant sects were added dramatically different religious groups. Idealistic utopian communes flourished during the nineteenth century. In 1825, socialist Robert Owen bought the town of New Harmony, Indiana, and created an experiment to change all of society; it lasted three years. Transcendentalist philosophy permeated the community at Brook Farm, Massachusetts. The Shakers, founded in colonial days by a self-proclaimed female messiah, Mother Ann Lee, did not believe in sexual relations yet lasted well into the twentieth century. John Humphrey Noyes started a "free love" community at Oneida, New York, which in 1837 declared its independence from the United States because of the latter's oppression of blacks and Native

Americans. One by one, these utopian communities disappeared and were largely forgotten. The Shakers were remembered primarily for their furniture, Oneida for its silverwork, and Brook Farm for its connection with the transcendentalism of Emerson and Thoreau. Nevertheless, they represented a strikingly alternative model of community life, tested and advanced America's ability to tolerate countercultural ideas and practices, and anticipated later utopian communes, such as those that developed in the 1960s and 1970s.

A much larger and longer-lasting religious experiment began in 1830 when Joseph Smith founded the Church of Jesus Christ of the Latter Day Saints—the Mormons—who under the leadership of Brigham Young journeyed west and created the state of Utah. One of Smith's many revelations mandated the return to Old Testament polygamy. Young wrote that at first he would have preferred to die, but he humbly complied with the revelation, taking thirty-five wives. Young was named governor of the Territory of Utah by President Millard Fillmore, beginning a long tradition of closeness between church and state in Utah. Mormon emphasis on family and group solidarity and tithing produced one of the most effective mutual assistance and group welfare efforts in American history. Even in periods of economic crisis, such as the Great Depression, few Mormons went without the basic necessities of life.

Mary Baker Eddy founded the Christian Science Church in 1879. Holding that "Jesus of Nazareth was the most scientific man that ever trod the globe," Eddy and her followers emphasized faith healing rather than standard medical treatments. Probably alone among American religious leaders, she had the distinction of being attacked by the *Journal of the American Medical Association*. In spite of its offensiveness to the religious and medical establishment of the nineteenth century, Christian Science became a large, highly literate, and financially successful religion. Probably no religiously inspired periodical in the history of American journalism has achieved the prominence of the nonprofit *Christian Science Monitor*.

The Seventh Day Adventists provide another nineteenth-century example of the connection between religious and health interests. Founded principally by Ellen Gould White, the Adventists, or "Millerites," first formed in response to preacher William

Miller's predictions of the Second Coming of Christ in 1843 and 1844. Christ did not come, but the new group continued, refining its beliefs and taking up interest in natural and faith-related healing. In a rare instance of the commercial value of a religious idea, two Seventh Day Adventist brothers, John and Will Kellogg, converted this health interest into the invention and marketing of a new health food, cornflakes, and started the dry cereal empire that bears their name. The Kellogg Company in turn gave birth to the W. K. Kellogg Foundation, now the nation's third-largest private foundation, with assets of more than $2 billion.

The Civil War divided white Protestant religion along regional lines; it also highlighted the religious debate about slavery. By 1831, when William Lloyd Garrison founded the pro-abolition *Liberator,* no American religious group other than the Quakers had taken a clear stand on the slavery issue. The abolition movement was an ethical-moral movement that came more out of *Uncle Tom's Cabin* than the Bible. As one abolitionist put it, antislavery organizations must be "united together to do what *the Church* OUGHT to do" (Marty, 1984, p. 245). Another called the movement an "uncanonical church" (p. 246). Abolition and the women's suffrage movement were two of the nineteenth century's great moral issues, but churches did not play a leadership role in either, and many church leaders opposed both.

Throughout the century of immigration and westward expansion, Protestantism multiplied, grew, and made its influence felt in nearly every area of American organizational life, founding colleges, social welfare agencies, and hospitals; supporting or opposing social movements from temperance to women's suffrage; and shaping the values of families, communities, and even governmental agencies, such as the new public schools.

World War I, for all its horrors, taught Americans some lessons about liberty, equality, and fraternity. Protestants of myriad sects attended the same battlefront services and fought side by side with Catholics, who constituted 15 percent of the nation's population but 25 percent of the army and 50 percent of the navy and marines. A quarter of a million Jews, many of them immigrants fresh from the pogroms of Russia and Poland, served in the war. When the soldiers got back, it was not quite to business as usual:

they had seen too clearly at Verdun and on the Marne the consequences of hate and division. But the trauma of World War I also
led the United States into isolationism, escapism, and fear of
foreigners; and a series of laws in the 1920s brought large-scale
immigration to a halt. For the next quarter century, the religions
principally survived the Roaring Twenties, the Great Depression,
and World War II and consolidated the numerical and organizational gains they had made during the growth spurt of the immigration century.

The churches did find time and energy, however, to argue
about alcohol. Following a century-old temperance movement,
supported in great part by Methodism and other mainline Protestant religions, Prohibition became part of the Constitution in 1919
and lasted until 1933. Before and during the Prohibition era,
churches battled over the bottle issue. Sometimes it looked like a
WASPs versus ethnics contest, with the "drys" led by English
Protestant middle-class, rural, and Southern religionists and the
"wets" led by Northeastern and Midwestern urban Catholic, Jewish, and Lutheran immigrants. This period also saw a major struggle between liberals and conservatives, culminating in the famous
"monkey trial" pitting former presidential candidate and fundamentalist Christian leader William Jennings Bryan against
American Civil Liberties Union lawyer Clarence Darrow in a battle
over Darwinism and literal interpretation of the Bible. Millions
listened to the proceedings on the newly invented radio. Bryan died
a few days after winning the case, unaware of the extent to which his
behavior at the trial had exposed him and his cause to ridicule. The
fundamentalist movement receded from the public eye but would
reappear with impressive strength in the 1970s and 1980s.

Religion thrived in the period following World War II. The
Depression had ended, Hitler and Hirohito had been defeated, and
America was the economic, military, and moral leader of the free
world. Americans wanted babies, suburban homes, automobiles,
television sets, and religion. Church attendance soared. Thousands
of young men and women went into the ministry. When Trappist
monk Thomas Merton wrote of his conversion from the life of
Greenwich Village to the life of Gethsemani Abbey in *The Seven
Story Mountain,* the book became a best-seller. Jews exulted in the

new state of Israel, which resolved the wrenching debate over
Zionism within the Jewish community. Billy Graham thrilled
Protestants with his Baptist eloquence, and Norman Vincent
Peale's *The Power of Positive Thinking* was read by millions.
Church building and donations to religion reached all-time highs.
But the effect was not confined to churches. Religious schools and
colleges, hospitals, nursing homes, social service agencies, and
international assistance efforts also expanded dramatically.

The 1960s brought yet another era in American religion. The
decade began with the election of the first Catholic president in
United States history. John F. Kennedy's intelligence, idealism, wit,
and good looks mesmerized many Americans. The Kennedy
Camelot, as well as the popular Pope John XXIII and the historic
Second Vatican Council, made American Catholics look better to
their neighbors than ever before and gave Catholics a new depth of
self-confidence. Protestant, Catholic, and Jewish leaders marched
together for civil rights, a nuclear test ban treaty, and other causes.
There seemed unlimited possibilities for good if all believers
labored together to seek justice and peace.

Then came Vietnam. Only the Civil War had been so
disruptive of American religious unity. Many congregations split
into pro- and antiwar groups. Sermons ended in shouting matches.
Evangelical Protestants bitterly criticized the liberal National
Council of Churches for "meddling in politics" by opposing the
war. Conservative Catholics were shocked when priest brothers
Daniel and Philip Berrigan poured blood on Secret Service files.
Rabbis, ministers, and priests were arrested for antiwar protests. A
Catholic Worker Movement peace activist burned himself to death.
Many well-intentioned church leaders did not know which way to
lead and remained immobile and invisible. Fear, anger, and
cynicism swept through the nation's youth, which only a few years
earlier had been volunteering for the Peace Corps and registering
black voters in Mississippi. "I have a dream," Martin Luther King
had cried in 1963, but King and others increasingly had to turn their
attention from the hopes of the civil rights movement to the horrors
of the Vietnam War, and by the late 1960s King's dream had turned
into a nightmare of napalm and body counts.

Hard on the heels of Vietnam came Watergate, and once

again the American value system suffered a massive shock. There had been corrupt and weak presidents, but never before had an American president resigned in disgrace, nearly all his top staff on their way to prison. The religiosity of the 1940s and 1950s and the idealism and ecumenical spirit of the early 1960s gave way to the shaken cynicism of the late 1960s and 1970s. Church attendance declined. New quasi-religious sects appeared. In California and elsewhere, human potential movements such as Werner Erhard's "est" became the new religions. Thousands of men and women left the ministry. Attendance at religious schools and colleges dropped off. Individualism, materialism, drugs, and "good sex" became more respectable pursuits than social or religious idealism. President Kennedy's inaugural words "Ask not what your country can do for you—ask what you can do for your country" stirred young hearts in 1961 but would have brought hoots of derision only ten years later.

The church connection with the civil rights movement survived the ups and downs of these years. One of the great puzzles in the history of religion is the fact that black slaves, torn from their African religious roots, devoutly adopted the religion of their European-American oppressors. That baptism offered some small protection to slaves is not an adequate explanation. In two thousand years of persecution and religious force-feeding, Jews never adopted Christianity in significant numbers. Christians under Moslem rule for centuries did not take up Islam. Native Americans never really embraced European religion. But blacks in America not only espoused Christianity but ultimately used its moral force to overthrow the oppression of white Christians. With a few exceptions, such as W. E. B. DuBois, black leaders have historically identified their struggle for liberation with that of the Jews in Egypt and their pain with that of Jesus on the cross. Black churches were the cells of the civil rights revolution, black ministers its cell leaders. Martin Luther King, Jr., a minister and the son of a minister, is only one of many examples. However great the influence of Tolstoy and Gandhi on King's message, the greatest influence was always the Bible.

The civil rights movement began in the catharsis of slavery and liberation, as Judaism had taken shape in liberation from

Egyptian and Babylonian slavery. Black Christianity's quest for
meaning was born of suffering, death, and resurrection. It redefined
God, church, salvation, sin, and grace not through exegesis but
through experience. But the movement had effects far beyond
religion and the black community. Civil rights led to religious and
moral questions on a broader scale. King, in spite of intense
criticism, spoke out not only on civil rights but also on Vietnam
and the whole issue of peace and war. The civil rights movement
helped reactivate the women's movement just as abolition had
helped create the nineteenth-century women's suffrage effort:
women who fought for the liberation of blacks then turned to the
task of their own liberation. All the advocacy movements of the
1970s and 1980s—the United Farm Workers movement, the environmental movement, the peace movement—owed their origin in some
way to the civil rights movement, which owed its origin to black
Christianity.

The late 1970s and the 1980s saw a rebirth of religious
fundamentalism, without the monkey trials or bumbling Bryans.
Fundamentalists had learned communications skills and were masters of the broadcast and print media. The marriage of old-time
religion and modern media technology may have been an improba-
ble one, but it worked extraordinarily well. Jerry Falwell, a Virginia
minister with a magnetic smile and an ambitious vision of religion
in politics, formed the Moral Majority and through highly successful fundraising and political organizing helped elect Ronald
Reagan and dozens of other conservative politicians. There were no
apologies for fundamentalist involvement with politics. If the left
can have the Reverend Jesse Jackson, it was argued, why can't the
right have the Reverend Jerry Falwell? Indeed, there was ample
historical precedent for the involvement of churches and religious
leaders in the political process. Still, the close connection of religion
and politics made many Americans nervous.

The religious history of the last three decades was also
marked by a return to utopian and sometimes bizarre religious
experiments not unlike some of the religious fringe movements of
the mid nineteenth century. A flurry of religious cults appeared,
some mild and peaceful communes and some, such as Jonestown,
paranoid and violent groups. Satanic cults and witchcraft, one of

the oldest forms of religious expression, reappeared on the fringes of American society. The Unification Church and its "Moonies," disciples of the Korean Sun Myung Moon, appeared with their fixed smiles, roses, and collection cups and became a familiar scene at airports. Hare Krishna devotees with shaved heads and safron-yellow robes chanted their way into America's consciousness.

But the churches and synagogues also took leadership roles in the nuclear arms control effort, the sanctuary movement and other immigration issues, and the struggle with problems such as AIDs, drug abuse, and homelessness. The issues and strategies had changed since Franciscan friars rose to condemn the enslavement of Native Americans nearly five centuries earlier, but the impact of religion on society had not.

Policy Issues

The relationship between religion and politics is an age-old issue that has not receded in importance. Church leaders were involved on both sides of the Revolutionary and Civil Wars. The temperance movement saw a mix of religious and legislative activities over a period of 150 years. The last 20 years have seen extensive religious involvement in such issues as civil rights, the Vietnam War, U.S. policy in Central America, nuclear arms control, abortion, and prayer in public schools. The one constant is that conservatives like it when churches back conservative positions and liberals like it when churches back liberal positions. Liberals praise Catholic bishops for opposing the nuclear arms race and condemn the same bishops for opposing abortion. Conservatives are pleased when ministers campaign for prayer in public schools and are upset when ministers campaign against American policy in Nicaragua. Liberals and conservatives who say that religion should stay completely out of politics are silent when asked whether they would have given the same advice to German churches during the rise of Hitler.

Tension between church and state is unavoidable outside a theocracy, since all religions hold that there can be immoral laws and that the state can never be the ultimate arbiter of individual or social conscience. The perennial question is what the individual believer and the religious group may or must do when confronted by a law or policy perceived to be deeply immoral. Most Americans today would probably hold that the Nazi holocaust was unspeakably, totally evil and that any form of resistance to this policy was morally justified. Should the same reasoning be applied by Americans who believe that abortion or nuclear weapons constitute today's Auschwitz? What political issues are also moral issues, and how is this to be decided, and by whom? Was Prohibition really a moral issue, as so many religious leaders at that time believed? Churches have in recent years debated the retention of the Panama Canal and the policies of the International Monetary Fund; are these therefore moral or religious issues?

A related policy question facing not only churches but many other nonprofit organizations is the proper balance between the interests of members and the needs of society. Nonprofit hospitals and nursing homes are sometimes accused of avoiding the poor, private schools of favoring students of a particular religious or social group, private colleges and universities of skimming off the academic elite, and church-sponsored international assistance agencies of mixing relief with religion. Prescinding from the accuracy of such charges, it is clear that many nonprofit organizations face conflicting client demands, some of which challenge their very mission. Part of the natural tension within organized religion comes from the competing demands of sacramental and social concerns. Countercultural religious movements such as the Great Awakening of the early eighteenth century and today's pentecostalism, charismatic healing, and Eastern spirituality make it clear that the established religions are not always successful in rendering to God the things that are God's. At the same time, American religions have often felt the need to become more involved in social issues. In recent decades, racial prejudice, Third World poverty, dictatorships of the right and left, and nuclear proliferation have created new urgency in justice and peace efforts by religious groups. How to balance these two impulses is a major policy question faced by organized religion but also one faced by other parts of the nonprofit sector: the conflict that can exist between the interests of members and supporters (including funders) and the needs of a world in distress. Indifference to human needs has always been unacceptable to the great world religions, yet so has indifference to the call to prayer and the quest for the Other. American religion, so character-istically practical and down-to-earth, has the challenge of nourish-ing and balancing both tendencies if it is to be true to itself and helpful to society. As so often in the history of the third sector in America, this challenge facing religion is symptomatic of a larger challenge facing the entire nonprofit sector.

One of the most important policy issues facing the third sector and American society is the role of women, particularly the role of women in professional and leadership positions. Women constitute two-thirds of all nonprofit employees as compared with 45 percent of the total workforce (Hodgkinson and Weitzman, 1988a, p. 2). The women's liberation movements of both the nineteenth and the twentieth centuries originated within the sector, and women have played major leadership roles in nonprofit health care, education, social service, and advocacy movements. Yet the position of women within the sector is still highly ambiguous. Nowhere is this clearer than in organized religion. With a few exceptions, religious leadership roles in major world religions have been limited to men. Judaism, Christianity, Islam, Buddhism, Hinduism, Confucianism, and the state religions of Egypt, Persia, Greece, and Rome differed in many respects but all barred women from leadership positions.

American religious history, like world religious history, is male-dominated, with a few exceptions. Anne Hutchinson un-settled the Puritans of Boston by her bold preaching. Mary Baker Eddy founded the Christian Science church. Ellen Gould White was the primary founder of the Seventh Day Adventist faith. Mother Ann Lee established the Shakers. Mother Elizabeth Seton, a widow with five children, founded an order of Catholic nuns and became the first American-born canonized saint. Protestant missionaries Narcissa Whitman and Eliza Spalding were the first white women to cross the continent. More recently, American Episcopalians voted in 1976 to admit women to ordination, and by 1988 there were more than 1,200 women priests and one bishop, Barbara C. Harris. In 1988, there were about 130 women rabbis in American Conservative and Reform Judaism. Some Pentecostal churches in the last twenty-five years have taken a pioneering role in the ordination of women. The Catholic church continues to bar women from ordination although nuns often hold positions of authority, such as college president, hospital administrator, and school principal, in institutions staffed by their orders, as well as positions such as school superintendent, chancellor, or director of Catholic Charities in dioceses. But these are isolated, exceptional cases. American religious leadership for five centuries has been overwhelmingly male, and attempts to deviate from this tradition have generally been met with stern disapproval from the male elders.

Most Americans believe that women and men should have equal political, economic, and social opportunities; however many exceptions there are to the realization of this norm, it has at least become the norm. This is not so in organized religion. It is questionable how long religion can hold out against what seems to be an irreversible trend in modern Western nations toward the recognition of equality for men and women. Historically, religion has not been successful in resisting broad social trends. A century and a half ago, churches could openly or quietly support slavery, and many did; no church could take this position today and survive. Similarly, marriage and sexual practices have greatly changed as a result of the increased longevity of women and men, modern communications and mobility, and changes in mores. Nearly all major religions have subsequently modified their teachings on sex and marriage, and even when the official position remains traditional (for example, the Catholic position on birth control), the attitudes and practices of church members are often quite different. The exclusion of women from leadership positions is a major policy issue facing American religion, the nonprofit sector, and the society as a whole.

PRIVATE EDUCATION AND RESEARCH
Quest for Ideas and Ideals

Even with free public education available to everyone, 8.5 million American students attend private educational institutions, paying from $500 a year at some religious elementary schools to nearly $20,000 a year at prestige private universities. That these schools and colleges attract so many customers at this price when there are free alternatives is striking evidence of the power and persistence of the private education idea.

Scope and Impact

Private education and research have had a major impact on American society. Private universities such as Harvard, MIT, Stanford, and Johns Hopkins produce much of the nation's basic and applied research and many of the nation's leaders. Private liberal arts colleges such as Swarthmore, Williams, Carleton, and Reed provide some of the country's best undergraduate education. Inner-city Catholic schools give thousands of black and Hispanic students the skills necessary to escape from the ghetto. Alternative schools create some of the most experimental forms of American education.

Private education is one of the most controversial parts of the nonprofit sector. When nineteenth-century Catholic leaders refused to accept the vaguely Protestant public schools, middle America was outraged. In our fiercely "common man" culture, elite prep schools such as Exeter and Andover are regarded with some suspicion.

43

When, after a hundred years of separate and unequal educational opportunity, public schools in the South were ordered to desegregate and public schools in the North were ordered to bus their way out of de facto segregation, private schools somehow became the problem, and television commentators spoke ominously of "white flight." Proposals for government aid to private schools have been castigated as assaults on the foundations of American democracy, in spite of the fact that the first three centuries of American education and the current policies of all other Western democracies contain many examples of such aid. And when sociologist James Coleman, whose massive *Equality of Educational Opportunity* study (Coleman and others, 1966) provided much of the rationale for busing in the 1960s and 1970s, published the "second Coleman report" in the 1980s saying not only that private schools were doing a better job than public schools but also that Catholic schools were more like Horace Mann's "common school ideal" than were modern public schools (Coleman, Hoffer, and Kilgore, 1982, pp. 185, 196–197), some public school advocates were nearly apoplectic. Private education in America has had its share of success and failure and more than its share of controversy.

Elementary and Secondary Education. The Center for Education Statistics of the U.S. Department of Education estimated that there were 5.7 million private school students in fall 1987, 12.4 percent of the nation's K-12 enrollment (National Center for Education Statistics, 1988, p. 9). An example of the pitiful government data collection on the nonprofit sector is the fact that the U.S. Census Bureau estimated 1983–84 private school attendance to be 4,868,000, 15 percent lower than the Department of Education's 1983–84 figure (Williams, 1986, p. 188). The Department of Education report notes gently, "The two national data sources—Center for [Education] Statistics and Bureau of the Census—on private school enrollment have not agreed upon the number and proportion of private school students in recent years" (p. 186). There are about 30,000 private elementary and secondary schools in the United States. Table 4 shows the distribution of private school enrollment in 1982-83.

About 90 percent of private school students attend religious schools, and two-thirds of the religious school students attend

Table 4. Private Elementary and Secondary Schools
and Students, 1982-83.

	Number of Schools	Number of Students
Roman Catholic	9,432	3,027,317
Evangelical	10,741	912,985
Independent[a]	873	336,797
Lutheran	2,480	280,539
Jewish	572	100,202
Seventh Day Adventist	1.324	81,507
Episcopal	527	78,214
Calvinist	382	74,541
Special education	2,600	298,999
Montessori	640	50,000
Other	526	63,945
TOTAL	30,097	5,305,046

[a]Members of National Association of Independent Schools.
Source: Cooper, 1988, p. 33.

Catholic schools. While Catholic school enrollment declined more than 40 percent from its peak of 5,574,000 in 1965-66 to the mid 1980s, all other segments of private education increased during the same period (Cooper, 1988, p. 33), with the result that private education's 1987 "market share" of 12.4 percent of total K-12 school enrollment was only slightly below its 13 percent share in the mid 1960s. The Census Bureau estimated that private education's 1985 market share of 10.9 percent was exactly the same as its market share in 1970 (Williams, 1986, p. 188).

Parents send their children to private schools for a variety of reasons, but the three most frequently mentioned are quality education, religious and moral formation, and an orderly and safe school atmosphere (Kraushaar, 1972; Greeley and Rossi, 1966; Greeley, McCready, and McCourt, 1976; Gratiot, 1979); a 1981 survey found the same pattern of answers in British Columbia (Erickson, 1986, p. 94). Families that send their children to religious schools tend, not surprisingly, to be more religiously active than families that do not (Greeley and Rossi, 1966; Greeley, McCready, and McCourt, 1976). Aside from the obvious consequences of the religious variable—students in Jewish schools tend to be Jewish,

and so forth—private school students are somewhat more likely
than public school students to come from higher-income families
and to be white (Coleman, Hoffer, and Kilgore, 1982; Catterall,
1988). The U.S. Department of Education summarized its findings
on the racial-ethnic composition of private schools: "Hispanic
children are as likely as whites to attend private schools, when
family income is taken into account. However, black children
generally are less likely to attend private schools than white
children, even when family income is taken into account" (Williams, 1986, p. 186). There were 550,000 employees of private elementary and secondary schools in 1984, 70 percent of whom were
women and 16 percent of whom were black or Hispanic (Hodgkinson and Weitzman, 1986, p. 126). The National Center for Education Statistics (1988, p. 9) estimated that there were 600,000 private
school employees in fall 1987.

Expenditures for private elementary and secondary education
in 1984 were $16.6 billion (Hodgkinson and Weitzman, 1986, p.
129). In virtually all private schools, tuition is the primary source of
revenue. Church-related schools often receive significant subsidies
from the sponsoring religious institution. A few independent and
other schools have large endowments. Nearly all private schools
engage in several forms of fundraising. Government support is
minimal to nonexistent and usually includes only marginal aid,
such as school lunch programs, bus transportation, library books,
remedial reading programs, and other specialized educational
services. More substantive forms of aid have consistently been
declared unconstitutional (Vitullo-Martin and Cooper, 1987).

Using unpublished IRS data, Hodgkinson and Weitzman
(1986, p. 43) estimated the 1982 assets of private elementary and secondary schools as $73.5 billion. Such figures, however, must be inter-
preted with caution. The physical assets of religious schools are often
part of the property, buildings, and equipment of the religious
congregations sponsoring the schools, with attendant difficulties in
allocating these assets to religion or private education.

Private schools play a variety of roles in American society.
They educate nearly six million students a year. The purely
financial contribution of this can be estimated by imagining that all
these students were in public schools at the 1987–88 per-student cost

of $4,500: the additional taxpayer burden would be more than $25 billion. Private schools emphasize values—such as morality, religious faith, discipline, responsibility, and care for others—that are considered important by the society. Private schools educate hundreds of thousands of low-income and minority students every year, and recent research suggests that private schools may be particularly effective with such students (Coleman, Hoffer, and Kilgore, 1982; Greeley, 1982; Cibulka, O'Brien, and Zewe, 1982). Private schools are widely perceived as providing a more orderly atmosphere for learning than public schools. Many Americans feel that private schools offer healthy competition to public schools. Some believe that private schools have more freedom to adopt new programs and practices and therefore provide a useful testing ground for educational ideas.

The classic criticism of private education is that it is divisive and separatist. Horace Mann and other proponents of American public education argued that the common schools were essential to bring together students of all backgrounds and to encourage democratic attitudes and behavior. Following this logic, private schools were viewed as undemocratic and even segregationist. Is this the case?

By definition, most private schools are "segregated" along religious lines, but that may be no more meaningful than to say that churches are "segregated" along religious lines, ethnic groups are "segregated" along ethnic lines, and millions of American families are "segregated" along both religious and ethnic lines. The "religious segregation" argument assumes that it is socially unhealthy for groups to have a particular religious identification, which is at least debatable and certainly goes far beyond any federal or state constitutional provision or public policy. There is some evidence to the contrary; for instance, Greeley and Rossi (1966, pp. 114-137) found that Catholic school graduates were more likely than Catholics who attended public schools to be socially well integrated as adults.

Many public and private schools are socioeconomically "segregated" in the sense of serving mostly higher- or lower-income students rather than a mixed clientele. In public education, school socioeconomic segregation is largely the result of residential socioeconomic segregation—school districts in affluent suburbs have higher-income residents and students; schools in poverty-stricken urban and rural areas have lower-income residents and students. In private education, socioeconomic segregation results from both geographic factors and tuition charges. The fact that private schools receive no significant government aid and therefore must charge tuition makes it unsurprising that private school students come from somewhat higher-income groups than do public school students. What is surprising is that the correlation of family income and private school attendance is not greater than it is. The stereotypical elite, upper-class private school represents a statistically small part of American private education, comparable to the proportion of highly affluent school districts within public education. The great majority of American private schools are religious schools serving a predominantly middle-class clientele. Coleman, Hoffer, and Kilgore (1982) argued on the basis of their research that private high schools are actually more socioeconomically integrated than public high schools. While in all probability a small percentage of private schools both historically and currently have intended to educate only or primarily upper-class students, family income differences between private and public schools seem to result primarily from the fact that private schools have to charge tuition while public schools do not.

Are private schools racially segregated? In their study of public, private, and Catholic high schools, Coleman and his colleagues found that the proportion of Hispanics and the Hispanic-white mix were about the same in public and private schools. Their conclusions about the black-white mix were more startling: "The results for black-white segregation are more complex. There is a substantially smaller proportion of blacks in the private sector than in the public sector. . . . But information on the internal segregation between blacks and whites tells a different story: The public sector has a substantially higher degree of segregation than the private sector (or either of its two components [Catholic and other private] separately)" (Coleman, Hoffer, and Kilgore, 1982, p. 36).

Coleman's conclusion that public high schools had "a substantially higher degree of [internal] segregation" than private or Catholic high schools was intensely controversial and still generates much debate (see, for instance, the November 1981 issue of the *Harvard Educational Review;* the April/July 1982 and October 1983 issues of *Sociology of Education;* and Haertel, James, and Levin, 1987). While evaluating or even summarizing the debate is beyond the scope of this chapter, the Coleman report underlines the fact that "private school segregation" is far from self-evident.

Higher Education. There were an estimated 2,838,000 students in 1,873 private colleges and universities in the United States in fall 1987 (National Center for Education Statistics, 1988, pp. 9, 182). These institutions enroll about 23 percent of all postsecondary education students, down from 50 percent in the early 1950s. This dramatic change is due not to a numerical decline in enrollment in private higher education, which actually doubled during this period, but rather to the expansion of enrollment in public higher education. Private institutions in 1985–86, however, still awarded 33 percent of all baccalaureate degrees, 41 percent of all Masters degrees, and 36 percent of all doctoral degrees (National Center for Education Statistics, 1988, p. 213).

Private higher education is far from homogeneous. General types include large research universities, such as Yale, Columbia, Chicago, and Cal Tech; liberal arts colleges, such as Wellesley, Oberlin, Smith, and Amherst; large religious "commuter" institutions, such as Fordham and Marquette; other religious colleges and universities, including seminaries and divinity schools; secular commuter institutions, such as Boston University, New York University, Adelphi University, and the University of Southern California; two-year colleges; and professional and special schools, such as the Juilliard School and the New England Conservatory of Music.

Private colleges and universities in the United States had current-fund revenues of $35.4 billion in 1985–86 (National Center for Education Statistics, 1988, p. 260). Tuition and fees accounted for 38.6 percent of the total; government contributed 19 percent (of which 84 percent came from federal grants and contracts); private gifts, grants, and contracts were 9.3 percent; endowment contributed 5.3 percent; and sales, services, and other revenue accounted for 27.7

percent. Most federal grants and contracts go to a small number of major research universities: in fiscal year 1987, 84 percent of all federal research and development funds went to one hundred institutions (Fact-File, 1988, p. A19). The typical private college or university is far more tuition-dependent than the 38.6 percent figure suggests. In 1985–86, American private higher education had endowments valued at $41.2 billion and physical plants valued at $39.7 billion (National Center for Education Statistics, 1988, p. 281).

Private higher education employed 770,200 people in 1984, of whom 49 percent were women and 12 percent were black or Hispanic (Hodgkinson and Weitzman, 1986, p. 126).

Private higher education may well be the most influential part of the entire nonprofit sector. The quantity and quality of research produced by the top-ranked private research universities would alone secure for private education a place among the most influential institutions in American society. Even more visible are the thousands of national, state, and local leaders who are products of private institutions. Harvard alone has graduated six American presidents—John Adams, John Quincy Adams, Rutherford B. Hayes, Theodore Roosevelt, Franklin Delano Roosevelt, and John F. Kennedy—and its alumni have often held key positions in American business, education, politics, and professions.

Private higher education has provided much of the best teaching and research in American colleges and universities. In the recent five-volume *Assessment of Research-Doctorate Programs in the United States* (Jones, Lindzey, and Coggeshall, 1982), six of the seven universities most highly rated in overall strength are private: Stanford, Harvard, Yale, MIT, Princeton, and the University of Chicago. (The top-ranked is the University of California, Berkeley.) (Webster, 1983, p. 18). Also, aggregating the results of seven major quality ratings covering the period from 1925 to 1982, Webster (p. 23) found that seven of the ten consistently top-ranked research universities were private: Chicago, Harvard, Columbia, Yale, Princeton, Johns Hopkins, and Cornell. In a less scientific but widely read study ("America's Best Colleges," 1987, pp. 53, 55), a national survey of college presidents who were asked to rank the best undergraduate institutions in the country, 85 percent of the top choices were private. While there is no fully satisfactory way to evaluate graduate education and research, much less undergraduate education, such rankings point to the strong leadership role played by private colleges and universities.

Private higher education provides a wide range of choices to American students: black colleges, women's colleges, religious colleges, specialized schools such as Juilliard, progressive education institutions such as Bennington and Sarah Lawrence, "Great Books" colleges such as St. John's, freestanding professional schools, and innovative institutions such as Adelphi, which among other programs offers M.B.A. courses early in the morning on Long Island commuter trains.

Private higher education plays a vital role in the economy of the United States, not only by its sizable direct economic impact but also by educating and training the people who make the economy more productive through better management methods, increased scientific and technological knowledge, and critical and creative thinking skills. Further, private colleges and universities are frequently engaged in productive partnerships with business. Private universities have been extensively involved in such products as computer software, genetic engineering, and the development of the Chicago futures market. Private university professors and researchers are often consultants to the business world. The university-industry linkage has become so productive that most major research universities have developed patenting policies—and some have even developed private companies—to capitalize on the commercial value of their research.

The economy of the United States and other modern nations is increasingly based on information-related productivity as distinguished from traditional farming, mining, and manufacturing productivity. This new "information economy," in turn, demands an educated work force; so educational institutions play an increasingly important and direct role in economic productivity. Formal education and the economic structure of a society are always interactive. Formal education did not appear until the economic and bureaucratic needs of societies such as Egypt, Mesopotamia, Persia, Greece, and China demanded it. The growth of formal education in America has been directly related to economic conditions: the relative absence of schooling in colonial times was a direct reflection of the colonies' largely home-based and agricultural economic system; the rise of common schools and bureaucratic systems of education in the nineteenth century was directly related to the changes brought about by the Industrial Revolution, immigration, and urbanization (Katz, 1971; Callahan, 1962); and the land-grant colleges and the development of state college and university systems were directly related to the rapidly developing economy of the Midwest and West. Today's information and service economy has become even more dependent on formal education. Quality education and research are economically more important today than they were one or two hundred years ago. The strong role that private institutions currently play in education and research suggests that their future role may be even stronger.

The line between public and private education is more blurred at the postsecondary level than at the elementary-secondary level (Bozeman, 1987; Levy, 1986, especially chap. 7). Johns Hopkins University, a private institution, receives $500 million a year from the federal government in research and development funds. Many private colleges and universities, especially those in states with tuition grant programs, are indirectly but significantly funded by government sources. In its relationship to and support by government, private higher education is somewhat more like the nonprofit health and social service areas, while private elementary and secondary education is somewhat more like religion, arts and culture, and advocacy organizations. Nevertheless, most private institutions of higher education are keenly aware of their nongovernmental status and of the funding and decision-making differences between themselves and public institutions.

Research Institutes. Although much of the nation's basic and applied research takes place within higher education, government, business, and professional associations, some of it takes place within a small but influential group of nonprofit scientific research and policy analysis organizations. These include "think tanks" such as the Brookings Institution, the Rand Corporation, the Urban Institute, the Hudson Institute, the American Enterprise Institute, the Heritage Foundation, the Institute for Policy Studies, and the Cato Institute. Also part of this world are scientific research agencies such as the National Opinion Research Center, loosely affiliated with the University of Chicago, and the L. S. B. Leakey Foundation, an anthropological research organization heavily supported by billionaire Gordon Getty, as well as organizations that bring scientific knowledge to the public, such as National Geographic, a one-hundred-year-old nonprofit organization whose familiar yellow-covered magazine with spectacular color photographs is sent to 10.5 million subscriber-members and whose television documentaries are watched by 30 million people a month.

In 1982, there were 1,946 "noncommercial educational, scientific, and research organizations" with 50,000 employees and revenues of $2.9 billion (National Center for Charitable Statistics, 1985, p. 5). These nonprofit research organizations, in spite of relatively small budgets, often have considerable influence on public policy, science, and popular education. The Brookings Institution, for instance, had a 1987 budget of only $15 million and the American Enterprise Institute only $12 million, yet their studies have shaped multibillion-dollar government programs. These institutes also provide a useful "gray area" between government, business, and education, facilitating the study of issues that the other organizations cannot deal with effectively for political or bureaucratic reasons.

Historical Development

It is misleading to speak of colonial "public education" or "private education," since, as Harvard historian Bernard Bailyn has said, "The modern conception of public education, the very idea of a clean line of separation between 'private' and 'public,' was unknown before the end of the eighteenth century" (Bailyn, 1960, p. 11; see also Cremin, 1970). The funding, operation, and control of colonial education came from a mix of governmental and private sources. Formal education in Virginia began in 1635 when Benjamin Syms, a wealthy planter, left two hundred acres of land and eight cows to endow a school. A few years later, Virginia surgeon Thomas Eaton donated five hundred acres of land, twenty hogs, twelve cows, two bulls, and two slaves to endow another school. In 1635, the town fathers of Boston created a Latin "grammar" school (roughly equivalent to our secondary school), which was to become famous as "Boston Latin." In 1636, the Massachusetts General Court appropriated £400 for "a schoale or colledge," and when Charlestown cattleman-minister John Harvard died two years later at age thirty, he left £800 and four hundred books to the college, which thereupon was named after him.

The concept of a privately supported institution serving a public purpose and the mix of private and public resources were familiar to the colonists from English law and custom. To the colonists, fearful that this strange, raw, and exciting new land would draw their children away from English civility and piety, the legal form of the enterprise was much less important than what it could do for their children. Further, formal education was much less widespread in America and England during the seventeenth and eighteenth centuries than it would be in the nineteenth and twentieth centuries. The powerful influence of family, church, apprenticeship system, and community provided considerable informal education, including all the skills and knowledge most people of that time needed for economic and social well-being. There was a great variety of formal education—from the "dame schools" conducted in widows' kitchens in Massachusetts to the "old-field schools" held on exhausted tobacco fields in Virginia— but schooling in colonial days was far more limited and less structured than it would later become. As Kraushaar (1976, p. 15) notes, "By the end of the colonial period, the school as an institution was firmly rooted on the American continent. But nothing resembling the modern concept of secular, free, compulsory, universal education had as yet appeared. . . . The colonial schools were conceived to be supplemental to the informal education that the child received in the home, in church, on the farm, in the shop, in commerce, in village life, and by reading and self-study."

The history of Harvard College illustrates the murkiness of the public-private issue in the seventeenth and eighteenth centuries. Following the initial government grant and private gift, the college was supported by legislative appropriations, private donations, and student fees. Harvard received its official charter from the Massachusetts General Court in 1650. The charter mandated that government officials sit on the Harvard board. Harvard received appropriations from the Massachusetts General Court on at least one hundred occasions between 1636 and 1789, and it almost surely could not have survived the colonial period without this assistance. Yet in the mid nineteenth century, following a long series of struggles with the commonwealth over money and control, Harvard terminated its relationship with the state government and declared that by virtue of its 1650 charter it was and had always been a private, not a governmental agency.

The growth of denominationalism played an important role in the development of formal education in the colonies. The English colonists had come from a country that essentially had two universities, Oxford and Cambridge, but religious and other conditions soon established a different pattern in America. The founding of institutions such as Harvard (Puritans), William and Mary (Anglicans), Yale (Congregationalists), Columbia (Anglicans), Princeton (Presbyterians), and Brown (Baptists) anticipated the much larger diversification of higher education along religious lines that took place in the nineteenth century.

The division of American education into "public" and "private" is a product of the nineteenth century. In 1819, in *Dartmouth College* v. *Woodward*, the U.S. Supreme Court decreed that government could not intervene at will in the affairs of private charitable corporations: though a creation of the state of New Hampshire, Dartmouth was not simply a department of the state government, it was a separate and distinct entity. The case for the college was argued by a then unknown lawyer named Daniel Webster (Dartmouth class of 1801), who closed his five-hour presentation before the Court with this famous passage:

This, sir, is my case. It is the case, not merely of that humble institution, it is the case of every college in the land. It is more. It is the case of every eleemosynary institution throughout our country . . . the case of every man who has property of which he may be stripped—for the question is simply this: Shall our state legislature be allowed to take that which is not their own, to turn it from its original use, and apply it to such ends or purposes as they, in their discretion shall see fit? Sir, you may destroy this little institution . . . but if you do . . . you must extinguish, one after another, all those great lights of science, which, for more than a century, have thrown their radiance over the land! It is, sir, as I have said, a small college, and yet there are those that love it [Rudolf, 1962, pp. 209–210].

Rudolf (1962, p. 210) has written, "For higher education in America, the Dartmouth College decision put on the way toward clarification the distinction between private and public institutions, a distinction that had not been made nor required a half century before." But the Dartmouth College decision was of great importance in clarifying the private nature of not only colleges but also, as Webster said, "every eleemosynary institution throughout our country." The separate legal position of private nonprofit corporations was further strengthened by the Court's *Girard Will* decision of 1844, which protected a $7 million bequest from merchant Stephen Girard for a college for orphans in Philadelphia. As Hall (1987, p. 6) concludes, "Thus, after 1844, private charitable corporations were securely established under federal law, although this did not affect the actions of states like Virginia and New York, which continued to limit their activities."

Meanwhile, the beginning of mass immigration, the sudden growth of cities, industrialization, and bewildering religious and ethnic diversity led cities and states to develop a variety of government agencies to meet new social needs. One of these agencies was the "common school." The diversity and informality of colonial education were wholly inadequate to meet the new urban society's needs, not the least of which was Americanization of the immigrant and corralling of potential young hooligans. Reformers such as Horace Mann, a former temperance activist and Massachusetts state legislator, Samuel Gridley Howe, founder of the first American school for the blind, and Calvin Stowe, husband of *Uncle Tom's Cabin* author Harriet Beecher Stowe, turned their Yankee zeal to the problem of education. Henceforth the well-being of America was to be based on free, nonsectarian, English-speaking, King James Bible–reading common schools.

The common school revolution was less one of philosophy than one of organization, consolidation, expansion, and exclusion.

There had long been government support of schools, and there had long been free schools. But now individual public schools and many denominational schools were absorbed by the common school movement, split into grades following the Prussian model of education that Mann admired so much, and organized into public school *systems*. In the aftermath of this highly successful administrative revolution, schools that did not go along found themselves, somewhat to their surprise, classified as "private" or "parochial," neither of which adjectives was meant as a compliment.

Although Mann himself was a deeply dedicated politician-reformer, clearly committed to the quality and universal accessibility of education, his efforts were attacked by immigrants who suspected that the common school was a devious strategy to erase their ethnic and religious heritage. The Irish and other immigrant groups had had precisely this experience with government schools in their homelands. The most vehement protest came from the Catholic community, which set up its own alternative school system (Cross, 1965; Lannie, 1968; Tyack, 1974). Although the official goal of "every Catholic child in a Catholic school" was never reached, Catholic elementary and secondary schools became the largest segment of private education in the United States.

Many of the grammar schools and academies founded in the seventeenth, eighteenth, and nineteenth centuries became public high schools, some became colleges, and still others became private high schools. The latter included prestigious prep schools such as Exeter, Andover, and Choate for young men and the Emma Willard School, the Hartford Female Seminary, and the Young Ladies Academy at Philadelphia for young women. Through their graduates, these schools have had an influence on American society and education far out of proportion to their numbers.

By the time of the Revolution, there were only eight colleges in the colonies: Harvard, William and Mary, Yale, Princeton, Columbia, the University of Pennsylvania, Brown, and Rutgers. The number of secondary institutions—the old grammar schools and the newer academies—was not much higher. By 1855, only seventy-five years later, there were 6,185 academies and 239 colleges, not counting 500 other colleges that had opened but failed. Most of these new schools and colleges were denominational, and most promptly demanded the traditional state support for their efforts. "But with the unleashing of hundreds of little colleges, the state governments were financially and emotionally in no position to support them all. Sectarianism, even before the end of the colonial period, had cut off some state support. In the years after 1820 the sectarian spawning of colleges and the tendency of many institutions to draw students from beyond state boundaries had the effect of diminishing the partnership of state and college, thus emphasizing the private rather than the public nature of the colleges" (Rudolf, 1962, p. 187).

"College mania" was rampant during the nineteenth century. In 1880, Columbia University president Frederick A. P. Barnard caustically remarked that England, with a population of twenty-three million, seemed to be faring well with four universities, while Ohio, with a population of three million, had thirty-seven institutions of higher learning. Rudolf (1962, pp. 48–49) comments, "College-founding in the nineteenth century was undertaken in the same spirit as canal-building, cotton-ginning, farming, and gold-mining. . . . All were touched by the American faith in tomorrow, in the unquestionable capacity of Americans to achieve a better world. In the founding of colleges, reason could not combat the romantic belief in endless progress." Most of the new colleges were denominational and small, and many lasted only a few years. In the newer Midwest and West, public higher education became dominant, while in the older East, private institutions remained the leaders, beginning a pattern of relative strength that remains even today: most of the top-ranked public universities— Berkeley, UCLA, Michigan, Wisconsin, Illinois, Minnesota, Washington, Indiana—are in the Midwest and West, while most of the top-ranked private universities—Harvard, Yale, Princeton, MIT, Columbia, Cornell, Carnegie-Mellon, Johns Hopkins, Rockefeller, Brown—are in the East.

A few women and blacks began to be admitted to colleges and universities during this period. In 1828, a student at Bowdoin College and a student at Ohio University became the first black college graduates. In 1837, Oberlin enrolled four women students and thus was the first American college to become coeducational. The same year, Mount Holyoke Seminary, the first American college for women, opened. As the century went on, many more women's colleges were founded, among them Vassar (1865), Smith (1875), Wellesley (1875), Bryn Mawr (1888), Trinity (1900), and the "sister colleges," such as Sophie Newcomb (Tulane) (1886), Barnard (Columbia) (1889), Pembroke (Brown) (1891), and Radcliffe (Harvard) (1893). All of these were private institutions. The most rapid development of coeducation and equal higher education opportunities for women, however, took place in the new public land-grant colleges and state universities of the Midwest and West, partly because of the greater economic and social independence of women in those areas, partly because of the absence of long traditions of male-only education.

In 1876, Johns Hopkins University opened in Baltimore, the beneficiary of the millions its namesake had made from his Baltimore and Ohio Railroad. Modeled on the German universities and dedicated to scholarly research, Johns Hopkins had a profound effect on the subsequent development of American higher education. Research-oriented graduate schools came to dominate many public and private universities. In a parallel development, private institutions such as the Massachusetts Institute of Technology (1865) and the Rensselaer Polytechnic Institute (1884) created higher education models particularly adapted to the new age of science and technology.

The growth of capitalism in the nineteenth century had a major impact on the development of private higher education. Besides the endowment that created Johns Hopkins, the University of Chicago was the beneficiary of oil king John D. Rockefeller's millions, and Andrew Carnegie's steel interests and Andrew Mellon's aluminum and oil businesses generated the funds for the institutions that would in 1967 combine as Carnegie-Mellon University. Another Carnegie philanthropy, the Carnegie Commission on Higher Education, developed a nationwide pension plan for college professors now known as the Teachers Insurance and Annuity Association and the College Retirement Equities Fund (TIAA-CREF), which with $63 billion in assets is the largest nonprofit financial institution in the country. Leland Stanford, another railroad baron, left the greater portion of his estate to establish Leland Stanford, Jr., University, in memory of his son. In

1867, banker George Peabody founded the Peabody Education Fund to support higher education for blacks, a cause continued by Julius Rosenwald, the creator of Sears Roebuck. Less imposing business figures could also have memorable effects, as Poughkeepsie brewer Matthew Vassar did when he donated a million dollars to launch Vassar College.

The nineteenth century had seen the emergence of a sharp public-private distinction in education, the great expansion of both private and public education at all levels, and the development of new forms of education such as the modern research university, scientific and technical institutions, and colleges for women. Many of the small private institutions founded during the college mania of the early and mid nineteenth century were closed or consolidated because of financial pressures, competition from the rapidly proliferating state higher education system, and changes in religious and social attitudes. Meanwhile, the common school came to dominate elementary and secondary education, the only large alternative being the Catholic parochial school system.

During the twentieth century, American higher education institutions continued to mature and started to take their place among the leading universities of the world. Economically and militarily, the United States had become the most powerful nation in the world by the end of World War I, but intellectually and culturally it was still subservient to its English and European ancestors. That relationship changed dramatically as the century went on, and by the 1960s American scholarly productivity, particularly in the physical and social sciences, was second to none. Private research universities played a key role in this development. Other private institutions, especially those with strong ethnic roots, such as Fordham and Notre Dame, expanded their offerings for the sons and daughters of immigrant parents who were beginning to stream into higher education. Most private schools and colleges suffered through the Depression years, as donations went down and families were hard pressed to come up with even modest tuition payments. Following World War II, the federal government began putting large amounts of money into research and development, much of which was awarded to private institutions. Another boost was the GI Bill, which paid the tuition of all veterans whether in public or private (including religious) schools and colleges, thereby simply ignoring the century-old public policy of government support for public but not private institutions. The religious revival of the postwar years also led to higher enrollments in religious schools and colleges. New educational markets were opened up, particularly for adult students returning to complete secondary or collegiate degrees or taking courses to prepare for career change. Adult education, the community college system, and the increasing numbers of "nontraditional" (older) students changed the face of American education. Private institutions responding to market opportunities were prominent in this movement, especially large urban universities such as New York University, Boston University, and the University of Southern California.

On the elementary-secondary level, private school enrollment fell during the Depression but otherwise grew steadily through the twentieth century and grew dramatically during the two decades following World War II, as a result of the baby boom and the resurgence of interest in religious values reflected in the growth of religious schools. In the late 1960s and early 1970s, however, Catholic schools suffered a precipitous decline in enrollment, apparently as a result of attitude changes on the part of some Catholic religious and lay leaders, a 40 percent decrease in the number of Catholic births from 1959 to 1975, and the shift of the Catholic population from central cities, where Catholic schools were plentiful, to outer-city and suburban areas, where Catholic schools were not built fast enough to accommodate the Catholic population. The rate of decline had leveled off by the mid 1970s, but by that time, Catholic schools had lost over two million students, a decline of 40 percent.

No such crisis was taking place in other private school groups, however. During the same years, all other types of private schools grew, and some grew phenomenally (Cooper, 1988, p. 33). The number of students in fundamentalist Christian schools grew from 110,000 in 1965–66 to nearly a million in 1982–83. Fundamentalist parents had become increasingly troubled by what they perceived as secularist U.S. Supreme Court decisions and godless public schools, which had eliminated prayer, Bible reading, hymn singing, and Christmas crèches. To fundamentalist parents, the public schools were no longer part of the solution of value formation but were now part of the problem. Many fundamentalist families withdrew their children from the public schools and set up their own schools.

The irony of the fundamentalist school growth is that prior to the 1960s, fundamentalist churches generally opposed the separate Christian school movement and urged members to expose their children to children of other faiths and indeed "give witness" in the public schools. The events of the 1960s and 1970s changed this completely. As private education scholar Donald Erickson has remarked, "If courts and public educators had conspired to alienate these one-time public school supporters, they could hardly have done a more thorough job" (Erickson, 1986, p. 90).

Calvinist Christian, Lutheran, Episcopal, and Seventh Day Adventist schools grew substantially during this period, though not at the same meteoric rate as those of the fundamentalist Christian groups. Other parents, not particularly troubled by the secularism issue but very concerned about the quality and safety of public education, turned to nondenominational independent schools. Enrollment in these schools went up by 69 percent between 1965–66 and 1982–83 (Cooper, 1988, p. 33). Jewish school enrollment grew by 37 percent during this period. The Jewish day school movement had begun in the 1940s, as the Nazi holocaust and the founding of the state of Israel highlighted Jewish identity and as Jews became more affluent and began to look for alternatives to the urban public schools that they had so long attended and supported.

The public policy debate on the role of private education continued. No one seriously questioned the need for private higher education, which was clearly a critical part of the American system. But paying for that education was another story. Some states, such as California, provided substantial assistance to private college and university students, but most state and federal programs left private institutions still heavily dependent on tuition and fundraising. There was considerable legislative and judicial activity on the elementary-secondary level. Several attempts were made to provide some form of state assistance to private schools; most were declared unconstitutional (Vitullo-Martin and Cooper, 1987). A few major proposals attracted considerable attention. Tuition tax credits, which would allow parents to reduce their federal or state income tax payments by some part of their children's tuition and fees, were endorsed by the Nixon and Reagan administrations but failed to pass Congress. Education vouchers, an idea that goes back to Adam Smith, were promoted by such unlikely bedfellows as conservative economist Milton Friedman and liberal sociologist Christopher Jencks. Under this plan, families would receive for each school-age child a voucher that could be "cashed" for educational services at any licensed public or private school. The education voucher idea received support from many parts of the political and intellectual spectrum but failed to develop a strong constituency among private educators, who feared the loss of control over admissions, and was vehemently opposed by public school groups. The constitutionality of tuition tax credits or education vouchers has not yet been determined by the courts.

The principal feature of twentieth-century American education has been the increasing dominance of government at all levels. At the elementary-secondary level, public education, with nearly 90 percent of the enrollment and 95 percent of K-12 expenditures, is now virtually a monopoly. In higher education, the statistical equality of public and private institutions was obliterated in the three decades after 1950; by 1988, nearly 80 percent of all students were in public colleges and universities. While private institutions still have a powerful role in higher education—far more so than their counterparts on the elementary-secondary level—some observers wonder how long this can last, given the extreme price differential between public and private tuition. At the University of California, Berkeley, for instance, 1988–89 undergraduate tuition was $1,531; fifty miles down the road at Stanford, the tuition was $12,564. Former Stanford president Richard Lyman has said, "There may come a time when choosing a private college is no longer a rational economic decision."

Policy Issues

In no other part of the third sector is there such direct competition and confrontation between public and nonprofit agencies as in the arena of education. The government does not operate churches or opera companies, and in health and human services, government funding mechanisms such as purchase-of-service contracts and Medicare tend to control the competition between public and private agencies. But in education, the competition is fierce and the conflict is always just beneath the surface.

Public and private education, in fact, present a classic case of competing values in American society. The strongest proponents of the public school system, such as Horace Mann and John Dewey, argue that public education is a cornerstone of American democracy, offering free education to all children and young people without regard to gender, race, religion, ethnicity, or socioeconomic status. They hold that public education has brought together the extremely diverse strands of American society, has given the poorest of the poor unlimited opportunity, and has faithfully mirrored America's commitment to democratic values. They feel that the nation's system of public education from kindergarten through graduate school is one of the principal reasons for the great success of the United States in all fields of endeavor.

Private education adherents, on the other hand, see themselves as upholding such values as freedom of choice in education, moral and religious values, commitment to excellence, and the importance of orderliness in the educational process. They see private institutions as more responsive to the wishes of students and parents, millions of whom "vote with their feet" for private education in spite of great financial pressure to choose public education. Some private education advocates feel that public institutions consciously or unconsciously undermine religious and moral values, substituting a quasi religion of Americanism or secular humanism. On the elementary-secondary level, some regard public schools as excessively given to fads and see them as disorderly places filled with violence and drugs, places where only the most committed students can get a good education. Finally, some observers see public education as a governmental quasi monopoly, a huge, unwarranted, and somewhat dangerous intrusion of the state into the institutionalized process of shaping ideas and values.

In short, both groups start from the same principles—commitment to the rights and well-being of individuals, families, and the society—and come to diametrically opposite conclusions.

Also, of course, there are many shades of opinion. Some feel that private higher education is important but that private elementary and secondary schools are nonessential or even unfortunate. Some look favorably on nondenominational but not on religious private education. Some are committed to the existence and well-being of both private and public education and want to see both healthy competition and cooperation between the two but are concerned that the actual funding of American education is undermining this relationship.

A related policy question is what balance there should be between public and personal investment in education. Never in American history has the state paid for all the education that individuals wished. Even today, government does not pay for ballet lessons or summer seminars at Oxford. The commonsense reason for limiting state support of education, aside from simple budget considerations, is that education benefits the individual as well as the society. This is true of "extracurricular" education, but it is even more true of basic elementary, secondary, undergraduate, and graduate education. The government itself keeps reminding us how much more money we will make if we graduate from high school and then from college. Given the fact of individual as well as societal benefit, it is reasonable to ask what investment in their education individuals and families should be expected to make at *all* levels. The great majority of American families using public elementary and secondary education have incomes well above the poverty level. The state does not provide such families with free housing, clothing, food, health care, insurance, retirement plans, or other necessities of life. All of these items, at least theoretically, could be provided free of charge and supported by general taxation. All of them are as essential to good human life as is education. What is the modern (as opposed to nineteenth-century) rationale for providing education services free of direct charge while other vital goods and services are charged 100 percent to the immediate consumer?

A related question is whether providing totally free educational services is the most effective way of creating student, family, and educator commitment to the value of education. Public educators, parents, and editorial writers frequently complain that students do not value education highly enough. The fact that education is both free and compulsory may have something to do with this. The structure of education funding, by effectively eliminating any direct sense of personal contribution and ownership, may be a more powerful teacher than the teachers.

The nation has never really faced the basic policy question of whether it wishes private education to survive. While a few well-endowed and prestigious private institutions, such as Harvard, Stanford, Exeter, and Andover, are in no serious danger of extinction, most private schools, colleges, and universities operate under enormous financial pressure and competition from state-supported institutions. The government now controls 90 percent of elementary-secondary education and 80 percent of higher education, as measured by student enrollment. General tax funds now pay for the lion's share of this $300 billion-a-year effort. To supplement their tax revenue, public schools and universities have recently entered the competition for private donations. Louis Morrell, financial vice-president at Radcliffe College, has said, "the slow death of American private higher education is a distinct possibility" (Morrell, 1987, p. A52), and the same is clearly true of American private K–12 education. Yet there is almost no serious discussion of this policy question at either national or state levels. Meanwhile, the relative financial position of private education, which educates nearly nine million students a year and is, because of changes in the economy and society, even more important to the country now than in earlier decades, continues to erode.

Private education, in addition to educating millions of students and producing much important research, is a useful reminder that large-scale government involvement in human services is not always necessary or even useful and in fact has characterized only about 125 years of America's three and a half centuries of educational history. Private education has kept alive the model of significant student and parental choice in education. Millions of families who for religious, academic, or other reasons desire something different from public education have exercised this freedom of choice, which, though limited by the costs of private education, is nonetheless a major extension of freedom in an important area of human life. The societal and economic significance of American private education continues to grow even as its future becomes more problematic.

HEALTH CARE

The Sector's Quiet Giant

While the state has completely disentangled itself from the church and has appropriated most of the nation's education, government gives private health care $50 billion a year and no serious competition. Private hospitals, which account for nearly 90 percent of nonprofit health expenditures, receive between a third and a half of their operating revenue from government. Private hospitals, medical schools, and other health care agencies receive government research and development grants, construction funds, and education and training contracts. In fiscal year 1987, the National Institutes of Health (NIH) awarded $5.4 billion in grants; 57 percent went to private institutions.

Nonprofit health care is also closely connected to the business world. Nonprofit hospitals contract with self-employed physicians, food-service companies, laundry companies, medical equipment companies, pharmaceutical firms, and research agencies working on artificial hearts and the treatment of AIDS. Nonprofit hospitals have developed for-profit subsidiaries, created private insurance plans, and codeveloped industrial parks.

Scope and Impact

Nonprofit institutions dominate the health care industry. Seventy percent of the short-term, acute-care hospital beds in the country are in nonprofit hospitals (American Hospital Association, 1987, p. 7). Half of the nation's physicians, dentists, and nurses are trained in private institutions. Besides direct-care and training institutions, the nonprofit health world includes a vast array of medical societies,

67

professional associations, publications, accreditation agencies, and research support funds such as the American Cancer Society, which in 1987–88 raised $304 million. Nonprofit associations such as Blue Cross and Blue Shield provide over 40 percent of the private medical insurance in the country.

Nonprofit health care institutions have had great impact on American society. Organized health care for the poor was primarily a nonprofit—mostly religious—phenomenon throughout most of the country's history until the 1920s and 1930s. Much of the important biomedical research has taken place at private medical schools, hospitals, and research institutions. Private foundations such as Kellogg and Robert Wood Johnson and national organizations such as the March of Dimes and the Epilepsy Foundation invest tens of millions of dollars every year in health care research, development, and dissemination.

Nonprofit institutions have historically played an important role in establishing and maintaining health care quality standards. Recently, there has been much debate about the question of how to define and assess "quality" of health care; partly as a result of this definitional problem, empirical studies comparing the quality of government, nonprofit, and for-profit institutions have been largely inconclusive. The degree to which physicians control the delivery of care seems a more powerful variable than the legal form of ownership. The increasing similarity of health care funding across the three sectors and the regulations that accompany this funding also play a standardizing role (Hollingsworth and Hollingsworth, 1986; Marmor, Schlesinger, and Smithey, 1987; Fuchs, 1986). "Teaching" hospitals tend to be highly regarded whether the affiliated medical school is public or private. Nevertheless, there remains a widespread impression among both consumers and health care professionals that nonprofit hospitals, nursing homes, and other health care agencies tend to provide higher-quality care than their government or for-profit counterparts. Whether this impression is supported by hard evidence is still a matter of considerable debate. In general, certainly the quantity and perhaps also the relative quality of nonprofit health care organizations make them the dominant force in America's $500 billion health care industry.

American nonprofit health work has also had a major impact internationally. American medical research has dramatically affected fertility rates, infant mortality rates, disease control, and health practices in the developing nations of the world. The Rockefeller, Ford, Kellogg, and other foundations have done extensive health care funding outside the United States. The work of medical missionaries such as Albert Schweitzer and Tom Dooley raised American consciousness about the Third World. Nonprofit medical schools in the United States have trained thousands of health professionals from other countries and have helped improve the quality of medical education around the world.

Perhaps partly because of its imposing presence, nonprofit health care in recent years has come under increasing scrutiny with regard to admission practices and tax-exempt status. Clark (1980) argued in a *Harvard Law Review* article that the nonprofit form and the modern hospital industry are incompatible. Herzlinger and Krasker (1987, p. 95) argued in a *Harvard Business Review* article that the traditional reasons for nonprofit hospitals do not hold water and that in fact "nonprofit hospitals operate primarily for their physicians' benefit." Representative Fortney Stark (D-California) recommended in 1987 that the nonprofit status of certain hospitals be removed, on the grounds that they had forsaken their historical role of helping the poor and were quietly sending low-income patients "down the road to the county hospital." Several states have taken a hard line on tax exemption for nonprofit hospitals. In 1985, the Utah State Supreme Court, upholding a county's challenge to the tax-exempt status of two nonprofit hospitals, laid down a strict set of guidelines that nonprofit hospitals had to meet in order to retain their tax exemption. California, Vermont, and Tennessee have also tightened legal strictures on nonprofit hospitals.

The question of equal access of rich and poor to quality medical care has become the focus of a major policy debate. Both nonprofit and for-profit institutions have been accused of "cream-skimming," favoring the more affluent patients. One recent summary of the evidence concluded, "In short, there was still inequality in access to hospitals for the country as a whole, with public hospitals continuing to be somewhat more accessible.

Although some voluntary hospitals were more accessible to the poor in the nation's largest one hundred cities than proprietary hospitals, for the nation as a whole there appeared to be only modest differences in equality of access to care between voluntary and proprietary hospitals" (Hollingsworth and Hollingsworth, 1986, p. 31). This study also found, comparing 1935 with 1979, that the three types of hospitals had become more similar in their mix of various income groups (p. 46). However, there is still a paucity of research and a great deal of debate on the question of access to quality medical care. Marmor, Schlesinger, and Smithey (1987, pp. 230–234) reviewed the studies in detail and concluded, in part, that "All these findings should be interpreted with caution" (p. 233).

In 1986, there were 3,338 nonprofit short-term general hospitals, which had 690,000 beds, admitted 23.5 million patients, recorded 168.3 million outpatient visits, employed 2,242,000 people, and had total expenditures of $104 billion. In addition, there were 119 nonprofit long-term general, psychiatric, and other hospitals (American Hospital Association, 1987, pp. 5, 10, 11). There were also 3,046 nonprofit nursing and personal care facilities and 6,964 nonprofit outpatient care and allied service facilities in 1982 (Hodgkinson and Weitzman, 1986, p. 110). In 1986, nonprofit health care institutions employed 3,272,400 people, 45.6 percent of all employees in the independent sector (Hodgkinson and Weitzman, 1988a, Table 10 [n.p.]). A 1988 Gallup poll indicated that about 11 percent of Americans did volunteer work in health care institutions. Nonprofit health care revenue sources in 1984 are shown in Table 5.

Nonprofit health care current operating expenditures in 1984 were $104.7 billion (Hodgkinson and Weitzman, 1986, p. 117). In 1986, nonprofit hospitals alone had expenditures of $103.6 billion (American Hospital Association, 1987, p. 5). The assets of nonprofit hospitals were estimated in 1982 as $95.1 billion (Hodgkinson and Weitzman, 1986, p. 43).

The proportion of nonprofit, government, and for-profit health care agencies differs greatly by the service provided, as Table 6 illustrates.

Historical Development

During the seventeenth, the eighteenth, and most of the nineteenth centuries, health care in America was largely home-based rather

Table 5. Sources of Annual Funds of Nonprofit Health Services, 1984.

Source	Amount (in Billions of Dollars)
Private payments	$ 60.8
Government payments	44.5
Private contributions	10.4
Church contributions	7.0
Endowment, investment income	1.4
Other	1.6
TOTAL	$125.7

Source: Hodgkinson and Weitzman, 1986, p. 117.

Table 6. Proportion of Health Care Providers by Service.

Service	Measure	For-Profit	Nonprofit	Public
Acute hospitals	beds	8.5%	69.6%	21.9%
Psychiatric hospitals	beds	6.0	4.7	89.3
Nursing homes	beds	67.6	21.3	11.0
Homes for the mentally handicapped	residents	46.2	37.7	16.5
Blood banks	facilities	63.3	5.8	30.9
Dialysis centers	facilities	38.5	44.3	17.2
Health maintenance organizations	enrollees	15.8	84.2	NA
Health insurance	enrollees	45.2	42.7	12.0
Home health agencies	patients	25.5	64.1	10.4

Source: Marmor, Schlesinger, and Smithey, 1987, p. 224. Reprinted from W. W. Powell, ed., *The Nonprofit Sector*, with the permission of Yale University Press.

than institutional and was provided by family members and doctors of often questionable training (Ludmerer, 1985). Those who could not afford physicians were cared for in public or religious infirmaries, often connected to the local almshouse. The first general hospital, Pennsylvania Hospital in Philadelphia, was founded in 1751 with considerable assistance from Benjamin Franklin; New York Hospital began in the early 1790s, and Boston's famous Massachusetts General Hospital opened in 1821. But as late as 1873, when the first hospital census was conducted, there were only 178 hospitals, about 50 of them public and private mental institutions, in the entire country. Many of the 178 were municipal hospitals connected with local almshouses or penal institutions. There were only a few nonprofit, community-based general hospitals.

Urban hospitals were, on the whole, unsafe places, populated mainly by the poor. Ignorance of the ways in which infection spread made hospitals a breeding ground for disease. A Scottish physician coined the word *hospitalism* to refer to the high mortality rate among postoperative patients in urban hospitals (Rosenberg, 1987). And it was in absolute seriousness that Florence Nightingale said in 1863 that whatever else a hospital did, it "should do the sick no harm."

The last quarter of the nineteenth century saw a major shift to institutional health care. By 1909, there were 4,359 hospitals with 400,000 beds, not counting tuberculosis institutions. The discoveries of biomedical science during the late nineteenth and early twentieth centuries radically changed the nature of health care. Medical education and practice and medical equipment and facilities improved dramatically. People came to have more confidence in hospitals, more patients were admitted, and fees were charged for the first time (Starr, 1982).

Religious organizations played a major role in institutional health care. Caring for the sick had always been a mandate of Christianity and Judaism. Medicine was one of the major disciplines of the medieval universities, and care of the sick was the main purpose of many religious orders in Europe. This tradition continued in America. Catholics, especially through "hospital orders" of nuns, opened many health care institutions. Presbyterian, Methodist, Baptist, Lutheran, and other Protestant hospitals appeared. Quakers made a small but significant impact on the development of care for the mentally ill. In 1813, at a time when Philadelphians could for a shilling visit the Pennsylvania Hospital to stare at lunatics chained in the hospital basement, Quakers in that city founded the first private psychiatric hospital in the United States, the Friends Asylum for the Relief of Persons Deprived of the Use of Their Reason. With a revolutionary set of practices, the Quakers released the insane from their chains, gave each a private room with a window, allowed them to walk around the wooded grounds and work in the hospital gardens, and made caring conversation the basis of treatment. When the State Lunatic

Hospital at Harrisburg was opened in 1851, the Pennsylvania General Assembly declared that the quality of care should be the highest and should be based on the Quaker model. Seventh Day Adventists saw health care as a central part of their "reform and cleanse yourselves" ethic and set up hospitals both in the United States and abroad; by 1988, the number of Adventist hospitals and other health agencies was five hundred. The Jewish community, with a long tradition of medical scholarship and facing discrimination in some American institutions, set up hospitals such as Mount Sinai in New York, Mount Zion in San Francisco, and Cedars of Lebanon in Los Angeles.

The development of private black medical institutions was a direct result of discrimination. For several decades, black doctors were not allowed to join the American Medical Association. Most medical schools openly or surreptitiously barred blacks from admission. Black physicians could not get internships or take continuing education courses at nonblack hospitals. Blacks were barred from local medical societies and often from community hospitals. There were a few black hospitals, but they were sorely underfunded and often could not get accreditation.

As in the field of education, there were clear regional differences in the distribution of nonprofit, government, and for-profit health care organizations. In the East, where there was a stronger religious and philanthropic tradition, the nonprofit hospital remained the dominant form. In the West and parts of the Midwest, with less philanthropic tradition and more familiarity with the newer practice of charging fees, the for-profit hospital became more common. The rapid increase of for-profit hospitals and medical schools in the late nineteenth century "significantly changed the ownership picture in American medicine: [by 1900] over half of the medical schools and 60 percent of the hospitals in operation were privately owned, in most cases by one doctor" (Marmor, Schlesinger, and Smithey, 1987, p. 225). However, almost as suddenly, these small for-profit institutions began to disappear in the 1920s when it became clear that they could not keep pace with the growing professionalism in health care.

Institutional philanthropy played an important role in the development of health care. In 1901, John D. Rockefeller created the Rockefeller Institute for Medical Research, later to become Rockefeller University, and appointed as its head Simon Flexner, a distinguished physician from the University of Pennsylvania. His brother Abraham Flexner was commissioned by the Carnegie Corporation of New York to report on the condition of medical education in the United States. Flexner's 1910 report stated that most of the nation's 147 medical schools—many of them small, for-profit entities—were so bad that they should simply close. The report had dramatic effect, with a little help from another Rockefeller charity, the General Education Board (GEB), on which Abraham Flexner was also a trustee. The GEB allocated $45 million in the next five years to support about two dozen medical schools— such as Johns Hopkins, Yale, Chicago, Columbia, and Harvard— that were willing to adopt the Flexner standards and that Flexner thought worthy of support. Within a decade, most of the institutions criticized by the Flexner report had ceased to exist.

In 1909, Rockefeller called together a group of eminent physicians and asked them, "Is there a disease affecting large numbers of people of which you can say, 'I know all about this and I can cure it, not in fifty or eighty percent of the cases, but in one hundred percent'?" One of the doctors mentioned hookworm, a disease that afflicted millions of cotton mill workers, mostly Southern blacks. The subsequent virtual eradication of hookworm by the Rockefeller Sanitary Commission and the Rockefeller Foundation was to become one of the heroic tales of philanthropic lore.

The Rockefeller Foundation, chartered in 1913 "to promote the well-being of mankind throughout the world," has had a major influence on health care both in the United States and abroad, including codesigning with Johns Hopkins University the nation's first school of public health and funding a medical school in Peking, which the foundation hoped would be "the Johns Hopkins of China." Through grants for buildings, equipment, research, and fellowships, the foundation played a leading role in the development of American and world health care until the 1950s, when the federal government largely took over that role. The Sloan Foundation funded the world-famous Sloan-Kettering Institute for Cancer Research. Other funders, such as the Robert Wood Johnson Foundation, the Kaiser Family Foundation, and the W. K. Kellogg Foundation, have had similar impact.

The Great Depression led to some of the most significant

developments in the history of American health care. Vastly improved medical science and education had made health care better but also more expensive. The sudden poverty caused by the Depression meant that millions of Americans could not afford medical care. Private and public health insurance programs, long opposed by the American Medical Association, which feared loss of physician control over medicine, were finally implemented; these included the Blue Cross and Blue Shield programs. The federal Social Security Act represented a major step toward making medical care affordable to all Americans, including giving older Americans the chance to escape the notorious "poor farms" or poorhouses run by county governments to house the low-income elderly. Title I of the Social Security Act "injected a substantial new flow of income into the hands of older people and those who sold services to them" (Vladeck, 1980, p. 39).

Another breakthrough came in 1946, when Congress passed the Hill-Burton Act, which provided federal funds to build and equip hospitals. The assistance was given to nonprofit and government hospitals, and from 1946 to the mid 1970s, well over half of Hill-Burton funds went to private nonprofit institutions. The Hill-Burton program had enormous effect. It subsidized one-third of all hospital construction projects during those years, supplying about 10 percent of the total capital expenditures.

In 1887, the federal government had established the Laboratory of Hygiene, which in 1930 became the National Institute of Health (NIH). The institute's 1938 budget was $464,000. Medical research increased greatly during and because of World War II; after the war, Congress discovered that funding such research was politically popular. The budget of NIH, renamed the National Institutes of Health, was dramatically increased. In 1950, the NIH budget was raised to $117 million; by 1987, it exceeded $6 billion. Much of the federally funded research took place at nonprofit institutions, expanding further the public-private partnership in health care.

The passage of the federal Medicare and Medicaid programs in the mid 1960s had far-reaching effects on American health care. These and similar state programs made quality health care more available to millions of elderly and low-income citizens. Medicare and Medicaid payments also had the effect of standardizing health organizations of all three legal types (Hollingsworth and Hollingsworth, 1986). Some observers wonder whether this aid has not also created "an industry that grew fat, sloppy, and uncontrollable in an era of increased subsidies for medical care, medical research, and medical tinkering" (Marmor, Schlesinger, and Smithey, 1987, p. 222). The growth of private health insurance programs and Medicare-Medicaid funding has engendered a much larger and more affluent consumer base for health care than ever before in American history. Meanwhile, the nonprofit health care sector has become both financially stronger and more like government and for-profit institutions.

For-profit hospitals, always a presence and in some eras and regions the dominant health care form, reemerged in the 1960s, 1970s, and 1980s as a serious competitor to nonprofit hospitals. The debate still rages as to the quality and mercy of the two forms; one critic of the for-profit hospitals even warned of a new "medical-industrial complex" (Relman, 1980). It is clear that the enlarged funding base of American health care stimulated the rise of the for-profits; what is less clear is whether the changing economics of health care will continue to provide that stimulus.

Policy Issues

American health care, unlike American education, has for at least a century been characterized by a balance of nonprofit, for-profit, and government service providers, even though the balance has varied in different historical periods, geographic areas, and types of health care. While the relative merits of nonprofit versus for-profit versus government providers continue to be debated, national health policy has always been more concerned with such issues as the general quality and cost of medical care; the availability of medical care to the poor, the elderly, and other vulnerable groups; and the appropriate roles of government, health care institutions, health care professionals, and consumers. Next to these issues—again, unlike the case with education—the legal form of health care providers has been a relatively uncontroversial matter.

However, major policy questions are being raised as to the role and status of nonprofit health care. Should nonprofit health organizations have the tax benefits that go with nonprofit status while for-profit organizations providing the same services do not receive such benefits? While nonprofits in the past certainly served the poor more effectively than government or for-profit agencies, is this still the case? Generally, do nonprofits provide health care services that, for instance, for-profit institutions cannot do as well or better? Since nearly all nonprofit health care revenue comes from government, health insurance, and fees, in what sense are they "charitable" institutions?

Ironically, the very success of nonprofit health institutions has helped stimulate these questions. Nonprofits have the dominant role in a $500 billion industry in which all three sectors compete; this situation is without parallel in the American economy. Power invites challenges. Recent economic, political, and legal challenges to nonprofit health care are hardly surprising; what is surprising is that it took so long for serious challenges to develop. Herzlinger and Krasker (1987, p. 104) say the problem with nonprofit hospitals is that they lack "market discipline": "[W]e believe nonprofit managers could perform even better if they were freed of the limitations imposed by the nonprofit setting and could operate in a for-profit environment with its clearer incentives and measures of performance." In other words, nonprofits could do better if they ceased to be nonprofits. While such suggestions will be upsetting to some nonprofit managers and at least puzzling to others, critiques such as this are in fact signs that a different kind of "market discipline" is developing for nonprofits, the discipline of having to support claims that have always been accepted without a murmur (for a response to such challenges, see Seay and Vladeck, 1988). Proponents of nonprofit health care have often claimed or implied that nonprofits are superior to government and for-profit institutions in quality of care, patient orientation, professionalism, selflessness, efficiency, and sensitivity to the less fortunate. Skeptics are now saying, "Prove it." Given the size and rapidly increasing costs of American health care, such a response is neither surprising nor unreasonable. Indeed, the new competition from for-profit providers and the new criticisms and political and legal challenges can and should be a healthy prescription for nonprofit health care.

Since nonprofit providers have the dominant role in American health care, and especially in the short-term general hospital industry, it is reasonable to expect them to play a leadership role in

dealing with the question of efficiency: giving the same or better
service for less cost. According to the U.S. Department of Health
and Human Services, Americans spent $500 billion on health care
in 1987, a 9.8 percent increase over 1986—more than twice the 4.4
percent inflation rate. Federal economists estimate the 1988 health
bill at $541 billion, up 8.2 percent from 1987. The total is projected
to rise another 9.1 percent to $590 billion in 1989. Health spending
accounted for 11.1 percent of the GNP in 1987, up from 9.1 percent
in 1980 and 7.6 percent in 1970, and some experts see it rising to 15
percent in the 1990s (Freudenheim, 1988). Recent efforts on the part
of government and private insurers have not capped the rising costs.
The increase in medical spending has a complex set of causes,
including the increased longevity of Americans, more aggressive
marketing on the part of health care providers, new medical
techniques and areas of care, the extension of medical insurance to
more people, increased costs of medical malpractice suits, and
generally skyrocketing demand for a wide variety of services.

Patients pay only 25 percent of medical costs; the other 75
percent is paid by government and, through medical insurance
plans, employers. Health care consumers are not likely to provide
powerful market incentives for institutional efficiency. With the
purchase of health care, unlike the purchase of a computer or car or
skateboard, the consumer usually has very little knowledge of
comparative quality and purchases the service at the time of
immediate need or crisis. Further, consumers who have govern-
ment- or employer-provided medical insurance may with some
logic think, "It's my body and their money," and so have little or no
incentive to shop for bargains. Finally, most consumers have little
control over where their major health care money comes from, since
that is largely a function of who their employer is, what state they
live in, and how old they are. For all these reasons, it is unrealistic to
expect that health care consumers will exercise choice in such a way
as to provide strong market incentives for efficiency.

Nor do individual health care professionals and employees
have the incentive to limit medical spending, since this would mean
sacrificing their personal well-being to an abstract goal. And
government alone may not have the political will to deal with the
problem effectively, especially given the increasing power of the
senior citizens' lobby, which consistently supports cost-contain-

ment measures but just as consistently opposes any cuts in benefits to its constituents.

Nonprofit groups lobby the federal government for increases in Medicare payments. The government looks for ways to cut the federal deficit and wonders why medical costs need to keep rising at twice the rate of inflation. Business, meanwhile, is increasingly concerned about its medical insurance payments. Probably only a broad coalition of government, business, and the health care community can make a major dent in the health costs problem. Nonprofit institutions could assume significant leadership in such an effort, given their prominence in the industry and their nonprofit mission, which presumably commits them to efficiency as well as effectiveness. With a $500 billion health care industry that some believe has become complacent and inflated, the efficiency question is a serious one, and one in which the nonprofit sector can play a centrally important role.

Finally, what policy lessons does the health care industry have for other parts of the nonprofit sector? The funding of American health care may have been discriminatory, elitist, ineffective, and inefficient a century ago, but it is now demonstrably more pluralistic, egalitarian, and quality-oriented than the funding of education, social services, the arts, and international assistance. Also, power in the health industry is much more broadly distributed than in other fields: doctors and other health care professionals, hospitals, health maintenance organizations, medical societies, accreditation agencies, government, medical schools, pharmaceutical and medical equipment companies, medical insurance groups, research agencies, private funders, and consumers all have significant power. The concentration of funds in American education, especially and increasingly at the state government level, makes such power distribution in that field impossible. International assistance programs are heavily influenced by federal government spending and policy. Social welfare programs, as we have seen in recent years, are significantly affected by federal funding. The rest of the nonprofit sector might learn a great deal from careful study of both the successes and the failures of the health services model.

One lesson might be the effect of the market principle in health care. Herzlinger and Krasker (1987) may well be correct when they argue that there is need for more "market discipline" in health care, but that field has vastly more market discipline than other human service fields, such as education and social services. The market principle is usually discussed only in relation to for-profit firms, but it clearly applies to a much broader range of activity (Steinberg, 1987; Young, 1983). Such governmental actions as allowing nonprofits or for-profits to enter a certain field and establishing rules for their operation in that field greatly expands or contracts the operation of the market principle. Similarly, government funding—through such policies as making funds available to three kinds of agencies in health care and limiting funds largely to government agencies in education—dramatically affects market mechanisms. There are countless examples in American history of government organizations, nonprofit organizations, for-profit organizations, families, and neighborhood groups entering a field and making it more competitive and more consumer responsive. The contrast between funding policy in health care and in other parts of the nonprofit sector raises important policy issues.

ARTS AND CULTURE

Supporting the Survival of Creativity

The nonprofit arts world is a convenient marriage of princes and paupers. Millionaire benefactors arrive at the opera in limousines to hear *La Bohème* while across town small arts groups, like Mimi and Rodolfo, struggle to pay the heat bill. Social class differences, downplayed in education and unmentionable in religion, grab the headlines in art. The symphony or ballet board may be the most exclusive club in town, but it is the archetypal starving artist who creates the world of nonprofit culture.

The marriage of wealth and artistic talent is hardly new. Lorenzo di Medici supported Michelangelo; popes and potentates funded artists long before Texaco, the Ford Foundation, and the National Endowment for the Arts got into the act. What is surprising is that high culture in America still includes this dramatic mix of the superrich and the creative poor, while the funding of health care, education, and social services has become bureaucratic and predictable. Whether it is H. Ross Perot giving $10 million to the Dallas Symphony Orchestra or Norton Simon apparently giving a $750 million art collection to UCLA and then apparently taking it back, arts funding makes news.

Scope and Impact

The arts world is one of the smallest parts of the independent sector. The American Symphony Orchestra League estimates that there are about 1,800 orchestras, of which about three-fourths are nonprofit. The Central Opera Service estimated that there were 841 nonprofit opera and musical theater companies in 1987–1988 and 409 university presenters, both public and private. There are nearly 900 nonprofit theaters, 2,500 nonprofit museums, 200 nonprofit radio stations, 120 nonprofit television stations, more than 700 nonprofit magazines, 150 nonprofit publishers, and more than 1,000 nonprofit local arts councils (DiMaggio, 1987, pp. 197–200).

Arts organizations employed an estimated 117,100 people in 1986 (Hodgkinson and Weitzman, 1988a, Table 10 [n.p.]). About 5 percent of Americans say they volunteer for arts organizations (Hodgkinson and Weitzman, 1988b, p. 7). In 1984, the arts world received volunteer help from the equivalent of 154,000 full-time workers, with one full-time-equivalent volunteer worker defined as 1,700 volunteer hours (Hodgkinson and Weitzman, 1986, p. 41).

The estimated 1984 operating expenditures of nonprofit arts organizations were $3.4 billion. The total annual funds received were estimated at $6.9 billion, less than 3 percent of the total annual funds of the nonprofit sector (pp. 117, 121). Nonprofit arts organizations receive their income from the source shown in Table 7.

Arts organizations in 1984 received $4.6 billion in contributions from foundations, corporations, and individuals (Hodgkinson and Weitzman, 1986, p. 117). By 1987, estimated private giving for "arts, culture, and humanities" (theaters, opera, dance, museums, public television and radio, symphony orchestras) had risen to $6.41 billion (American Association of Fund-Raising Counsel, 1988, p. 8). All three categories of private giving increased at a rate of more than 10 percent a year from 1980 to 1987, and most of the money from all three categories went to large, established arts organizations. While

Table 7. Revenue Sources for
Nonprofit Arts Organizations, 1984.

Source	Percentage
Private contributions	66.7
Government	13.0
Fees and charges	11.7
Endowment	2.9
Other	7.2

Source: Hodgkinson and Weitzman, 1986, p. 117.

a few of the very large foundations make carefully planned grants that include assistance for experimental groups, "most foundation arts dollars go quietly to major established institutions, in most cases symphony orchestras and art museums, for capital projects, endowment building, or operating support" (DiMaggio, 1986, p. 114). Corporate giving to the arts is driven by several factors: desire for good publicity (some of the biggest arts spenders have been oil and tobacco companies with major image problems), the personal interests of CEOs (Useem and Kutner, 1986), and the idea that the arts are healthy for the local and business community. The important connection of arts funding with high society leads major individual donors to give to the mainline organizations on whose boards they serve.

The nonprofit art world has many connections with the for-profit sector. Nonprofit theaters and festivals are often the de facto rehearsal grounds for future Broadway plays. August Wilson's *Fences* played at the Yale Repertory Theater before it moved to Broadway, winning both the Tony Award and the Pulitzer Prize in 1987. Michael Bennett's *A Chorus Line,* the longest-running musical in the history of Broadway, was developed in workshop at Joseph Papp's nonprofit New York Public Theater. Some theatrical productions go the other way, from minimal success on Broadway to long runs in nonprofit regional theaters. Recordings of symphony, opera, and other nonprofit musical productions are sold by for-profit firms. Musical instruments and sheet music used by nonprofits are produced and sold by for-profits. Actors, dancers, and choreographers move back and forth between the nonprofit and the for-profit stage. Paintings and sculpture are sold by commercial galleries and later exhibited in nonprofit museums. Television and radio broadcasting is dominated by for-profit firms, but there is some flow of personnel across these boundaries; Roger Mudd, Bill Moyers, and Daniel Schorr are examples of broadcasters who moved from commercial to public television or radio. National Public Radio's Garrison Keillor turned his "Prairie Home Companion" stories into major commercial success through *Lake Wobegon Days* and other books. Magazines such as *Harper's,* the *Nation,* and *National Review,* once for-profit entities, are now nonprofit; and if the Internal Revenue Service had been successful in a 1983 ruling,

Mother Jones would have been forced to change from nonprofit to for-profit status. Nonprofit literary journals are the stepping-stone for many fiction writers on the way to their first novel, published commercially. Robert Redford used some of his film profits to create the nonprofit Sundance Institute for independent filmmakers.

There are, however, dramatic contrasts between nonprofit and for-profit arts and entertainment. *Forbes* estimated that television comedian Bill Cosby made nearly $100 million in 1987 (Frank and Zweig, 1987, p. 120), and many other television, movie, and popular music stars make several million dollars a year. The highest-paid nonprofit performers—such as the music directors of major symphony orchestras—earn between a quarter and a half million dollars a year; the vast majority of nonprofit performers earn far less and often must take other jobs to make ends meet. Average salaries in the arts in 1984 were significantly lower even than in other parts of the nonprofit sector (Hodgkinson and Weitzman, 1986, p. 134).

Government gives far less to the arts than it does to nonprofit education, social services, and health care. About 13 percent of arts revenue comes from local, state, and federal government. In France the figure is 68 percent, in Germany 86 percent, in Austria 77 percent, in the Netherlands 73 percent, and in Sweden 90 percent (Montias, 1986). The difference is mitigated to some extent by the fact that the United States gives more favorable tax treatment than do other nations to corporations and individuals who donate to arts organizations; the resulting loss of tax income constitutes an indirect government subsidy. But even when this is taken into account, the United States is strikingly different from most industrial nations in government arts funding. Further, significant government support of the arts is relatively recent in the United States. The National Endowment for the Arts (NEA) was created in 1965, followed shortly by the establishment of state and local arts councils. The Reagan administration's annual attempts to cut the NEA budget, though generally unsuccessful, illustrated the political vulnerability of federal arts funding. Similarly, state and local government programs get immediate scrutiny any time there is a budget crunch.

Government also has much less operating presence in the arts than in health, education, and social services. The few government arts and culture agencies often look more like nonprofits than government operations. "Many public cultural organizations, especially public municipal museums, are pseudononprofits, buffered from city or county government by a volunteer board of trustees and, in some cases, considerable private patronage" (DiMaggio, 1987, p. 214). Museums are the principal area of government activity in arts and culture. About one-fourth of the museums in the country are under governmental auspices, including the Smithsonian Institution in Washington, the Museum of Natural Science in New York, and the Museum of Science and Industry in Chicago. Public school districts, community colleges, and state colleges and universities accounted for 34.3 percent of public television funding in 1983. Public colleges and universities and, to a much lesser extent, public high schools sponsor musical and theatrical groups. The military has many marching bands and other musical programs. The government at all levels has sponsored "public art" in the form of statues and occasional works of architecture.

Nonprofit arts organizations have significant economic impact on local communities. For instance, a San Francisco Bay Area study concluded that in 1985 local arts organizations brought $240 million into the local economy and drew more customers than the San Francisco 49ers, the San Francisco Giants, the Oakland Athletics, and the Golden State Warriors combined (San Francisco Arts Commission, 1987). Nonprofit arts organizations play a significant role in the tourism industry of cities such as New York, Los Angeles, Chicago, San Francisco, and Cleveland. Quality-of-life studies frequently point out the benefits that arts organizations bring to communities. Corporations find it easier to attract and keep top managerial and professional staff where there are thriving arts programs. As an executive now living in Los Angeles remarked, "When we lived in [a much smaller city], my wife and I would have to drive 100 miles if we wanted to see a good art exhibit or go to the theater. Now we have those opportunities all around us."

The contribution of the nonprofit arts world goes beyond the pleasure, enlightenment, and economic benefit it brings. While hospitals, mental health clinics, and remedial reading programs meet urgent human needs, art responds to needs that are less urgent but no less important. Both in normal times and in times of crisis, people turn to art to give expression to some of their deepest feelings and insights. Children create skits, lovers write poetry, armies march to music, Picasso paints the horror of war in *Guernica,* mourners at a wake sing, dance, and tell stories. These artistic expressions arise in private settings but are encouraged and to some degree stimulated by the nation's thousands of nonprofit arts organizations. If artistic performance was possible only when it was profitable, millions of Americans would be deprived of artistic opportunities. Nonprofit arts organizations provide the structure and stimulus for much artistic creativity that might otherwise be lost.

Arts and culture organizations not only provide an opportunity for individual and group artistic expression and appreciation; they also play a role in the enhancement of social, intellectual, and political discourse. Dictatorships are quick to suppress or co-opt artistic expression, as the fate of the arts in Nazi Germany and Maoist China illustrates. American courts have consistently held that art is a form of free speech and must, under the First Amendment, be protected as such. While the politicization of art can be deadly, as most of the seventy-year history of Soviet art shows, art is inescapably related to politics. The actions, values, and structures of the *polis* are as much the raw material of the artist as are nature, love, and death. Whether the artist celebrates or chastises the *polis* is not for government to decide or the market to determine. While the political impulse of art can survive even the most brutal suppression, it thrives only in societies where freedom of expression is not only tolerated but supported by the institutions of society. In the United States, nonprofit arts organizations play an important role in protecting and nourishing art even when it treads on politically dangerous ground.

Historical Development

The development of art and culture in colonial America faced almost insurmountable obstacles. The hardships of life and stern religious attitudes weighed heavily against cultural pursuits. Puritans and Quakers disagreed on many things, but both thought that plays were vain, wasteful, and immoral. The Pennsylvania Assembly passed several statutes prohibiting "stage-plays, masks, and revels," and a Boston judge noted in 1714, "Ovid himself offers invincible arguments against public plays. . . . Let not Christian Boston go beyond heathen Rome in the practice of shameful vanities" (Wright, 1957, p. 179). In 1774, the Continental Congress called for the suspension of "horseracing, gambling, cockfighting, exhibitions of shows, plays, and other expensive diversions and entertainments" (Nye, 1960, p. 263). Since the population was largely agrarian and isolated, there were few towns or cities with enough potential clients to sustain artistic productions. As late as 1800, there were only five cities of more than ten thousand people, and 97 percent of Americans still lived in smaller towns or on farms. As time went on, economic and demographic conditions changed and religious prohibitions relaxed, but even by the end of the eighteenth century, there were few established artistic and cultural institutions in the colonies; nearly all the productions were by traveling companies from Europe.

In spite of the hard days and dour preachers, however, the colonists enjoyed family and community celebrations. There was much dancing and a remarkable number of dance instructors. Ladies and gentlemen played musical instruments as a matter of course, sometimes well, sometimes badly. It was said that Thomas Jefferson was the worst violinist in Virginia, with Patrick Henry a close second.

In art as in the rest of the nonprofit sector, it was the nineteenth century that saw the most dramatic development. The rapid growth of cities, the wild mix of ethnic and religious groups, the spiraling economy, and the infusion of new ideas through immigration, increased education, and greatly expanded world trade led to a sharp increase in entertainment and artistic activity. Thespian societies flourished in the young nation's rapidly proliferating colleges. European touring groups were much in demand. Indigenous arts organizations were formed. The New York Philharmonic Society was founded in 1842, Boston's Handel and Haydn Society in the 1840s, and the Harvard Musical Association in the 1850s. After the Civil War, the development of cultural institutions quickened, increasingly aided by philanthropic gifts from the new capitalists. New York's Metropolitan Opera, the Boston Symphony Orchestra, and other major arts institutions appeared with great civic and social fanfare. Nor was this impulse limited to the older cities of the East. San Francisco, hell-bent for culture, hosted more than five thousand opera performances between the discovery of gold in 1848 and the great earthquake in 1906.

It was also this period that saw the gradual development of the distinction between art and entertainment, or "high" and "low" culture. Public presentations had often mixed the two. Actors in tavern theaters put on Shakespeare and bawdy skits with hardly an intermission between. P. T. Barnum's museum shows combined low and high art: "fine art was interspersed among such curiosities as bearded women and mutant animals" (DiMaggio, 1986, pp. 42–43). As Barnum said in his autobiography, "Show business has all phases and grades of dignity, from the exhibition of a monkey to the exposition of that highest art in music or the drama, which entrances empires and secures for the gifted artist a worldwide fame," or, more succinctly, "People cannot live on gravity alone. . . ." (quoted in Montias, 1986, p. 293). DiMaggio (1986) argues that in Boston, high and popular culture were almost inextricably mixed before the second half of the nineteenth century, when the capitalists moved in to buy high culture and set it apart from mass culture: "The distinction between high and popular culture, in its American version, emerged in the period between 1850 and 1900 out of the efforts of urban elites to build organizational forms that, first, isolated high culture and, second, differentiated it from popular culture" (p. 41). During this period, the Boston Brahmins created institutions such as the Museum of Fine Arts and the Boston Symphony Orchestra, which came to define and dominate culture in Boston. In other large cities, a similar process took place, and a select few cultural institutions became an important means of social differentiation for America's new rich.

Ethnic groups, meanwhile, were adding their own contributions to American culture. Art was a form of survival for the immigrant communities. Ethnic theater, dance, and musical presentations strengthened the bond with the home country and eased the adjustment to life in America. Ethnic art was a matter of group cohesion and pride as much as an expression of artistic impulse (Handlin, 1951, pp. 181-85. 198-200). Irish ballads, Italian arias, Jewish folk dances, Negro spirituals, and Chinese New Year parades all contributed to the growing richness of American art and culture. The first important form of distinctively American music—jazz—was the creation not of the new cultural elite but of the black community.

The twentieth century saw the coming of age of American art. For three centuries, it had been almost entirely derivative, but major socioeconomic and educational developments were laying the groundwork for a change. The accumulation of vast wealth by American entrepreneurs in the nineteenth and twentieth centuries, the rising level of education and income in the general populace, the increase in leisure time for most Americans, the mix of cultures from immigration, and the growing self-consciousness of the United States as the "leader of the free world" created conditions more favorable to the development and dissemination of indigenous art and culture. A few key institutions capitalized on this potential. The Carnegie Corporation of New York, under the leadership of Frederick Keppel, provided the lion's share of foundation support for the arts during the 1920s and 1930s (DiMaggio, 1986, p. 115). The Federal Theater Project, a Works Progress Administration (WPA) program established in 1935 to create jobs for actors and playwrights, had a short life of its own but a long-term effect on American theater. The project's controversial treatment of racism, unionism, and socialism led to its demise after only seven years, but it greatly strengthened the resident theater movement that had begun in the 1910s and 1920s with community theaters such as the Provincetown Players of Eugene O'Neill fame and that would later be developed by the pioneering work of the Arena Stage in Washington, D.C. (1950) and the Tyrone Guthrie Theater in Minneapolis (1963).

In 1957, the Ford Foundation, concerned about the health of America's cultural institutions, launched a program of major support. "The aim of the Ford program was nothing short of revitalizing the performing arts throughout the United States: in the case of orchestral music, stabilizing symphony orchestras around the country; in the cases of dance and theatre, creating new

industries where none existed. . . . [T]he Ford programs represented
an application of private funds to artistic development that was
unique in magnitude and scope and unusually broad in vision"
(DiMaggio, 1986, pp. 116–117). Under the leadership of program
officer W. McNeil Lowry, Ford poured $150 million into the arts
between 1957 and 1970. Ford also gave $292 million to public
television from the early 1950s to the mid 1970s. "During public
television's early years, Ford grants literally kept the system alive"
(Powell and Friedkin, 1986, p. 250). The Rockefeller Foundation,
under program officer Howard Klein, followed Ford's lead of in-
depth and discriminating arts funding, although at a lower dollar
level.

The spotlight then shifted back to Washington, D.C. In 1965,
the federal government established the National Endowment for the
Arts, and many states and local communities followed by setting up
state and local arts councils. Funding for the NEA grew from an
initial appropriation of $2.5 million to a 1987 level of $171 million.
State arts councils' funding rose to a total of $217 million by 1987
(American Association of Fund-Raising Counsel, 1987, p. 106). All
these triggering events combined with the underlying socioeconomic changes to produce a significant increase of activity and
interest in American arts and culture.

The nonprofit arts world took shape in the last half of the
nineteenth century and made a quantum leap in funding support
during the 1950s and 1960s. The patterns set in these two critical
periods essentially remained in effect through the 1970s and 1980s.
A few relatively minor shifts occurred: corporations started to give
more of their money to arts organizations and less, for instance, to
colleges and universities. The Ford Foundation, though still
prominent, withdrew from the dominant position it had held in the
Lowry years. While the National Endowment for the Arts stayed at
the same level of funding, state and local arts councils grew
significantly. The creation of the J. Paul Getty Trust, with 1987
assets of nearly $4 billion, added a major dimension to the study and
promotion of art. Nonprofit regional theater, largely a creation of
the Ford Foundation during the 1950s and 1960s, continued to
thrive, as did the regional and national dance companies started or
reinvigorated during that period.

Policy Issues

Government involvement is not as critical an issue in art as it is in education, social services, and health care, but the perennial money problems of arts organizations and the striking contrast between government support of the arts in the United States and in other Western nations make the issue one of some significance. While government provides about 13 percent of nonprofit arts revenue and operates some arts organizations on its own, the United States does not have a "national arts policy," as do several European nations, and arts funding is clearly not taken very seriously as a national priority.

Many feel that this is as it should be, that art and politics do not mix. As famed choreographer Agnes de Mille observed, "It is argued that in the United States church and state are separate, and that art and state should be separate, too" (DeMille, 1987, p. 26). Public television and radio stations sometimes find it awkward to carry programs critical of their government sponsors and funders. A former WNET executive said, "Most of [the state-operated stations] simply can't do public affairs shows that look critically at their own state government because of the funding constraint. There is a terrible baggage that comes with state money" (quoted in Powell and Friedkin, 1986, p. 249). But the examples of the National Endowment for the Arts, the National Endowment for the Humanities, the National Science Foundation, and the National Institutes of Health—all of which successfully withstood serious political pressure during the Reagan years—suggest that it is possible, through a careful peer review process, to protect the integrity of government grantmaking even under politically adverse conditions. European funding policies may also suggest workable models of government assistance for the arts, allowing for the different traditions of arts patronage in Europe and America (Montias, 1986; Schuster, 1986).

The "national policy" question is further complicated by the involvement of state and local as well as national government in arts support. Given the structure of American government, the absence of a national arts policy is no more surprising than the absence of a national education policy, a situation that continues to amaze other nations. Outside of the military, there are few areas of American life where national policy (or lack thereof) automatically dictates what will happen on the state and local levels. Further, since 1970, state and local government arts agencies have grown at a faster rate than federal funding. The recency, relatively small amount, and decentralization of government funding for the arts in the United States indicate the extreme unlikelihood of a national arts policy in the foreseeable future. Nevertheless, the importance of the arts makes this a useful question to discuss and debate. Specific policy questions include the following: Should there be more (direct or indirect) government support of the arts in the United States? If so, what forms should this take? What levels of government should be involved, and in what proportion? Would increased government support lead to a decline in corporate, foundation, and individual support? Would increased government support endanger the quality and freedom of artistic expression? Would it be possible to protect government support of the arts from undue political influence and budget uncertainties? Would art develop an unhealthy dependence on government? What have been the effects of large-scale government support for the arts in European and other nations?

Another policy issue concerns the distribution of wealth within the nonprofit arts world. It is a world of extremes, of rich and poor, of haves and have-nots. While even the Metropolitan Opera has budget problems, small ethnic arts groups struggling for survival are not apt to sympathize. Major arts funders—wealthy individuals, foundations, corporations, and government—tend not to be attracted to avant-garde or politically oriented arts organizations. DiMaggio's comments about corporate funders apply with some qualifications to all the major funders: "Corporations are generally ill equipped and little inclined to support serious innovation or experimental work, access beyond the middle class, or pluralism that extends beyond already popular or commercial forms. Nontraditional or highly innovative arts organizations, neighborhood arts groups, or arts organizations that serve minorities and the poor can expect little assistance from the business sector" (DiMaggio, 1986, p. 79). Even when a funder is not concerned about the smallness, newness, political orientation, and/

or artistic philosophy of an arts organization, there is still the difficult question of artistic merit. Very few funders—the NEA, a few large foundations, some state and local arts councils, an occasional wealthy individual—have the expertise to assess artistic merit. Even peer review is sometimes difficult to apply, especially when countercultural artists are challenging the work of their more established colleagues.

One possible way to deal with the distribution of wealth issue, analogous to federal education programs that focus on educationally disadvantaged students, would be to orient the NEA's funding more toward nonestablished arts organizations, on the grounds that the more visible and prestigious organizations are much more able than nonestablished organizations to secure funds from other major funders. The NEA, both with its own funds and in cooperation with interested state and local councils, could provide the resources and peer review expertise to support small arts groups that show organizational and artistic promise. Such a policy shift would be resisted by established arts groups and might also raise the specter of government control of new art forms, but it is difficult to imagine that a purely "free-market" approach to arts funding can solve the distribution of wealth problem.

SOCIAL SERVICES

A Nation of Helpers

Mother Hale of Harlem, an elderly black woman whom former President Reagan called "a true American hero," directs a home for infants infected through their mothers with AIDS or heroin addiction. Robert Hayes, a former Wall Street lawyer, files lawsuits on behalf of street people through his Coalition for the Homeless. Father Depaul Genska, a Franciscan priest, conducts a ministry to prostitutes in Chicago. Maxine Johnston, former head of health services for the 1984 Olympics, directs the Weingart Center in Los Angeles, a twelve-story hotel that holds six hundred homeless people a night.

The nation's sixty thousand nonprofit social services agencies respond to a vast array of needs. Some services are dramatic, such as those of Mother Hale's home or suicide prevention centers. Other services are simple but lifesaving, such as the food, clothing, and shelter provided by soup kitchens, Goodwill Industries, the Salvation Army, and Catholic Charities. Some agencies are highly complex, such as Local Initiatives Support Corporation (LISC), a Ford Foundation project designed to stimulate private and public funding for community development. Other agencies are straightforward, such as Guide Dogs for the Blind.

Scope and Impact

"Social services" is one of the most loosely defined areas of the nonprofit sector. Hodgkinson and Weitzman (1986, p. 111) give the following description: "Organizations in the social services subsector provide services to individuals and families, job training and related services, child day care, and residential care. The sub-

94

sector also includes major fundraising organizations, such as local United Ways, community action and development groups, social change organizations, youth self-help groups, and senior citizen associations." Kramer (1987, p. 240) describes the "personal social services" this way: "These services refer to the social care provided to deprived, neglected, or handicapped children and youth, the needy elderly, the mentally ill—in short, all disadvantaged persons with substantial psychosocial problems. It includes such services as day care and foster care, institutional facilities, information and referral, counseling, sheltered workshops, homemakers, and vocational training and rehabilitation. . . . Typical service providers are Family Service agencies, community or neighborhood centers, Planned Parenthood federations, associations for the retarded, centers for independent living, halfway houses, Visiting Nurses associations, Catholic Charities, and others usually included in the United Way."

The boundaries between social services, on the one hand, and health care (as in care for the mentally ill), education (as in day-care or preschool programs and job training), or religion (as in the welfare activities of many churches), on the other, are often hard to fix. Also, community development, social change, and legal-assistance activities are sometimes included under social services and sometimes treated as separate categories. Another complicating factor is that many social service agencies are multipurpose; the same agency might be operating direct service, advocacy, and education programs.

The 1982 Census of Service Industries provides the most recent comprehensive data on tax-exempt social service organizations, as shown in Table 8. These figures showed a dramatic increase in nonprofit social services since the 1977 Census of Service Industries: the number of organizations grew by 28 percent, the number of employees increased by 29 percent, and expenditures doubled (National Center for Charitable Statistics, 1985, p. 6).

In addition to the nearly one million employees of social service organizations, about 10 percent of Americans surveyed in 1988 said they volunteered in social service and welfare organizations (Hodgkinson and Weitzman, 1988b, p. 7). Volunteering added an estimated full-time-equivalent 416,000 workers to nonprofit

Table 8. Nonprofit Social Service Agencies, 1982.

	Number of Agencies	Revenue (in Thousands of Dollars)	Number of Employees
Child day-care services	12,676	$ 1,529,931	135,269
Individual and family services	17,236	5,459,576	244,034
Job training, vocational rehabilitation	4,425	2,277,531	209,507
Residential care	7,633	3,372,837	173,516
Other social services	10,601	7,319,062	141,552
TOTAL	52,571	$19,958,937	903,878

Source: National Center for Charitable Statistics, 1985, p. 5.

social service agencies in 1984 (Hodgkinson and Weitzman, 1986, pp. 72, 127).

Social service agencies are often small. The Urban Institute found that the median agency budget was $150,000 in 1982 (Harder, Kimmich, and Salamon, 1985, p. 21), and the median number of full-time employees was three. The funding base for different social services is shown in Table 9. The funding base of social service agencies has changed significantly in recent decades. Prior to the mid 1960s, these agencies were supported primarily by private donations, church funds, and the United Way. The Great Society programs of the 1960s and 1970s funneled massive amounts of

Table 9. Nonprofit Social Service Funding Sources, 1982.

Service Area	Source of Funding				
	Government	Fees	Giving	Endowment	Other
Mental health	62%	28%	6%	3%	1%
Social services	54	14	27	3	2
Legal service, advocacy	53	14	28	1	5
Housing, community development	52	27	18	3	1
Employment, training, and income support	51	10	13	3	23
Institutional, residential care	50	32	12	4	2
Multiservices	44	24	26	3	3

Source: Salamon, Musselwhite, and DeVita, 1986, p. 23.

federal, state, and local government money into the social services; much of this money went to nonprofit organizations through grants, contracts, and various purchase-of-service arrangements. Amendments to the Social Security Act in 1967 and especially Title XX of the Social Security Act in 1974 poured money into public and private social service agencies and in doing so revolutionized the funding base of the nonprofits. By 1977, government was providing 53.5 percent of the funds for nonprofit social service programs. In 1968, the United Way had provided 48 percent of its member agencies' revenue; by 1980, the figure was 15 percent.

Following these years of plenty, the lean years arrived with the inflation of the latter part of the Carter administration and the cutbacks of the Reagan administration. By 1984, government's share of nonprofit social service revenue had dropped to 43.9 percent (Hodgkinson and Weitzman, 1986, pp. 117–118). Social service agencies turned to more aggressive fundraising and higher fees to compensate for the loss of government dollars.

If opera companies and Ivy League universities represent the establishment side of the nonprofit sector, social agencies represent its street-smart, sometimes heroic, often heartrending side. Drug addiction, alcoholism, child abuse, schizophrenia, homelessness, immigration problems, wife battering, and teenage pregnancy are only a few of the problems that nonprofit social agencies deal with every day. Millions of Americans are directly affected by their work, and millions of others are indirectly affected: every drug addict cured means fewer people mugged, every marriage problem solved means fewer children emotionally scarred or physically abused.

Historically, nonprofit social service agencies have often played a vanguard role in responding to social needs. Child abuse is a recent example. Although the sexual and physical abuse of children is centuries old, it was one of America's darkest and most closely kept secrets until the 1960s, when medical evidence made it unavoidably clear that child abuse was a serious problem. Nonprofit agencies took the lead in caring for the victims and getting the public and the government to face the problem (Bremner, 1988). In the nineteenth century, voluntary agencies pioneered care for the physically and mentally handicapped. In a few cases, nonprofit programs have stimulated both government and for-profit activity.

Day-care programs, virtually nonexistent before World War II, now are strongly represented in all three sectors, with about 60 percent of the programs in the for-profit sector. While nonprofits are an important source of innovation in the social services, government—especially in the 1930s and 1960s—and more recently for-profit firms have also originated new programs. Further, as Kramer (1981, pp. 183–187) has pointed out, nonprofit innovations are by no means always adopted by government.

Social agencies represent a major example of "third-party government" (Salamon, 1987), whereby the state meets certain social needs through nongovernmental programs. Nearly half the operating revenue of nonprofit social service agencies comes from federal, state, and local government. Many agencies receive more than three-fourths of their funds from government. While it is often assumed that the entrance of government leads to the exit of nonprofits and that voluntary agencies largely pave the way for the arrival of the welfare state, the actual history of social welfare in the United States does not bear this out. The large increase in social services provided by local and state government during the nineteenth century ran parallel to the equally large development of nonprofit social services; and the Great Society programs of the 1960s and 1970s led to the expansion of both government and nonprofit efforts. The social services have, in fact, exhibited a strikingly different government-nonprofit relationship than have some other parts of the nonprofit sector. The nonprofit form has, since colonial days, completely displaced government in the provision of religious services; and government has largely displaced the nonprofit form in the provision of educational services, especially on the elementary-secondary level; but both the government and nonprofit sectors have steadily increased their social service offerings, with close funding and program development contacts between the two.

Historical Development

The transplantation of English life and customs to the New World was on the whole remarkably successful, but colonial conditions inevitably brought about changes. The colonies, beginning with

Rhode Island in 1647, adopted legislation modeled on England's "Elizabethan Poor Law" (An Act for the Relief of the Poor, 43 Eliz., 1601), which made local government the social service provider of last resort, gave help to the "impotent poor" while directing the able-bodied poor to get to work, and established residency requirements for welfare assistance. The American colonies, like England, also developed charitable agencies for helping the unfortunate, such as the Scots Charitable Society (1657), the Friends Almshouse of Philadelphia (1713), the New Orleans orphanage established by the Ursuline Sisters (1729), and St. Andrew's Society of Charleston, South Carolina, founded in 1730 "to assist all people in distress, of whatever Nation or Profession."

Economic and social conditions in the colonies, however, were quite different from those in England. The colonies did not face the problem of large unemployed and unemployable populations roaming the countryside, as did England. With the rich opportunities of the new land, American colonists felt there was little excuse for poverty, and the pervasive Calvinist theology led many colonists to suspect that misfortune might actually be a sign of personal guilt and God's disfavor. Problem families were not pitied but were perceived as economically and morally counterproductive. Poverty was not an excuse but a failing. The combination of economic opportunity and Calvinist theology encouraged hard work and frowned upon hard luck. Rugged individualists such as Benjamin Franklin thought that the Poor Laws were an open invitation to shiftlessness: "I have sometimes doubted whether the laws peculiar to England, which *compel the rich to maintain the poor,* have not given the latter a dependence, that very much lessens the care of providing against the wants of old age. . . . To relieve the misfortunes of our fellow creatures is concurring with the Deity; it is godlike, but, if we provide encouragement for laziness, and supports for folly, may we not be fighting against the order of God and Nature, which perhaps has appointed want and misery as the proper punishments for, and cautions against, as well as necessary consequences of, idleness and extravagance?" (quoted in Axinn and Levin, 1982, p. 29; emphasis in the original).

During the seventeenth and eighteenth centuries, church, local community, and charitable associations provided a modest amount of what would now be called social services. During the early nineteenth century, the growth of cities, periodic economic crises, and changes in religious attitudes produced a sharp increase in the number of associations dedicated to helping the less fortunate. In the 1830s, Tocqueville marveled at the multiplicity of such associations. Thoreau wondered whether America had not gone overboard in organized charity. One father counseled his daughter, "Marry thief! Marry murderer! But never marry philanthropist!" (quoted in Curti, 1983, p. 162). But attitudes had definitely changed. As Emerson wrote, "The ancient manners were giving way. There grew a certain tenderness on the people, not before remarked."

The incipient social service system was, however, completely unprepared for the tidal wave of European immigration that hit the country in the middle and late nineteenth century and the early twentieth century. The immigrants arrived poor, jobless, often sick, unaccustomed to urban life, and struggling to maintain family unity under the strains of radically different customs and conditions. Immigration and the rapid transformation of the nation from a rural and small-town, family-based economy into an urban industrial economy created social problems without parallel in American history. The response to these problems came in three major forms. Local and state governments expanded the traditional Poor Law assistance and developed new programs, such as "asylums" for the deaf, dumb, blind, and insane. Immigrant ethnic and religious groups created mutual assistance societies that dealt with everything from finding an apartment to finding a burial plot. Host-culture philanthropists and reformers founded organizations such as the American Red Cross, the Young Men's Christian Association, settlement houses, and Charity Organization Societies through which the upper classes and emerging social work professionals shaped and developed social services in urban areas. By the 1920s, all large American cities and many smaller communities were served by an intricate and interdependent complex of governmental and nongovernmental social service agencies.

High-minded and hardworking members of America's upper classes provided much of the leadership in the development of nonprofit social services (for example, see McCarthy, 1982, on the

Chicago experience). Care for the mentally ill was a case in point. In 1841, Dorothea Lynde Dix, a New England gentlewoman and teacher at a fashionable girls' school, visited the jail in East Cambridge, Massachusetts, and was shocked to see the insane inmates chained naked to the wall. Dix began a life of lobbying state legislatures and Congress for support of insane asylums. Almost singlehandedly, she persuaded Congress in 1854 to support this cause by a large land-grant bill, subsequently vetoed by President Franklin Pierce on the grounds that "I cannot find any authority in the Constitution for making the Federal Government the great almoner of public charity throughout the United States." Dix became a world leader in this cause, securing the personal backing of Queen Victoria and once telling Pope Pius IX that Rome's insane asylum was a disgrace.

Private welfare efforts cascaded forth in thousands of new organizations during the century of immigration. Thomas Gallaudet founded the American Asylum for the Education of the Deaf and Dumb in Hartford in 1817. In 1832, Samuel Gridley Howe opened the New England Asylum for the Blind. John Augustus, a Boston shoemaker, left cobbling to devote himself to repairing the lives of former prisoners; he is reputed to have helped rehabilitate two thousand men and women. In California, private orphanages receiving state subsidies cared for children abandoned in the gold rush. In 1851, the Young Men's Christian Association was founded, following the British YMCA model, and in 1866 the Young Women's Christian Association began. Clara Barton founded the American Red Cross in 1881, again following a British model. In the 1880s, the Henry Street Settlement in New York, the South End House in Boston, and Jane Addams's Hull House in Chicago opened, following the model of Toynbee Hall and other settlement houses in London. The Charity Organization Societies helped start the Community Chest movement, created family service agencies, and played a major role in the professionalization of social work and the establishment of social work education programs, such as those developed at Cornell, Bryn Mawr, Vassar, the University of Chicago, and Columbia (Lubove, 1965).

Meanwhile, important changes in attitudes were taking place. More and more, charity workers and theorists suggested that society, not sin, was the cause of poverty, alcoholism, delinquency, and other social ills. Even prisoners should be rehabilitated as well as punished, the National Prison Congress stated in 1870: "Punishment is suffering inflicted on the criminal for the wrongdoing done by him, with a special view to secure his reformation." Americans had always accepted that conditions such as blindness, deafness, and "idiocy" were beyond the control of the individuals and families affected and not a sign of God's disfavor, but viewing poverty as a societal rather than personal failing was a new and radical idea. The advent of this idea coincided with the Progressive Era's critique of unregulated capitalism and its abuses: sweatshops, inhumane and dangerous working conditions, and pollution, as chronicled in such works as Danish immigrant Jacob Riis's 1890 book, *How the Other Half Lives*. In the machine age, it was easier for people to see that economic and social structures might crush human beings. Such an idea would have gained little credence in the agrarian days of the seventeenth and eighteenth centuries.

Less visible but far more numerous than host-culture agencies were the mutual aid societies through which immigrants helped their own kind (Chambers, 1986). Besides providing food, clothing, shelter, jobs, apartments, legal assistance, and other basic services, these societies also played important intangible roles. As Oscar Handlin (1954, p. 28) has written, "In addition to the insurance functions, the mutual-aid organizations, through ritual and through elaborate patterns of social activity, also supplied their numbers with a sense of belonging, allowed some to play the role of leaders, and gave all the consciousness of common purpose." As the immigrants became more assimilated and secure, and as both government and voluntary agencies increased, the ethnic mutual aid societies disappeared or took on primarily associative functions. However, they played a highly important role in the provision of social welfare services during the nineteenth and early twentieth centuries. As Chambers (1987, p. 421) has written:

[M]any persons and families at risk avoided elite agencies of the host society, in some measure out of pride and the reluctance to throw themselves on the mercy of others; in some part from a revulsion against the intrusive, patronizing and controlling activities they had to suffer at the hands of their presumptive betters. To ask for public assistance, to beg for charity, to take the road over the hill to the poorhouse were paths to be considered only as a last resort. Dependence was first on support (economic, psychological, social) from family, extended and fictive kin, friends and neighbors, co-religionists and "landsmen." In Catholic and Jewish immigrant communities, help came from parish and synagogue, and from myriad societies created by the poor themselves within these religious and ethnic contexts. Left/liberal historians have made much of the pluralism and openness that characterized settlement houses in the early decades (and that surely is a story deserving of attention), but have all but universally neglected the equally significant and engaging experience of neighborhood institutions founded and sustained by immigrant groups themselves.

There were highly important regional differences in the philosophy and provision of social welfare. The urban areas of New England, the middle Atlantic states, and the Midwest were most directly affected by immigration and industrialization and thus were the primary centers of social service activity, much of which was provided by private and religious agencies. Settlers in the frontier West, like the earlier colonists, tended to rely on individuals and families to solve problems. The later growth of social service institutions in the West followed the then more prevalent model of government service provision. In the South before the Civil War, slavery made any serious discussion of social welfare dangerous, since those most clearly in need of social services—black slaves— were the foundation of the Southern economy. Even after the Civil War, the development of social welfare in the South was limited by the social, economic, and political division between whites and blacks.

By the end of the nineteenth century, there was little doubt that the voluntary agency was the dominant form in social service provision. The Charity Organization Societies, concerned about the corruption of city politics, actually succeeded in eliminating public relief as a municipal function in twelve large cities, including New

York and San Francisco (Kramer, 1981, p. 63). It was generally assumed—certainly by the voluntary agencies—that government social services were of lower quality and should supplement those of voluntary agencies, which, however, were increasingly supported by government funds.

The Great Depression of the 1930s permanently changed the alignment between public and private social service providers. The dominantly private system was unable to cope with the sudden and massive crush of human problems. State and local governments increased their efforts, and for the first time in American history the federal government became heavily involved in welfare assistance. Government social service went from kid sister to big brother. The Social Security Act of 1935 and other Depression programs significantly changed the balance between public and private and between federal, state, and local welfare provision.

The years after World War II saw a significant expansion in government social service efforts, and the Great Society programs of the Johnson era marked another great leap forward. From 1950 to 1975, government social programs grew four times as fast as those in the private sector, resulting in a ten-to-one spending ratio of government to nongovernmental organizations (Kramer, 1981, p. 67). Federal legislation during the Johnson and Nixon administrations funneled large amounts of money into nonprofit social service agencies, primarily through the mechanisms of grants and purchase-of-service arrangements.

The Reagan administration preached and to some extent practiced a philosophy of federal disengagement from the social services. The Reagan gospel was that such services are provided more effectively and efficiently by state and local governments and private agencies, both nonprofit and for-profit. The Reagan cuts in social service spending were much more severe than its actions in other parts of the nonprofit sector. Still, as the Urban Institute study (Salamon, 1984) demonstrated, the federal government remained a large funder of nonprofit social service agencies, and the state and local government roles continued strong. In spite of the impact of the Reagan cuts on some areas (for example, legal assistance and job-training services), the "Reagan revolution" brought about much less real change in social service funding than did the

Roosevelt programs of the 1930s or the Johnson programs of the 1960s.

Policy Issues

English colonization of America began shortly after England took a major policy stand on care for the needy. The Elizabethan Poor Law of 1601 shaped much of the history of American social welfare not only in colonial times but long afterward. Immigration, urbanization, industrialization, and shifts in religious and social attitudes led to major changes in both the philosophy and practice of welfare in the nineteenth and twentieth centuries. In sequence, local, state, and federal government became involved in social service provision. The voluntary sector, however, did not wither away; in fact, it remained dominant until the 1930s, when the sheer magnitude of Depression problems and the extent and creativity of the federal government's response changed the relationship between public and private social services. This relationship was further altered in the 1960s and 1970s, when the federal government again took a strongly activist role. During the Reagan administration, there was clear movement away from this role, but it remains to be seen how far-reaching the impact of the "Reagan revolution" will be.

In one form or another, the role of government in social service provision has been the dominant policy issue since the early colonial period. Closely related questions are what role nonprofit social service agencies should play and what their relationship to government should be. Some have argued that the private agencies should play the pace-setting, creative, experimental, and supplemental roles while government provides funds and basic services (Swift, 1934). Others have argued that government should take over more of the social service provider role, since private agencies have a tendency to be elitist and in any event cannot provide the vast array of social services that the society clearly needs. After more than a century of serious debate and experimentation on this issue, there is still no consensus.

Unlike education and religion, social service has been characterized by a relatively stable relationship with government. There has always been substantial government funding of private social service agencies, though the extent and focus of government funding have changed. Sometimes government has been the innovator, as in the 1930s and 1960s. At other times, it has played the residual role, limiting itself to bread-and-butter issues such as income maintenance, while nonprofits set standards of quality and pioneered new services. Sometimes the emphasis has been on federal funding, sometimes on state or local funding. But such changes should not distract from the basic stability of the partnership between government and voluntary social services that has characterized the American approach from the beginning.

The government-nonprofit relationship is thus not as volatile and controversial an issue in social service as it is in other parts of the nonprofit sector. Whether one agrees with the Great Society approach or the Reagan philosophy, it is clear that government funding in several social service areas is dependent to a significant extent on political philosophy, whereas national economic, military, foreign diplomacy, health care, and social security policies have to a large extent become "party-proof" and do not change dramatically whether Republicans or Democrats are in office. Can social services achieve more of this structural stability, or will they remain relatively fluid and more closely affected by political events? The related question is what *should* happen? Some would argue that the funding structure of public education has led to structural stability at the expense of quality and that the funding of health care has led to inefficiency and complacency. Others fear that heavy government funding of the arts would have the same effect.

More attention needs to be given to the role played by social service recipients. The history of social welfare has largely been written as the story of what the "haves" (government or the Dorothea Dixes) provided to the "have-nots." But it is clear that many groups in need—immigrants, minorities, women, gays and lesbians, physically handicapped people, alcoholics, drug addicts, former prisoners—have through self-help and mutual assistance organizations provided a wealth of social services to themselves and each other. It is quite possible if not probable that the cumulative effect of the social services provided by immigrant groups during the nineteenth century was greater than the combined effect of the government and host-culture voluntary agencies with respect to immigrant needs. The current work of groups such as the Center for Independent Living, an organization of and for physically handicapped people, and a host of refugee organizations that serve the new immigrants from Latin America and Asia indicates that mutual assistance social services are still alive and well. Not only historians but also social policy analysts have often ignored these groups (for a recent exception, see Glazer, 1988), yet such groups have long provided important social services, sometimes in situations avoided by government and established nonprofit agencies.

The challenge of privatization has been raised by the Reagan administration and, with more effect, by the Thatcher administration in Great Britain. This should raise profound policy issues for the nonprofit service sector. However politically unlikely, it is at least theoretically possible that the private sector (nonprofit and/or for-profit) could provide a much larger part of the social service system than is now the case. There has not been significant reform in the welfare system for fifty years. Should there be serious discussion of government contracting with nonprofit and even for-profit firms to manage the basic welfare system? Closely related is the issue of job training and retraining. Economic self-sufficiency remains the single most important solution to many social service problems, yet the society's mechanisms for matching jobs and people are crude and inefficient. In what is supposedly an "information society," nearly 80 percent of the jobs filled every year are not listed or advertised; they do not enter into any general information system. The nonprofit sector, working with the government and the for-profit sector, might play a role in this critical part of the economic and social equation. Nonprofits also have the networks and expertise to play a larger role in developing better systems for food assistance and housing assistance. Both nonprofits and businesses could work together to expand provision of social services to workers in the workplace. A few companies have developed exemplary programs to assist workers with substance abuse problems, and day care at the workplace is being tried on a limited basis. But we are far from tapping the full potential of cooperation among the three sectors in social service provision.

The relationship with government has always been the

classic policy issue for social service nonprofits, but the relationship with the for-profit world is a rapidly emerging issue. Although the serious reentry of for-profits into the health care field has been more widely publicized, there is now substantial for-profit presence in such social services as day care, job training, residential care, and substance abuse treatment. Instead of fearing or opposing such developments, nonprofits might explore cooperative relationships with the for-profits, working to achieve a productive balance of services and resources that involve all three sectors.

Another policy issue is the question of evaluation and quality control in the social services. Unlike the essentially public nature of artistic performances, foundation grants, education, and research, the "product" of many social services is necessarily private and elusive and therefore more difficult to evaluate in any objective way. Enrollment at private schools or colleges and attendance at artistic performances presume a relatively efficient market mechanism once enunciated by Yogi Berra when the New York Yankees were having a bad year and poor attendance: "If people don't wanna come, ya can't stop 'em." But individual satisfaction is harder to trace when the services provided are mental health care, refugee assistance, rehabilitation of prisoners, and day care for small children. Recent scandals in day-care centers provide only one example of how serious and complex the evaluation issue is in the social services. Some evaluation is provided by licensing and accreditation agencies, by government inspectors, and through routine supervisory work. Occasional oversight is provided by local government offices, the Better Business Bureau, the National Charities Information Bureau, and the United Way. But none of these methods is completely satisfactory. Accountability systems in nonprofit social service agencies should reflect the importance of their task as well as the intrinsic difficulties of evaluating such services.

ADVOCACY AND LEGAL SERVICES

Conscience of a Nation

Some parts of the nonprofit sector, such as health, education, and welfare, work closely with the other two sectors. Advocacy organizations thrive on making business and government uncomfortable if not furious.

Advocacy organizations are the most antiestablishment, independent part of the independent sector. Like political parties, they seek change; unlike political parties, they typically want no part in administering the changes they have lobbied for. Even when an advocacy group and a political party work for the same goal, their incentive systems are ultimately quite different, as more than one advocacy group has learned the hard way.

The dynamics of advocacy and direct service organizations are also fundamentally different. Jenkins (1987, p. 297) notes, "Advocacy focuses on changing policies and securing collective goods, whereas service delivery creates divisible or individual benefits and may be provided without actual changes in policies." Nevertheless, there has historically been a close relationship between advocacy and human service organizations, and often the same organization plays both roles. For instance, the Charity Organization Society of New York at the turn of the century not only provided social services but also campaigned for public health, housing, and welfare reform. The same mix of advocacy and service is evident today in many black, Hispanic, Asian, and other minority agencies. Nonprofit service organizations are often the training ground or retirement home of cause movement leaders. The civil rights movement depended heavily on black churches for leadership development. Schools and universities have historically been breeding grounds for social change efforts: student involvement in the civil rights, anti-Vietnam War, environmental, and antiapartheid movements are recent examples. Ralph Nader has made college campuses a principal base for his consumer advocacy campaigns.

Scope and Impact

Virtually all types of nonprofits engage to some extent in lobbying and public information campaigns. Advocacy organizations are primarily involved with lobbying and disseminating information directed toward broad societal objectives or collective goods rather than outcomes of benefit only to their own members. A trade association lobbying for the automobile industry and nonprofit hospitals lobbying to protect their tax-exempt status are working for the immediate interests of their member organizations, even though their products (transportation, health care) may be an important part of the society's well-being. A nonprofit advocacy organization lobbying for clean air is working for a collective good that will presumably benefit all members of society equally. Even when advocacy organizations represent a particular group—such as women, members of minority groups, physically handicapped people, victims of drunk driving, and potential victims of handgun attacks—there is an implicit assumption that actions benefiting these people will benefit all of society: voting rights for Southern blacks help guarantee voting rights for all citizens in all parts of the country.

While this characteristic of advocacy organizations generally deflects criticisms of excessive self-interest, it is scant protection against criticisms of excessive zeal. The first large, organized social movement in American history was the temperance movement. The activists of this movement had no doubt that their cause was in the public interest; but other Americans had a very different view of the matter, and some national and ethnic groups saw the temperance movement as thinly disguised bigotry. Both pro- and antiabortion leaders are convinced that their cause is in the public interest. Peace activists see the proliferation of nuclear weapons as the greatest threat to humanity in the history of the world; others see these weapons as the best way to preserve peace and protect the world from communism. Even social movements such as abolition, women's suffrage, child welfare, and civil rights were initially opposed precisely on the grounds that they would cause major disruptions in society and therefore were not in the public interest. The 1960s and 1970s gave rise to public-interest law groups, but "public interest" was defined by the lawyers involved. Unlike nonprofits that offer a service that people may take or leave, advocacy organizations attempt to change laws and public policies that affect millions of Americans; not surprisingly, their work is often intensely controversial.

For several reasons,there are no statistics on advocacy groups comparable to those on other nonprofit organizations. Advocacy groups are variously classified as "social welfare" entities, civic groups, membership organizations, and legal-assistance agencies. Many nonprofits whose primary activity is religion, health, education, or social services are also engaged in advocacy, within the limits on such activity imposed by the Internal Revenue Service. Advocacy organizations are often largely or exclusively volunteer-based and sometimes fall below the limit of $25,000 in annual revenue required for registering with the IRS. Some advocacy organizations with one tax identification number have dozens or hundreds of local subunits. The Sierra Club, for instance, has 440,000 members in 486 groups within 57 chapters, all of which use the same tax identification number and therefore are counted by the IRS as one organization. Many advocacy organizations come and go quickly; some live out their full life-spans between the five-year counting periods of the Census Bureau's Census of Service Industries, which would miss many anyway, because it includes only organizations with paid employees. Finally, it is possible that some advocacy organizations, by nature suspicious of government, exercise an old American tradition by declining to register with the authorities.

The 1982 Census of Service Industries listed 1,302 "legal aid societies and similar legal services" with 14,462 employees and revenue of $442,188,000 (National Center for Charitable Statistics, 1985, p. 5). But the great majority of advocacy organizations fall under other classifications, as "civic, social, and fraternal associations" and other membership and social service organizations. The

Urban Institute study of "nonprofit human service organizations" (social services, arts and culture, some education and health care, and advocacy and legal service agencies) reported that 3.5 percent of the organizations in the sixteen sites studied gave "legal services/ advocacy" as their primary activity (Harder, Kimmich, and Salamon, 1985, p. 17). If one adjusted and extrapolated this figure to the entire country by assuming that 3 percent of all nonreligious nonprofits are legal services/advocacy organizations, the national figure would be about 15,000 organizations.

Impressionistic evidence suggests that most advocacy organizations are characterized by low salaries and long work hours. Ralph Nader, once pictured on the cover of *Time* as literally a knight in shining armor, is a prime example of the high-work, low-pay ethic. Stories of Nader living in a low-cost boarding house and running down the hallway to answer the pay phone while taking on General Motors are a modern version of the tales of Sir Lancelot. Cause organizations thrive on the giant-slayer image even when they become large and sophisticated, such as the Sierra Club or Common Cause. In 1982, following stunning electoral victories in thirty-seven states and local communities, the nuclear freeze movement solemnly decided to retain its headquarters in St. Louis (the heartland) in spite of the fact that decisions on nuclear weapons tend to be made in Washington, D.C. Advocacy movements are often decentralized and suspicious of traditional forms of organization and authority. One study described the organization of a typical social movement as decentralized, cell-like in structure, based on charismatic rather than bureaucratic leadership, bound together by ideology, adaptive, and nourished by "personal ties between members and between local group leaders [and] by the activities of traveling evangelists" (Gerlach and Hine, 1970, p. 78).

Advocacy organizations receive their funding from a variety of sources. Some, such as the Sierra Club, Common Cause, and the National Association for the Advancement of Colored People (NAACP), have large memberships that provide most of the operational income. With a few exceptions, including the Ford Foundation, the Carnegie Corporation, and the Rockefeller Brothers Fund, mainstream foundations have been wary of contributing to advocacy organizations. Some smaller funders, such as the

Field Foundation, the Stern Family Fund, the Taconic Foundation, and the New World Foundation, supported black voter registration efforts in the South during the 1960s. Some of the "alternative" foundations, such as Haymarket, Vanguard, and Ploughshares, have funded advocacy efforts. Few corporations have donated to advocacy groups. Government has not been eager to fund some of its sharpest critics. As Nielsen (1979, p. 179) put it, "Because their essential purpose is social change, [advocacy organizations'] relationship with government and the established, conservative elements of society is inherently an abrasive one."

Although advocacy groups play the role of the loyal opposition, many causes later become government programs. Abolition led to the Emancipation Proclamation, women's suffrage led to the Nineteenth Amendment, the civil rights movement led to the historic Civil Rights Act and a host of government regulations and programs, and the environmental movement produced the Environmental Protection Agency. This transition is sometimes successful and sometimes not. When reform legislation is passed and government is no longer the enemy or the target, the clarity of social activism is sometimes followed by confusion, letdown, and even disappointment. The aftermath of the women's suffrage movement is an example: women got the vote but lost much of the impetus of their drive for equality.

All large organizations and complex societies build in checks and balances to protect individuals, guarantee a certain degree of freedom, and enhance the general well-being of the group. The U.S. Constitution did this in ways familiar to every high school civics class. Less obvious and rarely mentioned in civics textbooks is the powerful checks-and-balances system provided by the nonprofit sector, especially through advocacy organizations and social change movements. In the antebellum South, business and government interests had nothing to gain and much to lose from freeing the slaves. Neither the national government nor the business community fought for women's right to vote. The accomplishments of American business and government have been awesome, but many of the social and moral advances in American history have come from nonprofit advocacy efforts. Ironically, these moral advances have often brought great benefit to business and government. For instance, the women's and minority liberation movements brought a large supply of new talent into the labor force and political ranks.

Advocacy organizations have at times played a major role in institutionalizing the process of healthy social and political criticism. In some situations where government, business, the press, the universities, and the churches failed to meet a social or moral challenge, advocacy organizations took the leadership role. These organizations have become part of the collective conscience of the nation. Brian O'Connell, president of Independent Sector, has called advocacy "the quintessential function of the voluntary sector."

The legal, social, and economic accomplishments of advocacy movements have often been pointed out. Harder to measure but of great significance is the effect these efforts have had on the personal lives of activists. People who seek involvement beyond their family and work life and are not attracted to the religious, ethnic, and social organizations their parents and grandparents found so helpful sometimes turn to cause organizations. For many of these new-age Americans, involvement in a cause gives added meaning to their lives, expands their friendship groups, and gives them experiences not typically provided by business, leisure, and family life. Advocacy groups are often characterized by a particular feeling of community. The civil rights and women's movements exhibited a sense of family; the very words *sisterhood* and *brotherhood* took on a reality reminiscent of the early, charismatic phases of utopian communes, religious communities, revolutions, and some political campaigns. Advocacy organizations often give adherents not just a cause but a way of life.

Historical Background

Before the Revolution, America had no capacity for broad social movements. It was too consumed with bare survival, the exploration and development of the new land, and the increasing strain in its relationship with England. Moral and social reform was still largely within the province of religion. Even the tumultuous Great Awakening of the 1730s and 1740s, which added the new emotional energy of Methodists, Baptists, and "new light" Presbyterians to the older and more staid Quakers, Congregationalists, and Anglicans, only strengthened the notion that personal and social reform was a matter of faith. In short, neither economic nor political nor religious conditions were conducive to the growth of anything like the later social movements. However, the Great Awakening did teach Americans the power of a zealous cause, and both the temperance and abolition movements later used some of its techniques and certainly its moral fervor (Smith, 1957).

Like the rest of the nonprofit sector, advocacy organizations had their real birth in the nineteenth century. The first major issue was temperance. Tocqueville ([1835] 1969, pp. 242–243) was particularly intrigued by this aspect of American life and noted that "at the time of my visit [in 1831] temperance societies already counted more than 270,000 members." The number would rise to more than a million by the Civil War. By 1857, thirteen states had prohibited alcohol.

Alcoholism was no trivial moralistic issue but a severe social problem that brought poverty to families dependent on drinking spouses and parents. On the frontier and in the congested cities, a father's alcoholism could literally mean starvation for his wife and children. Women lobbied heavily against the saloons, which they depicted with some accuracy as the enemy of home life. Temperance crusaders adopted some of the revivalist tactics of the early Methodist preachers and succeeded in getting hundreds of thousands to "take the pledge." Like all social movements, temperance caused consternation. Immigrant groups such as the Irish and Germans were targeted by temperance crusaders in a way these groups found highly offensive. The New York Temperance Society reported in 1841 that this "refuse of European population, has been one of the most formidable obstructions to [the temperance] cause" (Billington, 1938, p. 195). In 1884, Presbyterian minister Samuel Burchard created a national sensation when he introduced Republican presidential candidate James Blaine by urging voters not to defect to the other party, "whose antecedents are rum, Romanism, and rebellion" (Ellis, 1952, vol. 1, p. 244). After a century of influence, the temperance/prohibition movement largely came to an end in the 1920s, the victim of changing mores and the excesses of a cause that had gone from persuasion to compulsion.

It was abolition, however, that became the prototype of social movements. The Founding Fathers had consciously avoided the slavery issue on the grounds that it would destroy any chance of union. The issue kept raising its head in the federal government, especially with regard to whether slavery should be allowed in the new frontier states; but aside from debating the issue, the federal government made no serious effort to eliminate the practice of slavery for seventy-five years following the Declaration of Independence statement that "all men are created equal." Business interests in both North and South accepted the practice; slavery was considered essential to the Southern economy and was of more than passing interest to textile and trading interests in the North. Organized religion's position on the issue was at best ambiguous. The impetus for abolition came not from the established institutions of society but from individuals and groups that came together to protest slavery on moral and social grounds.

The abolition movement not only won a great moral victory but also established patterns that many later advocacy movements would follow. The abolitionists to a large extent remained independent of particular churches and political parties. The movement used a secular voice to deliver a moral and religious message. It developed a coalition of activists who had come from other causes (such as temperance) and would go on to other causes (such as women's suffrage). The abolitionists made a long-term commitment to the cause; it was thirty years after the appearance of William Lloyd Garrison's *Liberator* in 1831 that slavery was finally abolished. Those three decades were filled with vehement opposition to the movement on the part of Northerners as well as Southerners. Abolitionists were beaten, tarred and feathered, banned from towns, burned from their homes. A few were murdered. Yet the movement kept growing, and by 1840 there were 150,000 members in antislavery societies.

The country's communication and transportation systems had advanced during the century since the Great Awakening and had increased the potential for broad social movements. The growth of cities made it possible to reach much larger audiences. The new circuit riders could ride the railroads. Garrison's main instrument was his newspaper, *Liberator*. Harriet Beecher Stowe's novel *Uncle*

Tom's Cabin, published in 1852, sold 300,000 copies the first year
and had a powerful effect on the movement. The picture of Eliza
being chased across the ice was etched in the American consciousness. Just as the invention of the printing press had, four centuries
earlier, greatly assisted the Protestant Reformation, so urbanization,
new technology, and the emerging mass media helped the abolition
movement. The connection between mass communication and
social change would not be lost on later reformers.

The reform impulse that produced abolition, temperance,
common schools, utopian communes, and new religious sects also
was creating a movement for women's liberation. Lucretia Mott and
Elizabeth Cady Stanton were among those who launched the
movement for women's suffrage during a meeting at Seneca Falls,
New York, in 1848. The women temporarily postponed their efforts
in order to assist the men in the abolition movement, and while they
gave assistance they got combat experience. Many of the leaders of
the women's suffrage movement came out of the abolition movement. One, Angelica Grimké, was married to Theodore Weld, who
may have been a more influential abolitionist even than Garrison.
Following the Civil War, the women's movement began again in
earnest, and women such as Susan B. Anthony and Lucy Stone were
added to the leadership ranks. The string of victories began in 1869,
when the territory of Wyoming gave women the vote, and extended
to 1919, when the Nineteenth Amendment to the United States
Constitution was overwhelmingly ratified by the states. The
crowning achievement of this seventy-year effort read simply: "The
rights of citizens of the United States to vote, shall not be denied or
abridged by the United States or by any State on account of sex."

The Progressive movement of the late nineteenth and early
twentieth centuries brought social activism to a new peak. The
emancipation of women, child welfare legislation, the union
movement, and welfare reform were just a few of the causes that
advocacy organizations pressed. Not coincidentally, this was also
the peak of the immigration period. The reformers, however, ran
into the realities of the new urban politics. Organizations such as
Tammany Hall had their own agendas and, representing primarily
the ethnic groups, were often suspicious of the high-minded Yankee
reformers. The differences and divisions were deeper than many

reformers suspected. Hofstadter (1955, p. 185) has written: "While the boss, with his pragmatic talents and his immediate favors, quickly appealed to the immigrant, the reformer was a mystery. Often he stood for things that to the immigrant were altogether bizarre, like women's rights and Sunday laws, or downright insulting, like temperance. His abstractions had no appeal within the immigrant's experience—citizenship, responsibility, efficiency, good government, economy, businesslike management. The immigrant wanted humanity, not efficiency, and economies threatened to lop needed jobs off the payroll. . . . Progressives, in return, reproached the immigrant for having no interest in broad principles, in the rule of law or the public good. Between the two, for the most part, the channels of effective communication were closed."

World War I, the Depression, World War II, and the Eisenhower era made social reform movements seem almost a thing of the past. The great break came, in a remarkable parallel to the abolition movement, with the advent of the black civil rights movement of the late 1950s and 1960s. This time, however, the liberation movement came from Southern black ministers instead of Northern white reformers. The new abolition movement was again met with hatred and violence and, like its predecessor, quickly gained broad-based support. The Southern Christian Leadership Conference, the Congress of Racial Equality, and many religious leaders, students, and women joined hands to march for an end to prejudice. The idealism of the civil rights movement and the charismatic leadership and then martyrdom of Martin Luther King, Jr., created one of the most powerful social movements in American history. Even with the setbacks of the Vietnam and Watergate era, the civil rights movement dramatically improved the position of blacks in American society and generated new energy for the reinvigorated feminist movement, the United Farm Workers and other Hispanic liberation organizations, the American Indian Movement, gay-lesbian liberation, and others. Although each of these has its own unique characteristics, all reverberate with overtones of the black civil rights movement. Not only are many of the organizing strategies similar, but sometimes even the songs, symbols, and language are the same. The civil rights song "We Shall Overcome" has become a universal hymn.

The increase in advocacy activity during the last thirty years is more the reflection of a mature society than of one in deep trouble. Jenkins (1987, p. 302) has noted: "In general, . . . the formation of nonprofit advocacy organizations depends heavily on the availability of entrepreneurs, elite patronage, and a favorable political environment." Leaders such as Martin Luther King, Cesar Chavez, Ralph Nader, and John Gardner have been the "entrepreneurs" of the advocacy industry. Several large foundations, the National Council of Churches, the Catholic church, White House conferences, and a number of wealthy individuals and celebrities have provided the elite patronage. A general climate developed that made advocacy more respectable than it has been in some periods of American history; by the 1970s and 1980s, charges of anarchism or communism were not automatically applied to activists as they had been at the turn of the century, in the 1930s, and again in the 1950s.

The structure and strategies of advocacy movements also matured. The movements began a self-propagating process, as activists trained in one movement went on to others. Strategies for the mobilization of volunteers and funds were developed and improved. Political lessons learned by one group were passed on to others. The advocacy movements of the 1970s and 1980s took on a more sophisticated, complex look. The issues turned from civil rights and the Vietnam War to cleaning up the environment, controlling the spread of nuclear weapons, reforming the financing of political campaigns, protecting consumers from faulty products, and eliminating apartheid from South Africa. A new development was that of conservative advocacy movements, promoting libertarian and free-market values, warning against pornography, and supporting anticommunist guerilla movements. Generally, advocacy groups became better organized, politically more astute, and highly skilled in the use of the media. Yet some of the passion had clearly gone. There was no burning issue like abolition, civil rights, or Vietnam that could unite many factions. For a short time, it seemed that the peace movement had this potential; but the public's attention wandered, and no one with the single-minded fervor of a William Lloyd Garrison, Susan B. Anthony, or Martin Luther King emerged to give the movement the charismatic leadership and staying power it needed against a military-industrial complex at least as entrenched as the institution of slavery had been in the South a century earlier.

Policy Issues

While nonprofit health care, education, social services, and international assistance are partially funded by government and directly influenced by public policy, advocacy, like religion and art, has an arm's-length relationship with government and is less directly an object of policy consideration. Social action movements are by definition outside the government establishments that embody public policy. Ironically, advocacy groups exist to shape public policy but themselves are not directly part of the result. Yet there are few more important issues in the American nonprofit sector than the society's stance toward cause movements. The ultimate defining characteristic of the nonprofit sector is its ability to disregard political and economic mandates and march to a different drummer. Advocacy groups highlight the nation's central policy toward the nonprofit sector: the guarantee of a private group's freedom to exist, believe, express values, speak out, and protest the policies and actions of government and other established organizations.

There is, however, a price for free speech. "Charitable" nonprofits—roughly, those exempt under Section 501(c)(3) of the Internal Revenue Code—may not "substantially" engage in attempts to influence legislation and may not actively support particular candidates for political office. Nonprofits, such as the Sierra Club, that are extensively involved in attempts to influence legislation have Section 501(c)(4) status and thus are not able to receive tax-deductible donations. Concretely, this means that thousands of nonprofits become extremely leery of speaking out on legislative issues for fear of slipping into the vague forbidden territory of "substantial" activity and thus losing their Section 501(c)(3) status. This effectively leaves serious lobbying to the "professionals," the nonprofits that can afford to organize as Section 501(c)(4) groups, and deprives the government and the society of a broader spectrum of opinion. While IRS definitions and rulings have demonstrated that there is a good deal of leeway in the meaning of "substantial," most nonprofits simply do not have the time or expertise to assess this.

Independent Sector president Brian O'Connell has argued that this is not a trivial legal issue and that it in fact goes to the heart of nonprofit-sector activity. Historically, advocacy has come not only or even primarily from "advocacy organizations" but from churches, social welfare agencies, and other nonprofits whose primary task is providing services but that occasionally feel impelled to speak out on an issue directly related to their mission. To quiet this voice is to lose a major part of the conscience of the nation.

A policy question more internal to the nonprofit sector relates to the personal lives of advocacy workers. The funding of advocacy organizations is a chronic problem. Government and corporations understandably do not fund causes of which they are the target. Foundations received a strong warning from Congress in 1969 not to get involved in advocacy funding; the great majority of foundations had never shown any such inclination to begin with. Religious groups have supported many social action movements, but the support rarely takes the form of large-scale transfer of funds. A few wealthy individuals and celebrities lend their support from time to time, but this has never been an adequate funding base for advocacy efforts. A few "entrepreneurs," such as Ralph Nader, are ingenious at maintaining long-term funding, and a few organizations, such as the Sierra Club, have developed a membership base and a sufficient variety of activities, products, and causes to keep members satisfied; but these are more the exception than the rule. The principal support of social action has typically come from the small donations of believers in the cause. One result is that the believers who work for the cause are terribly underpaid. Advocacy organizations test the theory of psychic income to the extreme. An added problem is that major social change often takes several decades. While most advocacy workers can hang on for a short time, few can endure low wages and long hours for the ten, twenty, or thirty years that it usually takes to make a real difference. "Burnout" is a common problem in advocacy efforts, and few workers stay with these organizations past the age of forty.

Advocacy groups, like all organizations, sooner or later have to deal with the problem of how to attract and keep first-rate leaders and workers, which in turn depends in part on the organizations' ability to obtain adequate and stable funding. More institutionalized support is greatly needed in advocacy circles. One answer might be specialized funders such as Ploughshares, which annually gives over a million dollars to peace organizations. Such intermediary funding mechanisms provide a regular means of support for advocacy efforts while assuring donors of the merit of particular groups. Another answer is building coalitions of service-producing nonprofits around particular issues and "taxing" each organization for a small percentage of its operating budget to support advocacy work on those issues. However, the principal funding and political strength of advocacy movements will probably always come from mass participation and multiple small donations from members and true believers—conscience money from the nation's millions of reformers.

INTERNATIONAL ASSISTANCE

The World Role of America's Nonprofits

We expect American business and government to shape world events but tend to view the nonprofit sector as local and homey, like the neighborhood Boy Scout troop. Yet nonprofit organizations have a major international presence. American religious, educational, health care, grantmaking, and international assistance agencies annually spend hundreds of millions of dollars abroad, primarily in Third World Countries. These efforts range from public health projects in Brazil to famine relief in the sub-Sahara and agricultural research in the Philippines.

Scope and Impact

American nonprofit organizations spent an estimated $1.8 billion for international assistance in 1986, not counting the government funds that also flowed through these agencies (U.S. Bureau of the Census, 1987, p. 825). Two hundred American foundations made over 2,500 grants for "international and foreign programs" worth $178 million in 1985–86 (Foundation Center, 1987b). Two-thirds of the grant dollars came from six foundations: Ford, A. W. Mellon, Kellogg, MacArthur, Rockefeller, and Carnegie. Religious organizations such as Catholic Relief Services, Lutheran World Relief, Church World Service, the American Jewish Joint Distribution Committee, and World Vision spent more than a billion dollars in program services in 1987. Catholic Relief Services alone had 1987 expenditures of $241 million, 93 percent of which went to program services reaching more than ten million people in seventy-four countries (Catholic Relief Services, 1988, pp. 1, 35). World Vision had 1987 expenditures of $146 million, of which $110 million went to program services for thirteen million people in eighty countries (World Vision, 1988). Half of the 485 national religious organizations surveyed in the Council on Foundations' 1984 study of religious philanthropy indicated that they had operations internationally (McDonald, 1985, p. 129). Over 70 percent of the 350,000 local religious congregations in the United States are active in supporting international relief work (Hodgkinson, Weitzman, and Kirsch, 1988, p. 18). Groups such as Amnesty International and Americas Watch have pressured totalitarian governments into releasing thousands of political prisoners.

As Bolling (1982, p. 35) notes, religion is particularly well organized for international assistance work: "The church-related agencies that work abroad have natural grassroots constituencies both in the United States and abroad, and, in most cases, a long tradition of denominational support for overseas projects to draw upon. Most of them operate within formal church structures: Baptists, Methodists, Episcopalians, Presbyterians, Catholics, Seventh Day Adventists, Salvation Army, Mormons, Pentecostalists, Lutherans, and many others. They have central administrative offices (once generally called missionary boards), church publications, and local women's societies that carry on activities to inform their fellow church members about programs overseas and to solicit funds. Their programs of relief, education, hospital services, and training in agricultural and industrial skills are usually related to those areas and peoples identified with the churches' missionary projects, some of which go back more than one hundred years."

Research and development projects have been one of the most important forms of nonprofit international assistance. The Rockefeller Foundation's legendary efforts to eradicate hookworm, yellow fever, and malaria in foreign countries have already been noted. In the 1960s, the Rockefeller Foundation and the Ford Foundation combined efforts with the federal government's Agency for International Development (AID) to launch a major attack on the world food problem by developing high-yield forms of rice, wheat, and other grains. Organizations such as the International Rice Research Institute (IRRI) in the Philippines and the International Maize and Wheat Improvement Center (CIMMYT) in Mexico

City, the latter headed by Nobel Peace Prize winner Norman Borlaug, led to the "Green Revolution" and have had a major impact on the food production capacities of developing nations. Rockefeller, Ford, and AID also joined forces to develop family-planning programs in foreign countries. The Kellogg Foundation committed 17 percent of its total grantmaking of $89 million in 1987 to Latin America, southern Africa, and other foreign countries in support of agricultural, health, education, and other projects. Environmental organizations in the United States work with foreign groups and governments on issues such as saving the rain forests of the Amazon, limiting the killing of whales and dolphins in international waters, and documenting the ominous depletion of the ozone layer. The American peace movement has extensive connections with similar groups in Europe and other parts of the world. The 1985 Nobel Peace Prize was awarded to the International Physicians for the Prevention of Nuclear War, an organization that included many American physicians.

American nonprofits have played a major role in resettling hundreds of thousands of refugees from Cambodia, Vietnam, Nicaragua, El Salvador, Guatemala, Ethiopia, and other nations. Groups such as Oxfam America, American Friends Service Committee, International Rescue Committee, and American Red Cross were particularly effective in meeting the needs of refugees when the Cambodian holocaust of the late 1970s was revealed. Similar efforts reduced suffering and death among refugees from the war between Ethiopia and Somalia. Nonprofits facilitate the entry of refugees into the United States. Bremner (1988, p. 199) notes that "the American government, voluntary organizations, and, in particular, churches, made it possible for more refugees to find homes in the United States in the decade 1975–85 than in any earlier half century of American history."

Changes in popular culture and media have led to some new forms of international philanthropy. When BBC films of the famine in Ethiopia appeared on NBC "Nightly News" in October 1984, they caused a sensation. The NBC telephone lines were jammed for hours. By morning, there were lines of people standing in front of international relief agency offices, waiting to make contributions. Thousands of contributions flowed into relief organizations, most of which did not even have operations in Ethiopia. Irish rock star Bob Geldof had watched the pictures on the BBC in England and was deeply moved. He decided to get personally involved and persuaded many of his colleagues in the music world to do the same. The result was the simultaneous "Live Aid" concerts on July 13, 1985, which were watched by 162,000 fans in London and Philadelphia and by an estimated 1.5 billion television viewers, the largest audience in history. The concerts raised $80 million for famine relief. The African famine also led to the "We Are the World" record, which sold fifty million copies worldwide and generated $52 million for relief of the African famine. Just as television had brought home the plight of Southern blacks and the horror of the Vietnam War, television showed Americans the reality of mass starvation in Africa and created a new form of philanthropy.

It may be too early to tell whether either the medium or the message of "Live Aid" and "We Are the World" will have any serious, long-term effect on international philanthropy or the involvement of young Americans in humanitarian causes. There is also the question of how many attendees at "Live Aid" were there for the concert rather than the cause. Rock producer Bill Graham said after the concert, "People are concerned about the plight in Africa, but if there was no famine we'd have sold as many tickets." But this Woodstock of philanthropy did at least raise some important questions about the potential of modern technology to galvanize large numbers of volunteers and raise large amounts of money in a short time.

The fact that the famine also quickly slipped from public attention highlighted the need for stable, long-term efforts in international assistance. Ethiopia, for example, is a Marxist-Leninist state involved in a civil war. Rock stars and mass television audiences are hardly equipped to solve hunger problems embedded in political and military struggles. International assistance experts know that even in more peaceful countries, solving the hunger problem is far more complex than raising money for food. As CARE executive director Philip Johnson put it, "It's not enough to feed the kid. . . . First you have to deworm him, so you also need a medical program. Otherwise you're just feeding his parasites and not the kid. And then you've got to dig wells so there's clean water instead of dirty river water to drink and he doesn't have to pick up new parasites or maybe die of the endemic intestinal diseases" (quoted in Bremner, 1988, p. 199).

Nonprofit organizations have often proved more effective than their government counterparts in international assistance efforts. The State Department's AID program has supported many worthy causes but has become increasingly tied to American foreign policy objectives and in some cases has been simply a conduit for military aid to regimes willing to take an anticommunist position. Even the highly regarded Peace Corps has been limited by the ebbs and flows of political support in the United States and recipient nations. Nonprofit organizations, for all their problems, at least do not have to fear that a presidential election will fundamentally alter their purpose. Religious and other nonprofit organizations that have been operating in Asia, Africa, Latin America, and the Middle East for several decades have had the opportunity to develop extensive knowledge of local cultures and traditions and have generally made it clear by their actions that they are not instruments of American business and foreign policy interests.

However, nonprofits are intimately involved with the federal government in international aid. Two-thirds of Catholic Relief Services' 1987 revenue came from the U.S. government (Catholic Relief Services, 1988, p. 30), primarily the Food for Peace program. A similar percentage of CARE's revenue came from the federal government (CARE, 1988, p. 39).

Historical Development

The colonization of America was primarily the result of economic factors, but the missionary impulse played an important role in the Spanish, French, and English colonies. Along with the Massachusetts Bay Company and the Virginia Company, there were the Corporation for the Propagation of the Gospel in New England (1649), the Society for the Propagation of the Gospel in Foreign Parts (1701), and its parent Society for Promoting Christian Knowledge (1699), which were active and influential in the development of colonial religion and education. More generally, the exploration and settling of the Americas came at the zenith of

European missionary activity, which also extended to the Far East, Africa, and India.

The missionary zeal that played such an important role in the colonizing of America planted the seeds for an American missionary movement in later decades. The Revolutionary War had hardly ended when American churches started looking for spiritual victories around the world. A missionary society was formed at Williams College in 1808. Andover Theological Seminary, founded in 1807, became a launching pad for missionary efforts. Presbyterians began sending missionaries to Arab countries in the early 1800s and founded a college in Lebanon that became the American University of Beirut. Before the Civil War, American missions were established in Burma, India, Ceylon, the Sandwich Islands (later Hawaii), China, and Africa. As Marty (1984, p. 186) said, "the mission *to* America from colonial days had now become the mission *of* America to the world."

Throughout the rest of the nineteenth and into the twentieth centuries, the American missionary movement grew rapidly. Catholics, Presbyterians, Methodists, Baptists, and such newer sects as Seventh Day Adventists and Mormons opened missions, hospitals, clinics, schools, and colleges in Africa, Latin America, India, and the Far East. The missionary efforts generated heroic tales of Dr. Tom Dooley in his Laotian jungle hospital, Dr. Albert Schweitzer in his African clinic, and such horrors as ministers and priests being tortured in communist Chinese prison camps and nuns being raped in the Belgian Congo. Sometimes the missionaries became part of a heavy-handed imposition of American culture; at other times they joined local guerrilla forces to fight against military regimes supported by the United States.

The missionary effort laid the groundwork for American government and nonprofit international assistance programs. At the turn of the twentieth century, Frederick Gates, John D. Rockefeller's chief philanthropic aide and a former Baptist minister, became impressed by the extent of American missionary work abroad and saw the possibilities of using this as a base for Rockefeller commercial and philanthropic efforts. Gates wrote to Rockefeller:

The fact is that heathen nations are being everywhere honeycombed with light and with civilization, with modern industrial life and applications of modern science, through the direct or indirect agencies of the missionaries. Quite apart from the question of persons converted, the mere commercial results of missionary effort to our own land is worth . . . a thousand-fold every year of what is spent on missions. For illustration: Our commerce today with the Hawaiian Islands . . . is, I am told, $17,000,000 per year. Five per cent of that in one year would represent all the money that ever was spent in christianizing and civilizing the natives. . . . Missionaries and missionary schools are introducing the application of modern science, steam and electric power, modern agricultural machinery and modern manufacture into foreign lands. The result will be eventually to multiply the productive power of foreign countries many times. This will enrich them as buyers of American products and enrich us as importers of their products. We are only in the very dawn of commerce, and we owe that dawn, with all its promise, to the channels opened up by Christian missionaries [quoted in Collier and Horowitz, 1976, p. 101].

It is not known whether the world's oil czar was impressed by this argument, but the various Rockefeller philanthropies have always included ambitious international programs. The Rockefeller Institute for Medical Research developed a vaccine for yellow fever, which the Rockefeller Foundation carried to the four corners of the earth, along with its antimalaria and antihookworm campaigns and other medical and public health innovations. The foundation also created the Peking Union Medical College, which it intended to make "the Johns Hopkins of China," developed international fellowship and leadership training programs, assisted in the international war relief effort during and after World War I, and was the principal initiator of the international grain research and development centers that created the Green Revolution.

Other foundations later joined Rockefeller in the international philanthropy effort. The Carnegie Corporation, founded in 1911, was an early and major leader in international grantmaking,

primarily—by direction of its Scottish-born founder—concentrated
on British Commonwealth countries and colonies. The W. K.
Kellogg Foundation, formed in 1930, specialized in the dissemination of agricultural and public health knowledge in foreign lands
and also invested heavily in leadership development programs
abroad. The Ford Foundation, created in 1936 but not substantially
funded until 1951, started its international efforts with $16 million
for agricultural development in famine-threatened India from 1951
to 1956 and soon launched agricultural, educational, and other
programs in Pakistan, Burma, Indonesia, the Middle East, sub-
Saharan Africa, the Caribbean, and Latin America. Ford quickly
became the giant among international funders; by 1966, it had spent
$1.7 billion on international programs, most of which went to the
Third World. Ford also took major initiative in funding programs
to enhance arms control and world peace; a world order of law and
justice; better understanding of the Soviet Union, African, Asian,
and other non-Western cultures; and the development of professionals, scientists, and government managers in many foreign countries.
Other foundations active in international assistance include the
Lilly Endowment, the Rockefeller Brothers Fund, and the Kettering
Foundation (Bolling, 1982, pp. 82–90).

The two World Wars triggered many private international
assistance programs. The American Red Cross raised and distributed $400 million during World War I. The Rockefeller Foundation
established a War Relief Commission in 1914 and with other
Rockefeller charities spent $22 million on war relief. Immigrants set
up numerous war relief organizations to aid members of their
ethnic, religious, and national groups in Europe. The American
Friends Service Committee was created in 1917 as a Quaker response
to the war's devastation and provided services not only in the Allied
nations but also in Germany and Russia. The Unitarian, Lutheran,
Catholic, and other churches began international assistance
programs that would grow and develop long after the war ended.
Trade unions such as the International Ladies Garment Workers
Union sent money.

After the isolationism and domestic economic problems of
the 1920s and 1930s, private relief agencies again proliferated during
World War II. Private agencies sent nearly $400 million in funds

and supplies between 1943 and 1945 (Bolling, 1982, p. 17). CARE (Cooperative for American Relief Everywhere), founded in November 1945, started by distributing food packages to starving Europeans and later became the largest private international relief agency. Catholic Relief Services, founded in 1943 as War Relief Services, would become the largest religious international relief agency. American Jews were particularly generous in assisting victims of the Nazi Holocaust and citizens of the new state of Israel.

A mixture of American altruism and concern over Soviet expansionism led to the federal government's Marshall Plan, which poured billions of dollars into European countries devastated by the war. In 1954, the United States created the Food for Peace program, which became a staple of American foreign assistance, much of which was provided through private agencies. The rapid decline of European colonialism in Asia, Africa, and South America left a military, diplomatic, and philanthropic vacuum that the United States was quick to fill. During the 1950s and 1960s, aid to "underdeveloped countries" became part of the American creed. Private agencies worked closely with the U.S. government to provide this assistance and carry the gospel of Americanism abroad. President Kennedy created the Peace Corps, the Agency for International Development (AID), the Alliance for Progress, and other foreign assistance programs. While Kennedy's death, the Vietnam War, and the increasing militarization of American foreign aid sharply curtailed the development of government assistance programs, private agencies continued their steady growth that had begun during and after World War II.

Policy Issues

In education, health care, social services, and art, while government and nonprofit efforts may take different forms and have different specialties, the basic goals are the same. That cannot be said of international assistance. Government programs bear the stamp of U.S. foreign policy interests and often bear the additional stamp of a particular administration. The European Recovery Program, or Marshall Plan, gave $12.5 billion to the nations of Europe from 1948 to 1951, but the effort was motivated at least as much by concern about Soviet expansion as by altruism. The Food for Peace program began in 1954 partly as a way to use agricultural surpluses, partly as a way to win friends among developing nations, and partly as an effort to help people in need. AID has often been heavily influenced by foreign policy interests. Federal funding of family planning through the Population Council and the International Planned Parenthood Federation was jeopardized during the Reagan era.

The collaboration between government and nonprofits, or "PVOs" (private voluntary organizations), as they are known in international assistance circles, is considerably more treacherous than in other nonprofit service areas. Some critics of CARE, for example, feel that the organization is too beholden to U.S. foreign policy goals. On the other hand, the federal government unquestionably has more resources to put into international assistance than do all PVOs combined. There are countless reasons to maintain good relationships between PVOs and the U.S. government in foreign countries, and international assistance programs are neither an effective nor an appropriate place to debate American foreign policy. Nonprofits engaged in international assistance work often find themselves walking a tightrope between program integrity and cooperation with the American government, and some PVOs, such as World Vision and Oxfam America, sharply limit the amount of government money they will take. Government funding to nonprofit arts, health care, social service, and educational organizations has never seriously threatened to compromise those institutions, but government funding in the international assistance area presents this threat constantly. The irony of this situation is that the work of PVOs in Third World countries may have more long-term benefit for the American government than some of the government's own policies and practices in those countries.

The government-PVO relationship has increased in importance as the PVO share of AID funds has steadily increased through the 1970s and 1980s. Both executive and legislative branches seem to look with increasing favor on the arrangement whereby federal dollars are disbursed through PVOs. Government has the big money; PVOs have the networks, local trust, and flexibility to put the money to best use. Still, the question remains of how separate

U.S. dollars can ever be from U.S. foreign policy objectives, including military and intelligence objectives. Should assistance to Nicaraguan earthquake victims, for instance, be contingent on the U.S. government's attitude toward the Sandinista government? As Bolling (1982, p. 194) points out, the dilemma is often more subtle: "Some PVOs are also concerned that by subtle or overt ways they may shift their priorities against their principles or better judgement because AID funds are available. On their own, they might go into Upper Volta, where the need is great and the United States has no vital political or economic interests; but, because of AID, they could decide to go into the Philippines instead. Or they may be encouraged by the offer of government funding to attempt to operate on a large scale when their common sense tells them they should stick to the work they have slowly developed in a few villages."

The other side of the argument is that by staying "within the system," PVOs are more likely to influence American foreign aid policies and programs, thus helping to direct the vast resources of the federal government toward areas with the most need and potential. The work of Rockefeller, Ford, and AID in the Green Revolution presents a striking example of what can be done through close PVO-government cooperation. Thousands of less visible but highly productive cooperative programs operate daily in the Third World. Clearly, a complete divorce between government and PVO international assistance would be harmful to the world's poor, as would complete capitulation of PVOs to U.S. foreign policy interests. A natural and inevitable tension exists between the two; their proper relationship will be continually defined and redefined in practice.

The American nonprofit presence abroad is dwarfed by the American business, military, diplomatic, and intelligence presence around the world. But the international activities of the U.S. nonprofit sector have a unique importance, not captured by quantitative measurements. Economic and military prowess is certainly part of the American reality and message, but it is not always the best message. Democracy, freedom of the press, freedom of religion, freedom of association, and the application of science and technology to meet human needs are all values that America has exemplified to the world. Nonprofit organizations, by legal definition lacking economic self-interest and largely independent of government, may often embody these American ideals abroad more effectively than American businesses, embassies, military installations, and intelligence networks. Before the United States was the world's dominant economic and military power, it was highly admired for its more idealistic qualities. In a world increasingly cynical about the intentions of all superpowers, American nonprofit organizations working in other countries may well be playing an important role in helping the United States maintain its moral and spiritual leadership.

Government foreign aid at least has the advantage of being relatively coordinated and consistent. The same can hardly be said for PVOs working abroad. Private efforts abroad have sometimes degenerated to the level of religious sects bickering with each other about territoriality and conversion methods. Less depressing but equally problematic is the very multiplicity of PVOs. Instead of working together on long-range economic development, changes in public health practices, and agricultural self-subsistence, PVOs have sometimes duplicated each other's short-term relief efforts. Some of the smaller agencies have fielded programs that are here today and gone tomorrow, leaving only increased expectations behind. On the home front, international relief fundraising appeals have multiplied, inevitably attracting a few dishonest or disorganized operations that have tainted the work of more reputable groups.

Some coalitions of PVOs have developed in recent years, including the American Council for Voluntary International Action (InterAction), Private Agencies in International Development (PAID), Coordination in Development (CODEL), Private Agencies Collaborating Together (PACT), and the older American Council of Voluntary Agencies for Foreign Service (ACVAFS). While these consortia provide useful coordination and communication functions, none of them has the influence to shape members' programs in a significant and long-term fashion. It is true that similar diversity exists in American domestic social services, but the stakes are higher in foreign countries, because there are few or no backup systems to handle the failures and inconsistencies of a "free-market" approach to meeting human needs. Also, the needs are simply greater. Americans have real and sometimes critical problems, but they do not face the immediate prospect of mass starvation or uncontrolled epidemics. The dangers of discontinuity in international assistance strongly suggest that PVOs need to work more closely with each other as well as with American and foreign governments.

Assisting foreign nations to become self-sufficient, theoretically a goal of both the U.S. government and PVO programs, is in practice very problematic, for both technical and political reasons. There have been a few great successes, notably India, which benefited from massive financial and technical investment from the United States, Great Britain, the Soviet Union, the United Nations, and the Ford Foundation. But in many other countries, more than three-fourths of the people still live in extreme poverty, even after decades of international assistance; and the gap between the developed nations north of the equator and the underdeveloped nations south of the equator continues to grow. Much international assistance has necessarily been in the form of emergency relief, such as responding to African famine. While critically important, such aid does not develop local capacity to solve the problems that created the famines in the first place and, in the opinion of some assistance specialists, sometimes makes the situation worse. For instance, massive infusions of grain can depress local grain prices, further damaging an already weak agricultural economy. More recently, there has been a shift of emphasis to long-term development and self-sufficiency programs, including assistance to agricultural and small business enterprises. A significant part of this emphasis has been the encouragement of indigenous PVOs. American PVOs have in many areas turned over operational responsibility for assistance programs to indigenous PVOs. Some American funders, such as the Rockefeller Brothers Fund and the Asian Foundation, give priority to funding indigenous rather than American PVOs. More cautiously, AID has endorsed this idea.

Such programs have had limited success. American support has been tentative. Foreign governments have been even more ambivalent; in some countries, local development and indigenous PVOs mean decentralization of power, which is exactly what the emerging central government does not want. In a particularly striking example, though not in a Third World country, a $75,000 grant by the international arm of the AFL-CIO to Solidarity, the Polish federation of labor unions, enraged both the Polish and the Soviet governments. Political instability in countries such as Ethiopia has been another major barrier. But more than anything else, the simple magnitude of the problems has overwhelmed efforts to develop long-range self-sufficiency programs. A billion people live in what the United Nations terms "absolute poverty." Local conditions such as overgrazing, deforestation, and overpopulation and world conditions such as oil prices and arms spending contribute to this poverty and to a great extent put it beyond the control of any government or set of PVOs. Until the developed nations come to see solutions to Third World poverty as vitally related to their own economic and strategic self-interest or until these nations and the people of the world develop significantly more altruistic attitudes toward the plight of Third World citizens, American PVOs can play a limited but important role in relief and development in foreign countries and in educating Americans about the needs abroad.

FOUNDATIONS AND CORPORATE FUNDERS

The Money Trees

Foundations and corporations give ten billion dollars a year to nonprofit organizations and are a highly visible and much acclaimed part of the philanthropic landscape. But these funders were once suspected of fomenting capitalist plots to take over America's charities and at another time of leading the nation into Marxist socialism. Even today, the institutional funders are accused of everything from fostering old-boy networks to supporting radical causes. Funders have learned to appreciate the comment of Robert Maynard Hutchins, who, concerned about opposition to his Center for the Study of Democratic Institutions, asked a friend, "Why do they hate us? We haven't even given them a grant."

Scope and Impact

Institutional funders play a highly influential role in the nonprofit sector and society at large. The influence comes from their ability to concentrate millions of dollars on selected projects, give these projects an aura of importance, and do this with a minimum of political accountability. Foundation grants have played a major role in medical research and education, world food production, the development of public television and radio, and the vigor of the American arts world, to give just a few examples. Foundations, whose endowments and legal structure give them permanence and make them relatively invulnerable to sharp political or market changes, have the ability to fund new, untested ideas and programs for which there might initially be little public support. The fact that foundations do not always use this power wisely and courageously does not lessen its unique importance. Corporate funding, though generally tied to company goals, plays a vital role in strengthening major educational, cultural, and social welfare institutions and adds an important source of funding to the nonprofit sector.

Foundations. A foundation is a nonprofit organization that exists primarily to give money to other, service-producing nonprofits. There are four kinds of foundations: independent, corporate, community, and operating. The last is not primarily a grantmaker; its main purpose is to fund its own activities in areas such as social science research (the Russell Sage Foundation), the promotion of art (the J. Paul Getty Trust), or the improvement of public education (the Danforth Foundation). By law, operating foundations may not give more than 15 percent of their total income to other nonprofits. Corporate private foundations, while legally distinct from corporate giving programs, are discussed below with other forms of corporate philanthropy.

In 1986, there were 25,639 active grantmaking private foundations in the United States, holding $102.1 billion in assets and awarding $6 billion in grants. In 1987, foundations gave an estimated $6.38 billion (American Association of Fund-Raising Counsels, 1988, p. 8). A Foundation Center analysis of grantmaking by a sample of 473 foundations in 1986–87 showed the following pattern of giving by subject category: welfare, 27.1 percent of grant money awarded; health, 23.2 percent; education, 17.5 percent; cultural activities, 14.7 percent; social science, 8.2 percent; science, 7.6 percent; and religion, 1.7 percent. (Reprinted with permission from *Foundation Grants Index*, 17th ed., the Foundation Center, New York, 1988, Table 14. p. xx.)

Foundation wealth is highly concentrated. One-fifth of the twenty-five thousand foundations in the country hold 97 percent of the total assets and account for 92 percent of total giving; the one hundred largest foundations hold over half the assets; and the fifteen largest foundations control nearly 30 percent of the assets. Foundation wealth is also geographically concentrated, with more than half the assets in the Middle Atlantic and North Central states and 20 percent in New York City alone. In recent decades, however, the growth of foundations in the West and South has somewhat reduced the domination of the Northeast.

Foundation size creates great differences in funding purposes and operating style. The twenty to twenty-five very large foundations—those with assets of more than $500 million—tend to be concerned with broad regional, national, and international issues. Examples include the Ford, Kellogg, MacArthur, Robert Wood Johnson, Rockefeller, Sloan, Andrew W. Mellon, and Hewlett foundations, the Lilly Endowment, the Pew Memorial Trusts, and the Carnegie Corporation of New York. These funders tend to have large professional staffs and are often headed by eminent people from higher education, public service, or the professions. Board members of the very large foundations often include people of high visibility and influence, such as Robert McNamara (Ford Foundation), Henry Kissinger (Rockefeller Brothers Fund), Michael Blumenthal (Rockefeller Foundation), and Lawrence Tisch (Carnegie).

A second type is represented by a few of the very large funders and the approximately one hundred large funders—those with $100 million to $500 million in assets—that have primarily, though not exclusively, regional funding interests. Examples include the Duke Endowment (North and South Carolina), the McKnight Foundation (Minnesota), the Richard King Mellon Foundation (Pittsburgh and western Pennsylvania), the Irvine Foundation (California), the William Penn Foundation (Philadelphia), the Mabee Foundation (Oklahoma, Texas, New Mexico, Kansas, Missouri), and all the large Los Angeles foundations (Keck, Ahmanson, Weingart, and Hilton). These foundations are characterized by local and regional interests, relatively small professional and support staffs, and almost exclusively local board members.

Third, there are the smaller foundations ($10 million to $100 million in assets), which, with very few exceptions, have primarily local funding interests. Most of these funders support a wide variety of nonprofit activities, while some specialize in one or a few areas, such as immigration, public elementary and secondary education, and children's welfare. These foundations often operate with only an executive director and a secretary and have exclusively local boards, most of whose members have close familial or business relationships with the founder.

Finally, the very small foundations (those with less than $10 million in assets) typically have no staff and limit their funding to a few agencies with which the founding family and board members have some relationship. While the popular image of the foundation world is created by Ford, Rockefeller, and the other giants, more than 80 percent of the foundations in the country have less than $1 million in assets and bear about as much operational resemblance to Ford and Rockefeller as the corner gas station does to the Exxon Corporation.

The predominant type of foundation is the private or independent grantmaking foundation, which is typically created by a wealthy individual or family to provide ongoing support for particular institutions or broad social purposes. The foundation's governing board is usually composed of the donor's family, close friends, and business associates; in a few of the larger foundations, board members are selected more broadly. There are more than twenty-three thousand independent foundations in the United States, which in 1985 had assets of nearly $80 billion and gave $4 billion in grants to a wide variety of projects.

Community foundations, by charter, limit their grants to a particular geographical region, are funded by a variety of donors rather than by one person or family, and are governed by board members appointed by local leaders and trustee banks. These funders, because of their closer community ties and accountability, are accorded somewhat more favorable tax treatment than the private or independent foundations. There are now more than three hundred community foundations with assets of $3.5 billion. In 1984, community foundations made grants totaling $285 million. Three-fourths of these foundations are very small (less than $10 million in assets). The community foundation movement, though still small, is growing rapidly, and many observers see it as one of the most promising recent developments in organized philanthropy.

Corporate Funders. Corporate giving in 1987 amounted to $4.5 billion. Corporations can deduct from their taxes contributions of up to 10 percent of pretax profit, but few donate nearly this much.

Since World War II, corporate giving has typically equaled about 1 percent of profit. In the Minneapolis–St. Paul area, the recognized national leader in corporate generosity, firms give less than 2 percent. Many companies throughout the country do not give at all. A 1977 study of all U.S. firms found that only 35 percent of those that reported profits made any contributions (Useem, 1987, p. 340). The same study showed that one-tenth of 1 percent of the nation's corporations gave more than half the total amount of corporate money contributed.

Even though the ultimate source of funds—the for-profit sector—is the same for both foundation and corporate philanthropy, and even though the principal beneficiaries—universities, major arts organizations, and welfare agencies—are the same, there are great differences between foundation and corporate giving. Corporate philanthropy is a direct extension of a particular corporation's economic interests. Grants often go to programs with a direct connection to the business. Bechtel, Westinghouse, Chevron, and Atlantic Richfield fund engineering schools. B. Dalton concentrates on a nationwide literacy project. Weyerhauser supports reforestation and affordable housing for the elderly. IBM, Apple, and DEC give computer equipment. Pillsbury and Lucky Stores give to hunger projects. Corporations sponsor such causes as the U.S. Olympics team and the Statue of Liberty celebration, mindful of the excellent publicity this will bring. A summary of research on corporate philanthropy concluded: "A leading variable accounting for many of the differences is the firm's perception of its self-interest. If a firm's managers feel that making gifts will benefit employee morale, promote product sales, enhance the company's reputation, or reduce government interference, they are likely to do so; but if they see no payback for the company, they are far less likely to make contributions" (Useem, 1987, p. 348). Corporate giving takes place at the intersection of corporate interest and community interest. Or, as Texas oil billionaire T. Boone Pickens somewhat more graphically put it, "Company giving has to be related to the company's interests, not be a gift to the ballet because my wife likes ballet" (Teltsch, 1987, p. 30).

It would be a great mistake to see foundation and individual giving as "pure" and corporate giving as "tainted." Giving is a form of social and economic exchange; givers give, but they also receive. Through giving, foundations and individuals as well as corporations achieve publicity, respect, acclaim, and a sense of participating in projects with intrinsic value and social impact. John D. Rockefeller, Johns Hopkins, and Leland Stanford are remembered more kindly for their philanthropic creations than for some of their business activities. As AT&T Foundation president Reynold Levy has observed, "Acts of pure altruism are rarely encountered. Individual donors may seek to do good for institutions, causes and people. But why? Does the social status such acts confer, the business opportunities they create, the guilt they relieve, the impulse to immortality they satisfy, or the visibility with which they are associated often have something to do with donor motivation? Sure. And foundation executives and board members, or at least those I've been privileged to know, are not themselves without motives of institutional, personal and professional advancement. In short, the ambiguity and complexity of motivation driving charitable gifts are not confined to corporations" (Levy, 1985, p. 59).

A major difference between corporate and foundation philanthropy is that whereas foundations employ only a few thousand people, corporations employ tens of millions of people and often encourage them to give time and expertise to nonprofits. Corporate employees raise money for nonprofits, advise nonprofits on everything from marketing to computer applications, participate on nonprofit boards, and serve nonprofits as "loaned executives" in United Way campaigns. A 1978 survey of the presidents and chairs of more than five hundred large American corporations found that 80 percent served on the board of at least one nonprofit organization (Useem, 1987, p. 341).

Corporations, again unlike foundations, have vast physical resources and sometimes put these at the disposal of nonprofits. Businesses let nonprofits use corporate facilities for meetings and occasionally even provide office space. Businesses donate equipment and materials to nonprofits. The noncash contribution of business to nonprofits has been estimated as approximately 20 percent of deducted contributions (Useem, 1987, p. 341).

Foundations have been responsible for some of the great

success stories of the nonprofit sector. Earlier chapters have detailed the role of funders such as Ford, Rockefeller, and Carnegie in the virtual eradication of hookworm and yellow fever, the reform of medical education, the development of the arts, the Green Revolution, and the support of minority groups. Less visible but of great importance are the start-up grants that foundations and corporations give to thousands of nonprofit organizations that go on to self-sufficiency and many years of service. These quieter success stories have cumulatively matched the more spectacular effects of large-scale grantmaking.

Foundations and corporations often play the sustainer rather than the venture-capital role. Nielsen's study of the thirty-three largest foundations suggested that their funding is typically neither far left nor far right but more middle-of-the-road and if anything somewhat conservative: "[D]escriptively, not judgmentally, the profile of their activity is clearly conventional, not reformist. They are overwhelmingly institutions of social continuity, not change" (Nielsen, 1985, p. 423). Ylvisaker (1987, p. 371) similarly concluded: "Viewed in the aggregate, foundations do not emerge as a force out in front of—certainly not at odds with—American society and its other institutions."

Historical Development

The idea and practice of private philanthropy date back thousands of years. Ancient Egypt, Mesopotamia, Israel, Greece, and Rome all had laws and exhortations relating to the care of widows and orphans and other charitable causes, and legacies were sometimes set aside for these purposes. The rise of Christendom gave further impetus to this practice; in addition to organized religious charity, individuals set up charitable legacies. In the Anglo-Saxon world, the institution of the charitable trust was well established by 1601, when the English Parliament codified it in the Statute of Charitable Uses, companion legislation to the Elizabethan Poor Law. The legal mechanism of the charitable trust protected assets set aside to support charitable work. The normal pattern was that some asset (a piece of land or a few cows) would be dedicated for the support of a particular institution or effort, such as a school, an orphanage, or assistance for elderly widows. The charitable trust was a familiar mechanism of local giving in seventeenth-, eighteenth-, and nineteenth-century England and America. Most trusts were relatively small and limited to specific purposes.

The modern general-purpose foundation took shape in the early twentieth century. The accumulation of vast fortunes led some of America's new superwealthy to create permanent, general-purpose charitable trusts. Although there had been large philanthropic funds in the late nineteenth century, notably the George Peabody Fund (1867) and the John F. Slater Fund (1882) to support the education of former slaves, the first modern general-purpose foundation was the Russell Sage Foundation, established in 1907 by Margaret Olivia Slocum Sage for "the permanent improvement of social conditions." The Carnegie Corporation of New York was established four years later and the Rockefeller Foundation two years after that. Both Andrew Carnegie and John D. Rockefeller had already created more specific philanthropic organizations; their foundations, like Sage, were to be "for the good of mankind." Through these foundations and other mechanisms, these captains of industry put much of their wealth back into society. The "little Scotsman," five-foot two-inch industrial giant Andrew Carnegie, created an empire of steel, coal, and railroads; he then proceeded to give away $350 million during his lifetime. In addition to the Carnegie Corporation and other grantmaking agencies, he founded 2,500 libraries, started the research-oriented Carnegie Institution, opened the Carnegie Institute in Pittsburgh (later to become part of Carnegie-Mellon University), and established the Carnegie Foundation for the Advancement of Teaching and the Carnegie Endowment for International Peace. Carnegie also preached what he practiced. In an influential essay published in 1889, "The Gospel of Wealth," Carnegie warned his fellow capitalists about the "disgrace of dying rich" and laid out the principles for philanthropy on a grand scale. Today all the Carnegie charitable institutions combined have assets of $2 billion and spend or give away $100 million a year (Foote, 1985, p. 22).

John D. Rockefeller is estimated to have given away $530 million by the time of his death, including gifts to such charities as the Rockefeller Foundation, the Rockefeller Institute for Medical

Research (later Rockefeller University), and the University of Chicago. The examples of people such as Sage, Carnegie, and Rockefeller led other millionaires to donate their fortunes to society and escape the disgrace of dying rich.

The new foundations were also seen as a mechanism to apply to charity the principles of efficiency, scientific thought, good management, and national and international scope that had worked so well in the business world. Foundations, research institutes, and universities were to be the nonprofit arm of business and government in developing and implementing social policy. The grand result would be "a complex system of institutions devoted to the generation, communication and control of research with a bearing on public policy" (Karl and Katz, 1981, p. 248).

Some Americans, however, were suspicious of the intentions of these capitalist-philanthropists. Rockefeller tried for three years to gain a federal charter for the Rockefeller Foundation, but Congress saw the foundation as just another Rockefeller scheme to amass power, and it refused to grant the charter. (The New York legislature, more amenable to Rockefeller interests, chartered the foundation in short order.) Congress was not through with the matter, however. In 1916, the congressionally appointed Commission on Industrial Relations, more commonly known as the Walsh Commission, reported that a few wealthy families, having gained control over much of the nation's business and some of its political structures, were using foundations and other philanthropic mechanisms to gain control of education, social services, health care, and other sectors of American life. Congress took up the foundation issue several more times, sometimes looking for excessive capitalism, sometimes the opposite. In 1952, the House Select Committee to Investigate Tax-Exempt Foundations and Comparable Organizations (the Cox Committee) sent larger foundations a questionnaire including the question, "Have foundations supported or assisted persons, organizations, and projects which, if not subversive in the extreme sense of the word, tend to weaken or discredit the capitalistic system as it exists in the United States and to favor Marxist socialism?" The most important investigation took place in the 1960s under Representative Wright Patman (D-Texas), a Southern populist who had been elected to Congress in 1929 and had long mistrusted the large foundations. Congress felt that some foundations were improperly moving into the political realm. Patman and other members were particularly disturbed by the Ford Foundation's support of public school decentralization in New York City, black voter registration in Cleveland (which helped elect the nation's first big-city black mayor, Carl Stokes), and stipends for Robert Kennedy's chief staff members following the 1968 assassination. Congressional hearings sounded an ominous note; "as Congress began consideration of what was to become the Tax Reform Act of 1969, an atmosphere had evolved which was at best skeptical and at worst hostile" (Edie, 1987, p. 15). The foundations' case was not helped by the fact that some foundation executives, unprepared for the seriousness of the Patman attack, testified with more arrogance than insight. The 1969 Tax Reform Act created a large number of new regulations for private foundations, mainly aimed at keeping foundations out of politics, preventing them from controlling large business interests, and making them more open and accountable.

Controlling a business through a foundation had, in fact, been basically the intent of Henry Ford in creating the Ford Foundation. The Revenue Act of 1935 established a rate of 70 percent for estate taxes on estates of more than $50 million but allowed tax exemption of bequests to charitable, religious, and educational organizations. The Ford Motor Company and the Ford family fortune had clearly been one of the targets of this legislation. In response, the Ford family established the Ford Foundation on January 15, 1936, and in the next few months, Henry Sr. and Edsel Ford wrote wills that made the foundation the potential owner of 90 percent of the Ford Motor Company. For the next fifteen years, the foundation remained a small, local funder. After the deaths of Henry Sr. and Edsel Ford, Henry Ford II in the late 1940s determined that the foundation would become a national institution, separate from the company. When the lawyers and the government finally finished with the estate and separation issues, the Ford Foundation in 1951 had an endowment of nearly half a billion dollars, as compared with the Rockefeller Foundation's $122 million, the Carnegie Corporation's $170 million, and Harvard University's $191 million (Sutton, 1987, p. 52). There was a new kid on the block, and the kid was very big indeed.

Since 1951, the Ford Foundation has had an enormous effect on the nonprofit sector, American society, and the world. From 1951 to 1987, the foundation awarded $6.6 billion in grants. Ford grants reinvigorated American cultural institutions; played a major role in the Green Revolution; created a wide array of black, Hispanic, Native American, and Asian minority organizations; created public-interest law firms; created or cocreated such research and policy organizations as the Fund for the Republic, the Fund for the Advancement of Education, the Center for Advanced Study of the Behavioral Sciences, and the Urban Institute; assisted the development of business education and public policy programs; created the Wilson Fellowships and, with Carnegie, the National Merit Scholarship program; funded community development organizations; and became a major supporter of arms control efforts. Ford's individual grants helped thousands of promising scholars and practitioners develop their work. The foundation became a major source of consultants to government and business, as well as a temporary refuge for public servants, university leaders, and renowned scholars. When McGeorge Bundy retired from the wars of the Kennedy and Johnson administrations, it was to the presidency of the Ford Foundation. Ford became a second home for "the best and the brightest" and a part of the American establishment along with Harvard, the Brookings Institution, and the Trilateral Commission. As Karl and Katz note, more generally, "Administratively, foundations became one of the crucial foci in the training of the country's managerial élite and the creation of the research techniques and the data that the élite needed. They were part of a system which provided governments and universities with advice and staff, in turn drawing their own staffs from universities and government" (Karl and Katz, 1981, pp. 268–269).

As a result of tax policies, the expanding American economy, and new visions of national and world leadership, the post–World War II period was the heydey of foundation formation. The 1950s saw the creation of more than 1,500 foundations, more than had been started in the previous half century. This boom period was followed by a noticeable drop-off in foundation establishment during the 1960s and 1970s, apparently as a result of increasing regulations affecting foundations and decreasing tax advantages of establishing and donating to foundations (Odendahl, 1987).

The post–Vietnam/Watergate era saw the development of a number of small "alternative" foundations, often started by young heirs whose social philosophy differed sharply from that of their ancestors who had made the money. John D. Rockefeller and his son "Junior" started the Rockefeller Foundation, the grandchildren ("the brothers") started the Rockefeller Brothers Fund, and the great-grandchildren ("the cousins"), with a little help from their parents, started the Rockefeller Family Fund in 1968. The Family Fund soon became active in conservation, peace, and women's issues. George Pillsbury of the Pillsbury flour fortune donated much of his inherited wealth to the Haymarket Foundation, the prototype of the alternative funds. Maryanne Mott, a General Motors heiress, established the C. S. Fund to support peace and environmental issues. In a unique example of social recycling, the wealth created by particular corporations was sometimes used a few generations later to challenge the minority hiring practices or environmental impact of those very corporations.

However, the deep relationship between private foundations and the corporate world was not greatly disturbed by such actions. Foundations receive their wealth from money made in the business world, invest their wealth in the stock market, and award grants that are approved by trustees largely from the business world. The financial dependence of foundations on for-profit institutions is illustrated in the following list, which shows the primary funding sources of the nation's twenty largest independent foundations:

Foundation	*Corporate Source*
Ford Foundation	Ford Motor Company
W. K. Kellogg Foundation	Kellogg Cereal Company
MacArthur Foundation	Bankers Life & Casualty
Lilly Endowment	Eli Lilly Company
R. W. Johnson Foundation	Johnson & Johnson Company
Rockefeller Foundation	Standard Oil Company
Pew Memorial Trusts	Sun Oil Company

A. W. Mellon Foundation	Aluminum Company of America
Kresge Foundation	S. H. Kresge Company
Duke Endowment	American Tobacco Company
C. S. Mott Foundation	General Motors Corporation
Carnegie Corporation of New York	U.S. Steel
McKnight Foundation	3M Company
R. K. Mellon Foundation	Mellon National Bank
W. M. Keck Foundation	Superior Oil Company
Gannett Foundation	Gannett Publications
W. & F. Hewlett Foundation	Hewlett-Packard Corporation
A. P. Sloan Foundation	General Motors Corporation
Knight Foundation	Knight-Ridder, Inc.
Starr Foundation	Starr Insurance Company

The last few decades have also seen the resurgence of community foundations. The first community foundation, the Cleveland Foundation, was established in 1914. Although a few dozen communities followed suit in the next decades, the principal growth of community foundations came in the 1970s and 1980s, when several large independent and corporate foundations—principally Charles Stewart Mott, Kresge, Bush, Hewlett, Ford, Kettering, Aetna, Levi Strauss, and Gannett—contributed seed money.

In a separate development, businesses themselves started to contribute directly to the private nonprofit sector. Direct corporate philanthropy in some form can be traced back to colonial days but is usually thought to have begun seriously in the last quarter of the nineteenth century, when the railroad companies donated more than a million dollars for the construction of YMCA buildings around the country, not coincidentally in cities and towns with significant railroad business. World War I produced the first major effort in direct corporate philanthropy. The needs of American soldiers and others in war-torn Europe led to special legislation in several states allowing corporations to declare and give a "Red Cross dividend," and many corporations used this mechanism to make gifts. Following the war, corporations continued to donate to various charitable causes, especially through the Community Chests and United Funds, which later became the United Way. During the 1920s, thirty-five thousand corporations gave $300 million to Community Chests in 129 cities. Corporations also started to give major gifts to colleges and universities, libraries, museums, arts organizations, and health and welfare organizations. But business donations posed special legal and political problems. Nobody questioned the right of the physical person Andrew Carnegie to give away his money. But a corporation was a legal person, and the owners were the stockholders. Clearly, the corporate directors and officers were empowered to use the stockholders' money to make a profit for the stockholders, but were they empowered to give away the stockholders' money to a nonbusiness cause, even if worthy? Also, would corporate donations lead to corporate control of private charitable institutions?

In passing the Internal Revenue Service Act of 1919, Congress explicitly rejected the idea that corporations could give to charity. Within two years, however, the IRS gave a cautious green light provided that such donations immediately benefited the company or the company's employees, such as by building a hospital in a company town. Community Chests pressed for more latitude in business giving. The Depression and President Hoover's reluctance to let the federal government do anything about it created new pressure on business to give. In 1934, the United States Supreme Court struck down corporate contributions to Community Chests, citing 1919 congressional intent. The Community Chests organized a lobbying effort that resulted in amendments to the Internal Revenue Code of 1935, allowing corporations to deduct charitable donations of up to 5 percent of pretax profit from their corporate income taxes. World War II provided the impetus for yet another change. There were heavy business contributions to war-related charitable activities. The traditional "direct benefit" requirement was stretched to the limit. The question was tested when a stockholder of the A. P. Smith Manufacturing Company sued the company over its $1,000 contribution to Princeton University. The case was decided by the New Jersey Supreme Court, which held that the needs of society and the transfer of much wealth from individual to corporate persons had created a condition that made limited corporate charity reasonable (*A. P. Smith Manufacturing Co. v. Barlow,* 13 N.J. S. Ct. 147). The decision was later upheld by the U.S. Supreme Court.

Corporate philanthropy became an accepted part of both business and society following World War II. The consciousness raising of the 1960s led many corporations to make their corporate social responsibility programs more explicit, and courses on the topic began to appear in business schools. But with few exceptions, there was no serious deviation from the pattern of corporate philanthropy established by the railroads in the late nineteenth century: business would give in the manner and to the degree that business interests dictated. There did not have to be a direct connection with the bottom line, but ultimately it was expected that corporate philanthropy would benefit not just the receivers but also the givers.

Policy Issues

Institutional funders constitute the youngest but one of the most influential parts of the nonprofit sector. The earliest foundations—Rockefeller, Carnegie, Russell Sage—are barely seventy-five years old, and the Ford Foundation for all practical purposes did not begin until 1951. Corporate philanthropy is essentially a post-World War II phenomenon. Foundation and corporate grants amount to only $10 billion of the nonprofit sector's $250-300 billion yearly revenue. Yet institutional funders have a powerful role because of their financial security, their relative immunity from political or market constraints, and their ability to concentrate large amounts of money on particular programs and agencies.

The power of foundations aroused distrust from the beginning. Although congressional suspicions seem to have subsided, the power and independence of foundations and corporate funders remains an important issue. Private foundation and corporate philanthropy decisions are made by self-perpetuating boards and by managers hired by and accountable to those boards. Their decisions, made in private, normally are not subject to political accountability. Neither is there a market mechanism to govern their activity, since there are no "buyers" of foundation and corporate funding services as there are "buyers" of health, education, welfare, artistic, and even religious services. Public criticism of funders is rare, one reason being that potential critics are often potential grantees. Waldemar Nielsen, the author of two widely read books on America's largest foundations, may be the exception that proves the rule, but even he went to great pains to explain how he could objectively analyze the MacArthur Foundation in a book supported by a MacArthur grant (Nielsen, 1985, p. x). Other possible critics— such as newspapers and journals—rarely have the interest or resources to analyze the large and complex world of institutional funding. Congress's involvement has been sporadic and strongly ideological, especially under Senator Joseph McCarthy and Representative Wright Patman; and the IRS and various state agencies typically get involved only when there is evidence of a major ethical or legal violation. The peer review process within the funders' world consists more of backroom gossip at Council on Foundations meetings than systematic and constructive criticism.

This leaves these powerful institutions with no effective means of internal or external review. There has probably never been any serious danger that these institutions would lead the country either to the right or to the left, as McCarthy and Patman feared. The real concern is that funders cannot profit from serious professional evaluation or consumer/voter evaluation. "Philanthropoids" themselves worry about the tendency toward arrogance in the field. But arrogance is only a hint of the real problem. Americans tolerate a certain degree of arrogance in businesspeople, politicians, athletes, and artists who have to prove themselves in a highly competitive field. The problem is that grantmaking is almost totally noncompetitive. As one grantmaker said, tongue in cheek, "It's a great job: you're guaranteed 100 percent success, because no grantee will ever tell you it was a lousy grant, and certainly you're not going to tell your board that it was."

Conceivably, funders could develop procedures and even national and regional organizations to achieve some independent evaluation of grantmaking. There exist many models from other professions and organizations. No such process is ever perfect—even the sacrosanct peer review process in scholarly journals has been demonstrated to have limitations—but some serious (and well-funded) effort at systematic, high-quality, and truly independent evaluation of grantmaking would be a great service not only to the nonprofit sector but also to the grantmakers themselves.

An allied issue is the relevance of variables such as ethnicity and race, gender, and social class in grantmaking (Odendahl, Boris, and Daniels, 1985). It has frequently been charged that funders are a largely white, male, upper-class club and that their grantmaking inevitably reflects a predisposition toward people and institutions of the same characteristics. Groups such as Women and Foundations/Corporate Philanthropy and Hispanics in Philanthropy have been formed to work for a more diverse gender and ethnicity profile in the trustees, staff, and grant recipients of institutional funders. Unquestionably, some major advances have been made. The president of the Ford Foundation, Franklin Thomas, is black. The president of the $430 million Marin Community Foundation, Douglas Patiño, is Hispanic. Ford's vice-president and chief program person and the presidents of the MacArthur Foundation, Pew Memorial Trusts, and Commonwealth Fund are women. There has been a considerable increase in the number of women heading small and mid-size foundations and corporate giving programs. There are now a few minority people on the boards of the one hundred largest foundations. But there is still a long way to go before the staffs and boards of institutional funders reflect the ethnic and gender profile of the larger society. This issue is hardly unique to funders; a 1988 study showed that only 3 percent of the board members of the seven largest arts organizations in progressive San Francisco were minority people (Jones, 1988). However, the "white men's club" issue is of particular importance in the foundation world, whose grants play such a pivotal role in shaping the nonprofit sector and the society.

A constant policy question in the funding world is what role funders should play. The heroic tales of the profession have chiefly been told about cases where foundations put large sums into a new area, achieved spectacular results, and later moved on to other issues. But the actual grantmaking of most foundations and virtually all corporate funders is cautious, mainstream, and reactive rather than proactive. Further, nonprofit organizations seeking grants may be as thrilled as anyone else by stories of the conquest of hookworm, but they also must daily worry about their own programs, clients, staff, and budget. These organizations intellectually appreciate the "venture capital" idea but often feel they genuinely need funds for basic operations and for longer periods of time than one to three years. Grantees privately grumble about what they see as faddishness in the funding world—the "what's hot this year?" syndrome. There is, in short, a Catch-22 in the funding world: foundations and corporations that stay with the same agencies for long periods of time are accused of being dull and timid, while funders that move around from one issue or organization to another are accused of being faddish. Other nonprofit organizations are clear about their mission but often feel they do not have enough money. Institutional funders have the money but sometimes genuinely do not know what their role can or should be. Thoughtful funders realize this and puzzle over the issue with colleagues; but a broader cross section of the nonprofit community needs to join this discussion, since the issue importantly affects the entire sector.

Corporate philanthropy needs an additional type of role clarification. Although the interaction between altruism and self-interest quietly permeates the entire nonprofit sector, the connection is much more evident in corporate philanthropy. Both grantors and grantees need to be clear and direct about this dimension of corporate funding. Nonprofit workers often express surprise and disapproval regarding the self-interest evident in corporate giving programs. Such criticism often comes close to suggesting that business would be all right if it were not business. On the other hand, some corporate managers play the giving game as if their motives were totally altruistic. Both sides need to engage in more frank discussion and work toward a fuller appreciation of the dynamics of corporate philanthropy. Broader dissemination of the growing body of first-rate research on corporate philanthropy (Galaskiewicz, 1985; Useem, 1987) would be a good place to start. The nonprofit sector has considerable self-interest in such dialogue. Unlike foundations, corporate giving programs are often extremely vulnerable. When profits go down, such programs are frequently among the first to be reduced or eliminated. More thorough analysis and appreciation of the dynamics and objectives of corporate funding might help corporate boards, CEOs, and stockholders view the corporate citizenship function as more similar in importance to the production, financial management, legal, and marketing and sales functions and thus solidify the position of giving programs within corporations.

☆★★ 10
MUTUAL BENEFIT ORGANIZATIONS
A Nation of Joiners

Besides philanthropic nonprofits, there are thousands of tax-exempt organizations that exist primarily to serve their own members. In many states, these are legally classified as "mutual benefit" as distinguished from "public benefit" organizations. Mutual benefit organizations include golf and tennis clubs, service organizations (Kiwanis and Rotary), economic cooperatives (American Automobile Association, Blue Cross), business leagues and trade associations (American Association of Realtors), chambers of commerce, professional organizations (American Bar Association), fraternal organizations (Elks), burial associations, labor unions, political parties, ethnic societies, hobby groups, and such special associations as a club for former Copacabana chorus girls and one for former members of the CIA.

Scope and Impact

The 1982 Census of Service Industries found the distribution of mutual benefit organizations shown in Table 10. The actual number of mutual benefit organizations is in all probability far higher than that shown in the table. Associations with no payroll and with less than $25,000 in annual revenue would not appear in either IRS or Census Bureau figures. Sociological studies of specific communities suggest that government figures greatly underestimate the number of mutual benefit organizations and other types of nonprofits (Sills, 1968, pp. 365, 373).

The *Encyclopedia of Associations* (1988) lists nearly twenty thousand national and over fifty thousand regional, state, and local

Table 10. Mutual Benefit Organizations, 1982.

Organizational Type	Number of Organizations	Number of Employees	Revenue (in Thousands of Dollars)
Business associations	12,108	80,174	$ 4,640,115
Civic, social, and fraternal organizations	35,457	295,792	6,271,122
Professional membership organizations	5,194	41,391	2,565,829
Other membership organizations	8,577	75,566	2,813,219
TOTAL	61,336	492,923	$16,290,285

Source: National Center for Charitable Statistics, 1985, p. 5.

associations. Some of these are government agencies or belong to other nonprofit categories, such as religion and social welfare. But even subtracting these, the multivolume *Encyclopedia* presents a dazzling array of mutual benefit associations, including many examples of Tocqueville's "serious, futile, very general and very limited, immensely large and very minute" associations. The following list is a small illustration:

Absent-Minded Club
American Legion (2.7 million members)
American Association of Bovine Practitioners (also Equine, Feline, Swine, and Sheep & Goat)
American Association of Retired People (28 million members)
American Academy of Arts and Sciences (John and Samuel Adams were members)
American Association for Ethiopian Jews
American Medical Association (205,000 members)
American Petroleum Institute
American Philosophical Society (established in 1743)
Ancient Order of Hibernians
Bald-Headed Men of America
Batterers Anonymous
Bobs International

Boston Computer Society (26,000 members in fifty states and
    forty countries)
Christian Homesteading Movement
Consumers Union
Daughters of the American Revolution
Democratic Party
Estonian Relief Committee
Flower Essence Society
Former Stewardesses Club
4-H Club
Gamblers Anonymous
Habitat for Humanity (President Carter is a volunteer)
Hemlock Society
Homebrew Computer Club (Steve Jobs and Steve Wozniak,
    creators of Apple Computer, were members)
Impotents Anonymous
International Brotherhood of Old Bastards (387,439 mem-
    bers)
John Birch Society
Lefthanders International
National Association of Manufacturers
National Association of Seventh Day Adventist Dentists
National Association of Truck Stop Operators
National Odd Shoe Exchange
National Association of Realtors (750,000 members)
National Education Association
National Ready Mixed Concrete Association
Nurses for Laughter
Republican Party
Superwomen Anonymous (self-help group for overachieving
    women driven by the need to be everything to everyone;
    motto is "Enough is enough.")
Teachers Insurance and Annuity Association and the College
    Retirement Equities Fund (TIAA-CREF) ($63 billion in
    assets; financially the largest nonprofit organization)
Trilateral Commission (300 members only)
Triplet Connection
Turkish American Physicians Association

Veterans of Foreign Wars
Yokefellowship Prison Ministry

The thousands of listings in the *Encyclopedia* show that America's passion for association is, if anything, even stronger than in Tocqueville's day. Such associations provide opportunities to make friends and business contacts, communicate with like-minded people, celebrate one's heritage, learn leadership skills, find mutual support and protection, test ideas in a low-risk environment, have a "home away from home," relieve loneliness in an impersonal society, find partners for intimate relationships, and promote the interests of a particular profession.

The distinction between public benefit and mutual benefit organizations is based on the idea that the latter do not serve society's needs, at least not by direct intent. "There is frequently very little altruism about the motivation of [mutual benefit organization] members" (Douglas, 1987, p. 51). In practice, this distinction is not always so clear. Ethnic mutual assistance organizations have played a vital role in delivering social services to immigrants throughout American history, and they continue to do so. Minority mutual benefit agencies have provided valuable leadership training to people who had no other opportunities. Religious institutions, which have many of the characteristics of mutual benefit organizations, provide charitable services to members and nonmembers. Labor unions and farmers' organizations are driven primarily by the economic interests of their members yet historically have played a much broader social role. It should also be noted that many charitable organizations benefit their members socially, economically, and in other ways. Serving on the board of an arts organization, a college, a hospital, or a mainline social service agency can bring considerable economic and social benefit to upwardly mobile board members. Working in prestigious Section 501(c)(3) organizations such as a major research university or research institute can convey personal benefits that go considerably beyond the monthly paycheck. Altruistic and self-directed behavior coexist comfortably in every part of the nonprofit sector, and some of the greatest societal benefits produced by the sector have come through the self-directed behavior of immigrants, minority groups, and low-income working people. There is a legitimate distinction between "public benefit" and "mutual benefit" nonprofits, but they are points on a spectrum rather than opposites, and the characteristics that are manifest in one are often latent in the other.

There is even some reason to view mutual benefit organizations as the original nonprofit form. Anthropologists who have studied the emergence of voluntary associations in tribal life note that these groups had ceremonial and entertainment roles, informal governing roles, and informal economic enhancement roles (Banton, 1968)—not unlike modern American service clubs. The appearance of voluntary associations in preliterate societies is related to new forms of social and economic behavior, as when tribes link with other tribes or develop new crafts. When tribes are caught up in rapid social change—for instance, when they migrate to towns and cities—voluntary associations play even more important roles for the newly uprooted: "Voluntary associations in the cities have many features similar to those in villages, but they differ in that initially they serve only as substitutes for the traditional institutions with which the migrant has lost touch. The first kind of urban association to appear, therefore, is the bereavement benefit society, which takes over the kin group's responsibilities in the event of death" (Banton, 1968, p. 360).

Associations are particularly related to the growth of cities and urban economies, not only because of the proximity of people but more importantly because urban life and economy weaken the social, cultural, and economic role of kinship and tribal groups. Mutual assistance associations and "welfare societies" frequently lead, in urban contexts, to economic and political groups such as trade unions and political parties. The guilds of medieval Europe were a major nongovernmental, nonchurch organizational form that arose from the economic and allied interests of groups of craftsmen. In France, some of the oldest nonprofit organizations are associations of winegrowers or "confréries" (brotherhoods), which originally formed for mutual assistance in adverse times and later evolved into public benefit organizations donating to hospitals and other charities.

Associations play an important sociological role in American life. Adding to Tocqueville's seminal observations, German sociologists Ferdinand Tönnies ([1887] 1957) and Max Weber ([1910] 1972) observed that associations provide a bridge between large, bureaucratic organizations, including the government, and individuals. Berger and Neuhaus (1977) have called them "mediating institutions." Lerner (in O'Connell, 1983, p. 86) says: "It is through these associations that Americans avoid the excesses both of state worship and of complete individualism. It is in them, and not in the geographical locality, that the sense of community comes closest to being achieved. . . . [T]hrough the sum of these ways the American manages to achieve a functional set of social relations with like-minded people, the core of which is not propinquity of place but community of interests, vocations, preferences, and tastes."

Such claims go far beyond the hard evidence. As Sills (1968, p. 373) notes, "The extent to which voluntary associations serve social integrative functions in industrial societies has not as yet been satisfactorily measured." But this is a limitation more of social science research than of the reality to be measured. These are, after all, voluntary associations—groups that people do not have to join, and groups that for the most part have little or no immediate economic or political benefit. The fact that millions of people join such associations strongly suggests that at least some associations provide benefits to some members beyond the simple stated purpose of the organization, whether that is the enhancement of the nursing profession or the promotion of Armenian heritage.

Mutual benefit organizations also play important roles in the economic and political realms. Trade associations and business leagues, in effect nonprofit extensions of the for-profit world, collect and distribute information about industry segments, something that individual firms would not have the money or time to do and that government could do only at considerable extra expense to the taxpayer. These groups also serve as a useful link between the business community, the government, and the populace. Unions and political parties, two other major forms of nonphilanthropic nonprofits, play immensely important roles in the nation's welfare. Nonprofit pension funds, insurance agencies, and credit unions manage billions of dollars for millions of members. Studies of local communities have noted the strong role that voluntary associations, particularly mutual benefit organizations, play in local government. As sociologist Peter Rossi put it, "To understand what is happening within a contemporary community an investigator cannot confine himself to the official table of organization for municipal government but must add to it a host of voluntary associations which act on behalf of the community and which together with the formal structure of local government form the basic organizational framework of the local community" (Rossi, 1961, p. 301). Quasi-governmental functions such as the licensing of professionals and the accreditation of educational programs are handled largely by professional associations, another type of mutual benefit organization. These associations also provide important research and education and training services.

Historical Development

Associations were part of the English customs and culture that the colonists brought with them to the New World (Jordan, 1960). There were relatively few associations in colonial times, because of population dispersion and the power of the family, kinship group, church, and local community. However, there were a few self-help and mutual assistance groups, such as the Scots Charitable Society (1657), the Charitable Irish Society (1737), and a number of Quaker societies (James, 1963). There were mutual improvement associations, such as Benjamin Franklin's Junto; Franklin was also a founder of the American Philosophical Society, the Union Fire Company, and the Philadelphia Library Company, all private associations. There were the secret "committees of correspondence" and the famous Sons of Liberty that helped fan the flames of revolution. There was the nation's first veterans' organization, the Society of the Cincinnati, composed of Revolutionary War veterans and their descendants. There were the "Democratic Societies" and "Republican Societies"—political clubs that President Washington in 1794 found it necessary to condemn; Thomas Jefferson thought this condemnation a shocking "attack on the freedom of discussion" (Chambers, 1963, p. 63).

With the political freedom of the new republic and the increase of urbanization at the end of the eighteenth and beginning of the nineteenth centuries, associations developed so rapidly that by 1835, Tocqueville said Americans had gone far beyond England in their application of the "principle of association." Immigration added thousands of ethnic mutual assistance agencies to the Anglo-American groups. These immigrant groups exhibited all the functions now seen as major subsectors of the nonprofit world: religion, social service, education, advocacy, international assistance (such as sending money to Ireland to help the famine victims of the 1840s), and even primitive forms of health care and "grant-making" (Handlin, 1959, chap. 6). But above all, they had a bonding, community-building role: "The magnetic element at the core of all, however, was always the opportunity for sociability. With the occasional association dedicated to intellectual and physical self-improvement, these provided the means by which like men got to know each other. The balls and picnics had the additional virtue of raising money; but their true end was sociability. And the event that excited greatest enthusiasm was the parade, a procession which enabled the group to display before the whole world the evidence of its solidarity, which enabled the individual to demonstrate that he belonged, was a part of a whole" (Handlin, 1951, p. 177).

The thousands of new ethnic organizations caused no great surprise among Anglo-Americans, who themselves had been developing associations at a feverish pace: "Those many generations in the country as well as those recently arrived found the most important social concerns here considered the function of voluntary, autonomous combinations, free of the State and all on an equal footing. In this realm of spontaneous organization, the appearance of immigrant associations was taken as a matter of course; every aggregation of individuals acted so in America. This was the means by which all groups discovered the distinctive similarities within themselves, the distinctive differences that cut them off from the whole society" (Handlin, 1951, pp. 185–186).

As private charity organizations developed and as government increasingly entered the welfare picture, many of the earlier mutual aid societies became fraternal organizations and took on more symbolic, social, and sentimental roles. Sinclair Lewis's *Main Street* and H. L. Mencken's columns parodied the "joiner" of fraternal and civic organizations such as the Elks and the Boosters. But community studies such as *Middletown* (Lynd and Lynd, 1929) and *Middletown In Transition* (Lynd and Lynd, 1937) made it clear that "joining" was very much alive and well in the 1920s and 1930s.

The Depression and World War II changed the focus of many mutual benefit associations, as the nation battled first against poverty, then against Germany and Japan. Following the war, the resurgence of domestic and neighborhood values led to a sharp increase in the number and membership of mutual benefit associations. The picture changed again with the social activism and international consciousness of the 1960s and 1970s. Some mutual benefits continued to grow. Between 1969 and 1985, the number of business leagues doubled, social and recreation clubs went from 36,000 to 57,000, and war veterans associations rose from 14,000 (in 1976) to 23,000. But other types of mutual benefit organizations declined during these years. Fraternal beneficiary societies went from 142,000 in 1976 to 94,000 in 1985, and labor and agricultural organizations dropped sharply in the 1980s (Weisbrod, 1988, pp. 176–177).

The decades following the mid 1960s also saw a new generation of ethnic mutual benefit associations, as American immigration laws were changed and as economic and political conditions in Latin American and Asian countries brought millions of new immigrants into the United States. In the nineteenth and early twentieth centuries, 90 percent of the immigrants had come from Europe; in the 1970s and 1980s, 90 percent came from Latin America and Asia. These new immigrant communities formed mutual assistance societies very similar to those created by European immigrants a century earlier.

The 1970s and 1980s also saw the revival of self-help organizations, reminiscent of nineteenth-century temperance societies. In addition to modern temperance societies such as Alcoholics Anonymous, there were organizations to help people deal with problems of smoking, drug abuse, child abuse, spousal abuse, and gambling. Also added were victims' groups, such as Mothers Against Drunk Driving, parents of missing children, people with AIDS, families coping with suicide, and rape victims.

Policy Issues

All organizations arise because of common interests. In mutual benefit organizations, the interests focus on the members rather than on external clients or the society at large. Although group self-interest and altruism are often closely intertwined (for instance, in ethnic, minority, and immigrant associations) self-orientation has been the defining characteristic of mutual benefit organizations. Douglas (1987, p. 51) refers to "the mutual benefit organization—which is established to provide collective benefits more or less exclusively for its members," and Simon (1987, p. 69) says that these organizations "may be roughly described as carrying forward the private interests of the members but subject to the nondistribution constraint."

Why then should these groups receive tax exemption and other nonprofit benefits? Why, for instance, should some retirement funds and health insurance firms have nonprofit benefits and others not? Blue Cross and Blue Shield receive nonprofit status in some states but not in others; which states are right? Should for-profit Fidelity Investments have to compete with nonprofit TIAA-CREF when both provide pension plans? Further, are trade associations, business leagues, consumer cooperatives, condominium associations, and labor unions really part of the for-profit rather than the nonprofit sector, since they deal primarily with the economic activities of their members (Sills, 1968, pp. 363–364)? Clearly, the job of the American Tobacco Institute is to persuade the government and the public to act in such a way that the profits of tobacco companies will be maximized. Should the IRS treat such business leagues any differently from the way they treat the businesses themselves? One of the principal objectives of unions is to secure higher compensation for worker-members. Since the classic defining characteristic of a nonprofit is that "no part of the net earnings of [the organization] inures to the benefit of any private shareholder or individual" (Internal Revenue Code Section 501(c)(3)), don't unions depart from at least the spirit if not the letter of the law? Some also argue that private social clubs are often a subtle extension of the business world. Recent lawsuits attempting to open elite male and largely white clubs to women and minorities have frequently claimed that these clubs are "where business is done" and that to be excluded from them is to be unfairly excluded from business opportunities.

Similar questions have been raised about the relationship of mutual benefit organizations to the political world. Some colonial leaders had serious misgivings about secret political societies such as the Society of the Cincinnati. In the nineteenth century, Catholics suspected the semisecret Masons, and Masons suspected the semisecret Knights of Columbus. Some Americans are convinced that the Trilateral Commission, certainly one of the most exclusive clubs in the country, is a dark threat to American democratic values. Some private clubs are thought to control the political processes of their communities. It has long been recognized that "service clubs" play an important role in the governance of smaller to mid-sized cities. As Rossi (1961, p. 309) said about "Mediana," a Midwestern industrial city of about forty-five thousand, "There is a saying in Mediana to the effect that Rotary owns the town, Kiwanis runs it, and the Jaycees do all the legwork." There are some three thousand trade and professional associations in Washington, D.C., and their presence in the nation's capital is not accidental; one of their chief tasks is to lobby the federal government.

These questions, however legitimate, illustrate the need for more understanding of the complexities and roles of mutual benefit organizations. As suggested above, such organizations have deep historical roots and have often demonstrated the capacity to move easily from self-directed to altruistic activity. Even the self-directed actions of mutual benefit organizations often have significant value for society, such as the efforts of professional associations to improve the education and training of lawyers, doctors, architects, teachers, accountants, and clergy. It is an illusion to equate nonprofits with altruism and for-profits with selfishness. While in some nonprofits (for instance, Amnesty International) the donors, members, and staff seem as far removed as possible from the intended benefits (freeing political prisoners and preventing human rights abuses in foreign countries), in many other nonprofits it is quite clear that members, board, and staff benefit directly in many ways, including financially. Some major foundations pay directors fees to their board members and substantial salaries and benefits to their staff. Herzlinger and Krasker (1987) have argued that physicians benefit considerably from nonprofit hospitals. Some arts organizations and private schools and colleges provide important social and economic benefits to their clients. On the other hand, for-profit organizations and business and professional organizations representing them have made many contributions to social welfare, not the least of which is the development of healthy industries and professions. Legal theorists of the nonprofit sector are increasingly inclined to distinguish between "mutual benefit" and "public benefit" organizations (American Bar Association, 1986), but it would be a mistake to push this distinction too far. There is a great need for more historical, sociological, anthropological, and economic studies of mutual benefit organizations to clarify their goals, activities, and impact. Such research may well show that mutual benefit organizations and "philanthropic" nonprofit organizations are much more similar than is commonly supposed.

All mutual benefit organizations combined account for less than 10 percent of the employment and economic activity of the nonprofit sector (Rudney, 1987, p. 55). Partly because of their size and partly because of the sharp distinctions made between philanthropic and nonphilanthropic nonprofits, mutual benefit organizations have tended to get somewhat lost in the research, theorizing, and educational programming related to the nonprofit sector. As only one example, the otherwise excellent compilation *The Nonprofit Sector: A Research Handbook* (Powell, 1987), largely a production of Yale's Program on Non-Profit Organizations, contains no separate discussion of mutual benefit nonprofits and pays very limited attention throughout the book to this topic. The richness of the mutual benefit world is often lost to the sector as a whole, and the potential benefits of the philanthropic nonprofit world are often lost to the mutual benefit organizations. Some mutual benefit organizations have particularly strong relationships with the business world, others with local communities, others with ethnic and racial groups, and others with professional groups. If nonprofit organizations are "mediating institutions," as Berger and Neuhaus (1977) would have it, mutual benefit organizations could play a mediating role between the larger nonprofit sector and various publics critical to that sector. A closer relationship between mutual benefit and public benefit nonprofits could be highly useful to both sides. As James Douglas (1987, p. 53) has written of the government, business, and voluntary sectors and of various classes of nonprofits within the voluntary sector, "these are artificial and academic distinctions imposed on what is, in reality, the seamless web of the institutional fabric of society."

PROSPECTS FOR AMERICA'S NONPROFIT SECTOR

☆ ★ ★ 11

An Agenda

By any measure—size, economic impact, political influence, cultural role, effect on personal and social values, effect on public policy, or international presence—private nonprofit organizations hold a highly important position in American life. The striking thing about the third sector is that it is seldom seen as important and in a sense seldom seen at all. When John D. Rockefeller III called it "the invisible sector," he identified a key problem of nonprofits, that of not being taken seriously. Any other American industry that employed more civilians than the federal and fifty state governments combined and ranked eighth among the world's economies would be treated with awe, suspicion, and fear. The nonprofit sector is hardly noticed, relegated to a pleasant and harmless world of churchgoers, opera buffs, and Girl Scout cookie vendors. It is, in many people's minds, still the world of do-gooders. It is still neatly skewered by Thoreau's comment that philanthropy is the only virtue which is sufficiently appreciated.

A major cause of the nonprofit sector's invisibility is conceptual, even semantic. *Business* and *commerce* are clear, strong, no-nonsense words and ideas, as American as the flag. Government and politics have been a national fixation for nearly four centuries. There is no such semantic clarity and conceptual strength about the nonprofit sector. Its descriptors are negative, complicated, verbally boring. Its public image is weak, diffuse, inconsistent. Is the nonprofit sector charismatic, wimpish, creative, bold, reactionary, sober, responsible, demagogic, feminine, masculine, liberal, conservative? Any American on the street could characterize presidential candidates, the Chrysler Corporation, and the Teamsters Union in some such terms but would only be puzzled if asked to so characterize the American Red Cross or the Pew Memorial Trusts and would go absolutely blank if asked to characterize the nonprofit sector as a whole. Other traditional terms, such as *charitable*, *philanthropic*, and *voluntary*, evoke similarly vague responses. If, as many politicians have said, the illusion of power is power, perhaps one of the reasons the nonprofit sector is collectively weak is that it is all reality and no illusion.

The conceptualization and semanticization of the nonprofit sector are among its principal tasks and have only just begun. Lester Salamon (1987) and others have pointed out that the concept of the private nonprofit sector did not begin to emerge until the last half of the nineteenth century, when there developed in several quarters an interest in distinguishing between the government and the private sector. Until that time, the distinction made little difference; the important thing was what was done, not the legal form of the organization that did it. Government, business, and voluntary associations were closely related and in some cases almost indistinguishable in the service activities we now call the nonprofit sector. In this sense, not just the concept but the reality of the nonprofit sector was invented in the second half of the nineteenth century; the earlier period might be considered the prehistory of the third sector.

Little has been written about the sector as a whole until relatively recently. Particular subsectors (religion, private education, foundations, and so forth) have been studied in some detail; but with a few exceptions, analysis of the nonprofit sector in general is largely a phenomenon of the last two decades. Pioneering work was done in the mid 1970s by the Commission on Private Philanthropy and Public Needs (1975, 1977a, 1977b, 1977c, 1977d, 1977e, 1977f), known as the Filer Commission after its chair, Aetna chief executive officer John Filer. Yale University's Program on Non-Profit Organizations, established in 1978 under the leadership of Yale law professor John Simon, contributed more than one hundred working papers and dozens of articles and books during its first decade. By 1988, there were seventeen research centers on the nonprofit sector, and dozens of new scholars had come into the field *(Research in Progress,* n.d., 1985, 1986, 1987, 1988; Powell, 1987). About a dozen colleges and universities had started graduate programs for nonprofit organization managers (O'Neill and Young, 1988; Gray, 1987). Dozens of other higher education institutions had launched courses on American philanthropy. Major theories of the nonprofit sector had been put forward (Douglas, 1983; Hansmann, 1980; Salamon, 1987; Weisbrod, 1975; Young, 1983). Good bibliographies on the sector had been produced (Layton, 1987; O'Connell, 1983; Powell, 1987). Independent Sector, a national coalition of more than six hundred large nonprofit organizations, was formed in 1980 by John Gardner and others and almost immediately assumed a major leadership role. The Foundation Center, the Conference Board, and the Council on Foundations helped make the role of institutional funders clearer, and United Way of America vividly portrayed the social service world through sophisticated television advertising.

It is much too early to tell whether this movement, now all of ten years old, will become a significant long-term influence in American education and public perception. But at least the nation is finally following up the incisive comments made in the early nineteenth century by a French aristocrat whose only direct experience of the United States was an eight-month tour made at age twenty-six. Tocqueville ([1835] 1969, p. 517) wrote, "Nothing, in my view, more deserves attention than the intellectual and moral associations in America." A century and a half later, these associations are finally beginning to receive serious attention.

The classic challenge of the nonprofit sector has been its relationship with government. Both exist partly, in the words of the federal Constitution, to "promote the general welfare." Many of the major activities of the nonprofit sector are paralleled by government. Much has been written on which came first, government or voluntary associations, but it is not at all clear that the question is a meaningful one. In the prehistory of the nonprofit sector, governmental and nongovernmental activity and institutions often flowed back and forth into each other. For this reason alone, the past may not offer much guidance as to appropriate relationships between nonprofits and government today. Until the 1930s, for example, state and local governments' role in social service provision was generally smaller than that of nonprofits, and the federal government's role was almost nonexistent; this does not mean that the same should be true today. The Depression programs and the later Great Society programs made government the biggest player in this field but also funneled billions of dollars into nonprofit social service agencies. More recently, private for-profit firms have seriously entered the health, education, and social service fields. While the respective roles and proper balance of government and private effort are a matter of debate, there is no self-evident reason to recreate the balance of the past.

Four centuries of history and the current vigor of the private nonprofit sector provide no evidence that American voluntary organizations are merely a stepping-stone on the way to an American welfare state. Nor, on the other hand, is there any reason to believe that the past dominance of private institutions in fields such as education and social services will reappear. The more useful question today is how government and nonprofits can cooperate and compete in ways most beneficial to American society. Should the "Reagan revolution" of returning social service funding to state and local government and private charity be continued or reversed? Should the government do more arts funding, and, if so, at what level, in what way, with what specific goals? Should the government be more or less involved in education and research? Should government fund education services in the same way it funds health and welfare services? What role should nonprofit hospitals play with respect to government funding and public policy on health issues? How can private voluntary organizations working abroad cooperate with the U.S. government without becoming its conscious or unconscious foreign policy tool? More generally, should nonprofits supplement government effort, or vice versa? Should nonprofits play the vanguard role? In what situations can nonprofit organizations do things more easily and effectively than government? Very much in the Tocqueville tradition, Salamon has written: "For government to act, substantial segments of the public must be aroused, public officials must be informed, laws must be written, majorities must be assembled, and programs must be put into operation. By contrast, to generate a voluntary-sector response, a handful of individuals acting on their own or with outside contributed support can suffice" (Salamon, 1987, p. 39).

The interaction between government and nonprofits is one of profound societal implications. Americans have long appreciated the significance of the separation of executive, legislative, and judicial powers in government, as well as the distinction among federal, state, and local government roles. Much attention has also been given to the complex interactions between government and business. But little theoretical inquiry, research, or policy analysis has been devoted to the relationship between government and the nonprofit sector, which may well be of similar significance. There is great need for such study. Analysis of this type should include not only careful review of each subsector but also comparative study across subsector lines. For instance, the "third-party government" theory may be highly useful in studying social services and health care but may have little relevance to art and none at all to religion, grantmaking, and advocacy. The theory may also be too simplistic for government-nonprofit interactions in education and international assistance.

A larger look at the relations between government and nonprofits should highlight the influence of broad social phenomena such as immigration, population mobility, and shifts in political attitudes. For example, the century of large-scale immigration (1820s–1920s) had dramatic effect on the growth and development of the nonprofit sector, but at the same time it was radically reshaping the relationship between government and religion, education, and social services. The settling of different parts of the United States and the period and conditions of their settling importantly affected the government-nonprofit relationship; some of these geographical differences still exist. The political attitudes of different political parties, ethnic groups, economic groups, and geographical regions have also affected the government-nonprofit relationship. In short, not only particular service areas, such as art and health care, but also demographic, political, and other variables shape the government-nonprofit interaction. A better understanding of these factors would allow us to formulate more useful plans and policies.

We also need to better understand how nonprofits aid government. A large modern society has countless needs that go beyond the power of individuals and families but are not sufficiently lucrative to attract business and, if left to government, would so absorb its energies and resources as to cause neglect of more basic governmental functions. Many of these tasks are carried out by nonprofits. As Tocqueville ([1835] 1969, p. 515) asked, "what political power could ever carry on the vast multitude of lesser undertakings which associations daily enable American citizens to control?" Nonprofits can and do perform many tasks much more efficiently than government, tasks that are vital for the good functioning of the society. Nonprofit organizations may also unintentionally but effectively protect government from much hostility and opposition. As Robert Nisbet (1986, pp. 181–182) noted:

> Few things are so calculated to divert human inclinations from focusing on the capture of political power and on a consuming ideology as the necessary avenue to secular salvation as is the proliferation of intermediate, voluntary and autonomous associations. The American Revolution did not choke off voluntary association, as did the French and the Russian. Voluntary associations in America could become not merely a functional refuge of the individual but also a buffer against the invitations of political centralization. It is safe to say that a great deal of American passion that would otherwise surely have gone into political movements went instead into the innumerable intermediate associations which, along with local, regional and religious loyalties, made the American social landscape so different from the French in the nineteenth century.

A macro view of the government-nonprofit relationship would also place particular political events in perspective. Some foundation leaders felt that the Tax Reform Act of 1969 would be the death knell of private foundations, whereas its effects seem to have been rather modest and far from totally negative (Ylvisaker, 1987, pp. 362, 375). More recently, the Reagan era has been labeled a devastating blow to the nonprofit world, but the gloom and doom are not altogether supported by the facts. There have been significant increases in private philanthropy from 1981 to 1988, there is no evidence that state and local government support of nonprofit services declined during this period, and even the federal government picture is quite mixed. Federal support of health care, including nonprofit health care, has grown steadily during the Reagan era, including the most significant expansion of Medicare since the 1960s. The relatively tiny amount of federal government money flowing into private elementary and secondary education (for school lunches, library books, and certain specialized services) has not changed appreciably during the Reagan years. The monetary effect on private higher education has been slight, taking all federally funded education and research programs together. The federal government does not give money to private foundations and corporate funders, so there has been no change in that area; if anything, the performance of the economy and the stock market during most of the Reagan era has greatly increased the assets and grantmaking ability of institutional funders. The federal government is strictly prohibited from giving direct support to religious institutions, so there has been no change in that large area of the nonprofit sector. The Reagan administration has repeatedly tried to cut funding for the National Endowment for the Arts and other cultural programs, but Congress has prevented this from happening. There was an overall decline in inflation-free dollars for arts funding, but it amounted to only 1 percent of arts revenue nationally. Nonprofit international assistance programs have fared little better or worse under the Reagan administration than they did under earlier administrations. Advocacy organizations have never been supported by the federal government, for obvious reasons; legal assistance programs, however, were substantially reduced. In addition to legal aid programs, the Reagan cutbacks primarily affected employment and training efforts, housing and community development work, and other social services. In these areas, the cuts were quite significant, ranging from 15 to 50 percent. In some cases, state and/or local government took up the slack. To cope with the government cutbacks, nonprofit social service agencies increased fees and fundraising activities and started for-profit ventures. The total amount of revenue flowing into the nonprofit sector has not decreased during the Reagan years; it has increased even after allowing for inflation.

Whatever one may think of the Reagan philosophy and actions, the "Reagan revolution" has simply not led to the sudden, massive collapse of the nonprofit sector, even in the hardest-hit area of social services. Similar gloom and doom prophecies followed the 1986 Tax Reform Act and the 1987 stock market crash, but private giving still rose 6.5 percent in 1987, significantly more than the rise in the GNP or personal income. All of which suggests that we need broader and more sophisticated theoretical constructs and better data bases to study the interaction between government and the nonprofit sector. The importance of this task can hardly be exaggerated.

The Filer Commission (Commission on Private Philanthropy and Public Needs, 1975), Nielsen (1979), Smith (1987), Weisbrod (1988), and others have called for structured representation of the nonprofit sector within the federal government, in the form of a special office, a special assistant to the president, a congressional subcommittee, or all of these. It is time that such recommendations be taken seriously, not only by the federal government but also by national nonprofit agencies such as Independent Sector, the Council on Foundations, and United Way of America. The business sector, unions, and other major parts of the economy have de facto representation within the federal government, but the nonprofit sector has nothing. Such representation would have to be carefully structured so that it did not become, consciously or unconsciously, a mechanism for inappropriate government influence on the nonprofit sector; but such representation could help to improve the position of nonprofits within the governmental system and the society and could help make the sector more visible, one of its greatest needs. Included in this representation should be maximum effort to get government statistical agencies to collect regular and comprehensive data on the private nonprofit sector. Government representation of the nonprofit sector should not be limited to the federal level. Such representation should also be sought at the state and city or metropolitan levels.

Since both government and nonprofits are primarily in the business of producing public collective goods rather than individual consumer goods, the government-nonprofit relationship is more obvious and visible than the relationship between nonprofits and for-profits. Yet the latter relationship is far more extensive and important than commonly realized. As Rudney (1981) pointed out, business revenues *from* the nonprofit sector are ten times greater than business contributions *to* the nonprofit sector. The third sector is a major buyer, a major employer, and a major economic contributor in countless communities. Nonprofits employ millions of people, train future workers, help troubled people resume a productive role in the economy, and provide educational and cultural services that enable employers to attract certain types of employees. Nonprofit universities, research centers, professional associations, and foundations form a major part of the national research and development industry that benefits the for-profit sector in countless ways.

The nonprofit sector may also play an important and little recognized role in supporting business and government by providing mechanisms to relieve some of the natural tension between powerful institutions and individuals. Sociologists Max Weber, Emile Durkheim, and Talcott Parsons have suggested that this is a central function of voluntary associations in a society dominated by large bureaucratic organizations. Even the antiestablishment actions of advocacy groups may be highly beneficial to the establishment, by allowing for the release of social pressure and warning establishment institutions that some of their practices are particularly offensive. It has often been observed that Franklin Roosevelt's New Deal economic policies, condemned by some business leaders in the 1930s as radical and even communist, actually played a major role in saving the capitalist system. In the absence of serious theorizing and research, the nonprofit sector has sometimes been seen as a David fighting against the Goliaths of big business and big government. Such metaphors are very misleading. It may be more accurate to think of the nonprofit sector as a highly effective guarantor of democratic capitalism. Better understanding of the mechanisms and effects of this interaction would be beneficial to both parties. As Weisbrod (1988, pp. 86-87) commented, speaking particularly about the recent entry of nonprofits into for-profit ventures:

Knowledge about the nonprofit economy is growing, yet major gaps remain. Not much is known about its changing composition, or about how effective nonprofits are in meeting society's wants as part of a pluralistic economy. The paucity of data has restricted serious examination of relations among nonprofit organizations, proprietary firms, and governmental agencies and has left us with a weak information base from which to design and implement public policy toward the nonprofit sector. . . . Inadequate data is not the only source of problems of understanding how and how well the nonprofit sector performs. A theory of institutional behavior is needed that will indicate what kinds of data are needed and how to interpret them. Is private enterprise being stifled excessively by expansion of the nonprofit sector? Alternatively, are nonprofits filling important gaps in markets where neither private firms nor governments are responding adquately to consumer wants? Answers to such questions require a combination of a theoretical framework, with which to define "excessive" expansion of nonprofits and "gaps" in markets, and quantitative testing.

One of the perennial problems of the nonprofit sector is deciding who its clients should be. This problem does not exist in the same way for business and government. At the most basic level, a client of business is whoever might buy the product, and government's client is any citizen. Obviously, the client issue is more complicated than that in business and government, but in the nonprofit sector it is complicated to begin with. Should nonprofits serve only or primarily the poor, disadvantaged and vulnerable groups, clients who have money to pay for services and/or to donate to the organization, clients who live in a certain area, those who sincerely believe in the organization's purposes, those who will give some time to the organization, or those who belong to a certain ethnic, racial, gender, religious, or socioeconomic group? All of these selection principles have been used, alone or in combination. Nearly all of them have drawn criticism at various times.

The client selection issue goes to the heart of what the nonprofit sector is all about and also raises fundamental philosophical questions about the nature and functioning of society. For example, if one holds that the nonprofit sector's central function is to provide direct services to poor and disadvantaged people, this position would necessarily make certain assumptions about government's and business's roles (or lack thereof) in this problem area, as well as about the nonprofit sector's ability to do the job. The view that the nonprofit sector's mission is to be the innovator and the standard setter would similarly be based on certain assumptions. A philosophy of the nonprofit sector as the loyal opposition would also have necessary antecedents and consequences.

Like many of its agencies, the nonprofit sector has to some extent answered this question by adopting a multiservice position. Ultimately, however, this is no real answer, because the obvious question is where to stop. Business and government select certain activities and exclude others, reach out to certain clients and not others, because of the way each defines itself. The nonprofit sector has historically exhibited a high degree of fluidity as to its clients, programs, and self-understanding. It may in fact be that one of the chief roles of the nonprofit sector in society is to move into areas of social ambiguity and stay there until it becomes clearer what the issues, needs, problems, and client groups are. In medieval England and colonial America, voluntary agencies occasionally built bridges and maintained roads. These are now seen to be functions for government, but when there was a need, the nonprofit sector acted, without much bother about philosophy and policy. In several service areas—especially health care, education, and social services—nonprofits have agonized over the client selection and program selection questions. This "problem" may be caused by an oversimplified view of the sector's role. Conceivably, one of the sector's greatest contributions to society is precisely its tolerance of ambiguity, its unwillingness to limit itself to a particular, defined set of activities. Organizational theory has long held that informal groups and unofficial processes are necessary to make large organizations work; something analogous may be one of the central functions of the private nonprofit sector in American society. If so, the client and program selection issue will necessarily remain murky, troublesome, and a subject of continuous debate, both within and without the nonprofit sector.

What is the future of the American nonprofit sector? It is becoming increasingly evident from the trends of the last twenty-five years that the nonprofit world, far from being on the edge of extinction, remains very large and has been growing even faster than business or government in recent decades. It is certain that the Great Society programs had a lot to do with this, and it is probable that the general economic welfare of the nation had a good deal to do with it. But whatever the reasons, there seems to be no evidence that the nonprofit sector is in some immediate and critical danger. Absent another great depression or large-scale war, there is every reason to believe that the nonprofit sector will maintain the position it has achieved in recent decades. In many cases, it is simply unthinkable that the society would allow the nonprofit sector to go out of existence or be seriously cut back. How could a system that provides 70 percent of the hospital beds in the nation be allowed to fail? Or a system that educates eight million American children, young people, and adults, including many of the future leaders of the country? As for religion, with a national membership of 140 million and a deeply ingrained position in American society, it is as likely that Congress will go out of existence. Certain programs in the nonprofit sector may be "endangered," but there is no evidence that the sector as a whole or any of its major subsectors is genuinely endangered.

On the other hand, it seems unlikely that the nonprofit sector will continue to grow at the rates seen in the 1960s and 1970s. The nation's budget and trade deficit problems and its runaway costs for military programs and "entitlements" (Social Security, medical care, and so forth) make it unlikely that the next few administrations, whether Republican or Democratic, will launch major spending increases that would affect the nonprofit sector. While total revenue to the nonprofit sector will likely continue to increase at a relatively steady rate, as has been the case for nearly all of the past twenty-five years, this will come as a result of increased fees for service, the combined funding of federal, state, and local government, private institutional and individual giving, and for-profit ventures within nonprofit organizations, and not as a result of any one source, such as the federal government.

It also seems likely, again on the basis of recent trends, that the nonprofit sector will sharply increase its self-enhancement efforts through lobbying, public awareness campaigns, research, publications, graduate and undergraduate degree programs, and professional conferences. This new self-consciousness could also lead to more ambitious and aggressive public policy and social change activities on the part of the independent sector, acting more in concert than it has in the past, which is almost not at all. For the first time in American history, the independent sector as a whole is beginning to have the communication links, the organizational forms, and most importantly the collective self-consciousness that could create a multiplier effect for major activities within the sector. For instance, if something like the civil rights movement were to take place now, the current and developing structures and communication processes within the nonprofit sector might help make the movement more immediately effective. Perhaps some relatively noncontroversial and emotional issue such as the plight of the homeless will be the first grounds for this kind of united effort. The AIDS crisis is of such magnitude that it seems already to have transcended the life-style and sexual politics issue and may be another candidate. Nuclear arms control, however worthy a cause, may be too political and technical an issue to gain broad-based support. The women's movement may, ironically, already be too successful to qualify.

The future of the nonprofit sector, however, has more to do with ideas and ideals than with money, structures, and media expertise. Some of the sector's greatest accomplishments—abolition, care for the mentally ill, easing the transition of millions of immigrants into American society, creating theories and research that have revolutionized modern life—happened with, at first, little money and few structures but a great deal of courage, passion, intelligence, and energy. Max Weber's classic analysis of organizations that move from charismatic to bureaucratic forms should be pondered by leaders and students of the nonprofit sector. The sector is clearly moving toward better organization, better communication systems, better salaries and benefits for its employees, better data collection and research, more and better theories, and a higher degree of professionalization. These are as needed as they are inevitable, but it would be a tragic mistake if they were allowed to develop at the cost of the charismatic energy that has driven the sector from the beginning. The very shift in today's terminology, from "voluntary associations" to "nonprofit firms," is a somewhat ominous indication of the intellectual and organizational change that is taking place within the third America. The great philosopher and mathematician Alfred North Whitehead once wrote that the ideal process of a human being's educational development is to go from a "stage of romance" through a stage of discipline to a stage of synthesis. America's nonprofit sector is clearly moving into its second stage. How it is led and inspired will greatly determine how successfully it arrives at its third.

☆ ★ ★ References

American Association of Fund-Raising Counsel. *Giving USA: Estimates of Philanthropic Giving in 1986 and the Trends They Show.* New York: AAFRC Trust for Philanthropy, 1987.

American Association of Fund-Raising Counsel. *Giving USA: The Annual Report on Philanthropy for the Year 1987.* New York: AAFRC Trust for Philanthropy, 1988.

American Bar Association, Committee on Nonprofit Corporations. *1986 Revised Model Nonprofit Corporation Act.* Chicago: American Bar Association, 1986.

American Hospital Association. *Hospital Statistics: 1987 Edition.* Chicago: American Hospital Association, 1987.

"America's Best Colleges." *U.S. News and World Report,* October 26, 1987, *103* (17), 49–90.

Axinn, J., and Levin, H. *Social Welfare: A History of the American Response to Need.* (2nd ed.) New York: Longman, 1982.

Bailyn, B. *Education in the Forming of American Society: Needs and Opportunities for Study.* Chapel Hill: University of North Carolina Press, 1960.

Bailyn, B. *The Ideological Origins of the American Revolution.* Cambridge, Mass.: Harvard University Press (Belknap Press), 1967.

Bailyn, B. *The Peopling of British North America: An Introduction.* New York: Knopf, 1986.

Banton, M. "Voluntary Associations: Anthropological Aspects." In

D. L. Sills (ed.), *International Encyclopedia of the Social Sciences*. Vol. 16. New York: Macmillan, 1968.

Ben-Ner, A. "Non-Profit Organizations: Why Do They Exist in Market Economies?" In S. Rose-Ackerman (ed.), *The Economics of Nonprofit Institutions: Studies in Structure and Policy*. New York: Oxford University Press, 1986.

Berger, P. L., and Neuhaus, R. J. *To Empower People: The Role of Mediating Structures in Public Policy*. Washington, D.C.: American Enterprise Institute for Public Policy Research, 1977.

Billington, R. A. *The Protestant Crusade, 1800–1860: A Study of the Origins of American Nativism*. New York: Macmillan, 1938.

Bolling, L. R. *Private Foreign Aid: U.S. Philanthropy for Relief and Development*. Boulder, Co.: Westview Press, 1982.

Bozeman, B. *All Organizations Are Public: Bridging Public and Private Organizational Theories*. San Francisco: Jossey-Bass, 1987.

Bremner, R. H. *American Philanthropy*. (2nd ed.) Chicago: University of Chicago Press, 1988.

Callahan, R. E. *Education and the Cult of Efficiency: A Study of the Social Forces That Have Shaped the Administration of the Public Schools*. Chicago: University of Chicago Press, 1962.

CARE. *1987 Annual Report*. New York: CARE, 1988.

Catholic Relief Services. *1987 Annual Report*. New York: Catholic Relief Services, 1988.

Catterall, J. S. "Private School Participation and Public Policy." In T. James and H. M. Levin, *Comparing Public and Private Schools*. Vol. 1: *Institutions and Organizations*. Philadelphia: Falmer Press, 1988.

Chambers, C. A. "Toward a Redefinition of Welfare History." *Journal of American History*, 73 (2), 1986, 407–433.

Chambers, C. A. "The Public and Independent Sectors: Separate Strategies or Partnership?" In *The Constitution and the Independent Sector*. 1987 Spring Research Forum Working Papers. Washington, D.C.: Independent Sector, 1987.

Chambers, W. N. *Political Parties in a New Nation: The American Experience, 1776–1809*. New York: Oxford University Press, 1963.

Cibulka, J. G., O'Brien, T. J., and Zewe, D. *Inner-City Private*

Elementary Schools: A Study. Milwaukee: Marquette University Press, 1982.

Clark, R. C. "Does the Nonprofit Form Fit the Hospital Industry?" *Harvard Law Review,* 1980, *93* (7), 1416-1489.

Coleman, J. S., Hoffer, T., and Kilgore, S. *High School Achievement: Public, Catholic, and Private Schools Compared.* New York: Basic Books, 1982.

Coleman, J. S., and others. *Equality of Educational Opportunity.* Washington, D.C.: U.S. Department of Health, Education, and Welfare, 1966.

Collier, P., and Horowitz, D. *The Rockefellers: An American Dynasty.* New York: Holt, Rinehart & Winston, 1976.

Commission on Private Philanthropy and Public Needs. *Giving in America: Towards a Stronger Voluntary Sector.* Washington, D.C.: Commission on Private Philanthropy and Public Needs, 1975.

Commission on Private Philanthropy and Public Needs. *Research Papers.* Vol. 1: *History, Trends, and Current Magnitudes.* Washington, D.C.: U.S. Department of the Treasury, 1977a.

Commission on Private Philanthropy and Public Needs. *Research Papers.* Vol. 2: *Philanthropic Fields of Interest. Part I: Areas of Activity.* Washington, D.C.: U.S. Department of the Treasury, 1977b.

Commission on Private Philanthropy and Public Needs. *Research Papers.* Vol. 2: *Philanthropic Fields of Interest. Part II: Additional Perspectives.* Washington, D.C.: U.S. Department of the Treasury, 1977c.

Commission on Private Philanthropy and Public Needs. *Research Papers.* Vol. 3: *Special Behavioral Studies, Foundations, and Corporations.* Washington, D.C.: U.S. Department of the Treasury, 1977d.

Commission on Private Philanthropy and Public Needs. *Research Papers.* Vol. 4: *Taxes.* Washington, D.C.: U.S. Department of the Treasury, 1977e.

Commission on Private Philanthropy and Public Needs. *Research Papers.* Vol. 5: *Regulation.* Washington, D.C.: U.S. Department of the Treasury, 1977f.

Cooper, B. S. "The Changing Universe of U.S. Private Schools." In

T. James and H. M. Levin (eds.), *Comparing Public and Private Schools*. Vol. 1: *Institutions and Organizations*. Philadelphia: Falmer Press, 1988.

Cremin, L. A. *American Education: The Colonial Experience, 1607-1783*. New York: Harper & Row, 1970.

Cross, R. D. "Origins of the Catholic Parochial Schools in America." *American Benedictine Review*, 1965, *16*, 194-209.

Curti, M. "American Philanthropy and the National Character." In B. O'Connell (ed.), *America's Voluntary Spirit: A Book of Readings*. New York: Foundation Center, 1983.

De Mille, A. G. "Martha Graham's Art Is Worth Preserving" (letter to the editor). *New York Times*, Dec. 15, 1987, p. 26.

DiMaggio, P. J. "Cultural Entrepreneurship in Nineteenth-Century Boston." In P. J. DiMaggio (ed.), *Nonprofit Enterprise in the Arts: Studies in Mission and Constraint*. New York: Oxford University Press, 1986.

DiMaggio, P. J. "Nonprofit Organizations in the Production and Distribution of Culture." In W. W. Powell (ed.), *The Nonprofit Sector: A Research Handbook*. New Haven, Conn.: Yale University Press, 1987.

Douglas, J. *Why Charity? The Case for a Third Sector*. Newbury Park, Calif.: Sage, 1983.

Douglas, J. "Political Theories of Nonprofit Organization." In W. W. Powell (ed.), *The Nonprofit Sector: A Research Handbook*. New Haven, Conn.: Yale University Press, 1987.

Edie, J. A. *Congress and Private Foundations: An Historical Analysis*. Washington, D.C.: Council on Foundations, 1987.

Ellis, J. T. *The Life of James Cardinal Gibbons, Archbishop of Baltimore, 1834-1921*. 2 vols. Milwaukee: Bruce, 1952.

Encyclopedia of Associations. (22nd ed.) Detroit: Gale Research Company, 1988.

Erickson, D. A. "Choice and Private Schools: Dynamics of Supply and Demand." In D. C. Levy (ed.), *Private Education: Studies in Choice and Public Policy*. New York: Oxford University Press, 1986.

"Fact-File: Trends in Student Aid, 1980-81 to 1985-86." *Chronicle of Higher Education*, September 24, 1986, 28.

"Fact-File: The Top 100 Institutions in Total Research-and-

Development Spending for Fiscal 1987." *Chronicle of Higher Education*, November 23, 1988, A19.

Foote, J. "You Name It, They Do It." *Foundation News*, Sept.-Oct. 1985, 14-25.

Foundation Center. *The Foundation Directory, 11th Edition.* New York: Foundation Center, 1987a.

Foundation Center. *Grants for International and Foreign Programs.* New York: Foundation Center, 1987b.

Foundation Center. *The Foundation Grants Index.* (17th ed.) New York: Foundation Center, 1988.

Frank, A. D., and Zweig, J. "The Fault Is Not in Our Stars." *Forbes*, September 21, 1987, 120-128.

Freudenheim, M. "U.S. Health Care Spending Continues Sharp Rise." *New York Times*, Nov. 19, 1988, pp. 1, 8.

Fuchs, V. *The Health Economy.* Cambridge, Mass.: Harvard University Press, 1986.

Galaskiewicz, J. *Social Organization of an Urban Grants Economy: A Study of Business Philanthropy and Nonprofit Organizations.* Orlando, Fla.: Academic Press, 1985.

Gerlach, L. P., and Hine, V. M. *People, Power, Change: Movements of Social Transformation.* Indianapolis, Ind.: Bobbs-Merrill, 1970.

Glazer, N. *The Limits of Social Policy.* Cambridge, Mass.: Harvard University Press, 1988.

Goldsmith, R. W. *The National Balance Sheet of the United States, 1953-1980.* Chicago: University of Chicago Press, 1982.

Gratiot, M. H. "Why Parents Choose Non-Public Schools: Comparative Attitudes and Characteristics of Public and Private School Consumers." Unpublished Ph.D. dissertation, Stanford University, 1979.

Gray, S. T. *An Independent Sector Resource Directory of Education and Training Opportunities and Other Services.* (2nd ed.) Washington, D.C.: Independent Sector, 1987.

Greeley, A. M. *Catholic High Schools and Minority Students.* New Brunswick, N.J.: Transaction Books, 1982.

Greeley, A. M., McCready, W. C., and McCourt, K. *Catholic Schools in a Declining Church.* Kansas City, Mo.: Sheed and Ward, 1976.

Greeley, A. M., and Rossi, P. H. *The Education of Catholic Americans.* Chicago: Aldine, 1966.

Gronbjerg, K. A., Kimmich, M. H., and Salamon, L. M. *The Chicago Nonprofit Sector in a Time of Government Retrenchment.* Washington, D.C.: Urban Institute Press, 1985.

Grossman, D. A., Salamon, L. M., and Altschuler, D. M. *The New York Nonprofit Sector in a Time of Government Retrenchment.* Washington, D.C.: Urban Institute Press, 1986.

Gutowski, M., Salamon, L. M., and Pittman, K. *The Pittsburgh Nonprofit Sector in a Time of Government Retrenchment.* Washington, D.C.: Urban Institute Press, 1984.

Haertel, E. H., James, T., and Levin, H. M. *Comparing Public and Private Schools.* Vol. 2: *School Achievement.* Philadelphia: Falmer Press, 1987.

Hall, P. D. "A Historical Overview of the Private Nonprofit Sector." In W. W. Powell (ed.), *The Nonprofit Sector: A Research Handbook.* New Haven, Conn.: Yale University Press, 1987.

Handlin, O. *The Uprooted: The Epic Story of the Great Migrations That Made the American People.* Boston: Little, Brown, 1951.

Handlin, O. *The American People in the Twentieth Century.* Cambridge, Mass.: Harvard University Press, 1954.

Handlin, O. *Boston's Immigrants: A Study in Acculturation.* (Rev. ed.) Cambridge, Mass.: Harvard University Press, 1959.

Hansmann, H. "The Role of Nonprofit Enterprise." *Yale Law Journal,* 1980, *89,* 835-901.

Harder, W. P., Kimmich, M. H., and Salamon, L. M. *The San Francisco Bay Area Nonprofit Sector in a Time of Government Retrenchment.* Washington, D. C.: Urban Institute Press, 1985.

Herzlinger, R. E., and Krasker, W. S. "Who Profits from Nonprofits?" *Harvard Business Review,* 1987, *65* (1), 93-106.

Higham, J. *Strangers in the Land: Patterns of American Nativism, 1860-1925.* (2nd ed.) New Brunswick, N.J.: Rutgers University Press, 1963.

Hodgkinson, V. "Slowdown in the Sector." *Foundation News,* Sept.-Oct. 1986, pp. 56-58.

Hodgkinson, V. A., and Weitzman, M. S. *Dimensions of the Independent Sector: A Statistical Profile.* (2nd ed.) Washington, D.C.: Independent Sector, 1986.

Hodgkinson, V. A., and Weitzman, M. S. *Dimensions of the Independent Sector: A Statistical Profile; Interim Update: Fall 1988.* Washington, D.C.: Independent Sector, 1988a.

Hodgkinson, V. A., and Weitzman, M. S. *Giving and Volunteering in the United States: Findings from a National Survey.* Washington, D.C.: Independent Sector, 1988b.

Hodgkinson, V. A., Weitzman, M. S., and Kirsch, A. D. *From Belief to Commitment: The Activities and Finances of Religious Congregations in the United States.* Washington, D.C.: Independent Sector, 1988.

Hofstadter, R. *The Age of Reform: From Bryan to F.D.R.* New York: Vintage Books, 1955.

Hollingsworth, R., and Hollingsworth, E. J. "A Comparison of Non-Profit, For-Profit and Public Hospitals in the United States 1935 to the Present." Working Paper no. 113, Program on Non-Profit Organizations, Institution for Social and Policy Studies, Yale University, 1986.

James, S. V. *A People Among Peoples: Quaker Benevolence in Eighteenth-Century America.* Cambridge, Mass.: Harvard University Press, 1963.

Jenkins, J. C. "Nonprofit Organizations and Policy Advocacy." In W. W. Powell (ed.), *The Nonprofit Sector: A Research Handbook.* New Haven, Conn.: Yale University Press, 1987.

Jones, J. *San Francisco's Prominent Arts Organizations: Why Aren't They Equal Opportunity Employers?* San Francisco: J. Jones, 1988.

Jones, L. V., Lindzey, G., and Coggeshall, P. E. (eds.). *An Assessment of Research-Doctorate Programs in the United States.* 5 vols. Washington, D.C.: National Academy Press, 1982.

Jordan, W. K. *The Charities of London, 1480-1660: The Aspirations and Achievements of the Urban Society.* New York: Russell Sage Foundation, 1960.

Karl, B. D., and Katz, S. N. "The American Private Philanthropic Foundation and the Public Sphere, 1890-1930." *Minerva,* 1981, *19,* 236-270.

Katz, M. B. *Class, Bureaucracy, and Schools: The Illusion of Educational Change in America.* New York: Praeger, 1971.

Kramer, R. M. *Voluntary Agencies in the Welfare State.* Berkeley: University of California Press, 1981.

Kramer, R. M. "Voluntary Agencies and the Personal Social Services." In W. W. Powell (ed.), *The Nonprofit Sector: A Research Handbook.* New Haven, Conn.: Yale University Press, 1987.

Kraushaar, O. F. *American Nonpublic Schools: Patterns of Diversity.* Baltimore: Johns Hopkins University Press, 1972.

Kraushaar, O. F. *Private Schools: From the Puritans to the Present.* Bloomington, Ind.: Phi Delta Kappa, 1976.

Lannie, V. P. *Public Money and Parochial Education: Bishop Hughes, Governor Seward, and the New York School Controversy.* Cleveland: Case Western Reserve University Press, 1968.

Layton, D. N. *Philanthropy and Voluntarism: An Annotated Bibliography.* New York: Foundation Center, 1987.

Levy, D. C. (ed.). *Private Education: Studies in Choice and Public Policy.* New York: Oxford University Press, 1986.

Levy, R. "Caught Between Two Poles." *Foundation News,* May–June 1985, pp. 58–59, 63.

Lippert, P. G., Gutowski, M., and Salamon, L. M. *The Atlanta Nonprofit Sector in a Time of Government Retrenchment.* Washington, D.C.: Urban Institute Press, 1984.

Lubove, R. *The Professional Altruist: The Emergence of Social Work as a Career, 1880–1930.* Cambridge, Mass.: Harvard University Press, 1965.

Luckermann, B., Kimmich, M., and Salamon, L. M. *The Twin Cities Nonprofit Sector in a Time of Government Retrenchment.* Washington, D.C.: Urban Institute Press, 1984.

Ludmerer, K. M. *Learning to Heal: The Development of American Medical Education.* New York: Basic Books, 1985.

Lynd, R. S., and Lynd, H. M. *Middletown: A Study in Contemporary American Culture.* New York: Harcourt Brace Jovanovich, 1929.

Lynd, R. S., and Lynd, H. M. *Middletown in Transition: A Study in Cultural Conflicts.* New York: Harcourt Brace Jovanovich, 1937.

McCarthy, K. D. *Noblesse Oblige: Charity and Cultural Philanthropy in Chicago, 1849–1929.* Chicago: University of Chicago Press, 1982.

McDonald, J. A. "The Philanthropic Activities of Religious

Organizations." In V. A. Hodgkinson and R. Sumariwalla (eds.), *Giving and Volunteering: New Frontiers of Knowledge.* 1985 Spring Research Forum Working Papers. Washington, D.C.: Independent Sector, 1985.

Marmor, T. R., Schlesinger, M., and Smithey, R. W. "Nonprofit Organizations and Health Care." In W. W. Powell (ed.), *The Nonprofit Sector: A Research Handbook.* New Haven, Conn.: Yale University Press, 1987.

Marty, M. *Pilgrims in Their Own Land: 500 Years of Religion in America.* Boston: Little, Brown, 1984.

Montias, J. M. "Public Support for the Performing Arts in Europe and the United States." In P. J. DiMaggio (ed.), *Nonprofit Enterprise in the Arts: Studies in Mission and Constraint.* New York: Oxford University Press, 1986.

Morrell, L. R. "The Survival of Private Colleges May Well Depend on Their Willingness to Accept Aid from State Governments." *Chronicle of Higher Education,* Nov. 11, 1987, p. A52.

National Center for Charitable Statistics. *Non-profit Service Organizations: 1982.* Washington, D.C.: National Center for Charitable Statistics, 1985.

National Center for Education Statistics. *Digest of Education Statistics: 1988.* Washington, D.C.: U.S. Department of Education, 1988.

Nielsen, W. A. *The Endangered Sector.* New York: Columbia University Press, 1979.

Nielsen, W. A. *The Golden Donors: A New Anatomy of the Great Foundations.* New York: Dutton, 1985.

Nisbet, R. A. *Community and Power.* New York: Oxford University Press, 1962.

Nisbet, R. A. *The Making of Modern Society.* New York: New York University Press, 1986.

Nye, R. B. *The Cultural Life of the New Nation, 1776–1830.* New York: Harper & Row, 1960.

O'Connell, B. (ed.). *America's Voluntary Spirit: A Book of Readings.* New York: Foundation Center, 1983.

Odendahl, T. J. (ed.). *America's Wealthy and the Future of Foundations.* New York: Foundation Center, 1987.

Odendahl, T. J., Boris, E. T., and Daniels, A. K. *Working in*

Foundations: Career Patterns of Women and Men. New York: Foundation Center, 1985.

O'Neill, M., and Young, D. R. (eds.). *Educating Managers of Nonprofit Organizations.* New York: Praeger, 1988.

Powell, W. W. (ed.). *The Nonprofit Sector: A Research Handbook.* New Haven, Conn.: Yale University Press, 1987.

Powell, W. W., and Friedkin, R. J. "Politics and Programs: Organizational Factors in Public Television Decision Making." In P. J. DiMaggio (ed.), *Nonprofit Enterprise in the Arts: Studies in Mission and Constraint.* New York: Oxford University Press, 1986.

Relman, A. S. "The New Medical Industrial Complex." *New England Journal of Medicine,* 1980, *303,* 963-970.

Research in Progress, 1982-83. Washington, D.C.: Independent Sector, n.d.

Research in Progress, 1983-84. Washington, D.C.: Independent Sector, 1985.

Research in Progress, 1984-85. Washington, D.C.: Independent Sector, 1986.

Research in Progress, 1985-86. Washington, D.C.: Independent Sector, 1987.

Research in Progress, 1986-87. Washington, D.C.: Independent Sector, 1988.

Rosenberg, C. E. *The Care of Strangers: The Rise of America's Hospital System.* New York: Basic Books, 1987.

Rossi, P. H. "The Organizational Structure of an American Community." In A. Etzioni (ed.), *Complex Organizations: A Sociological Reader.* New York: Holt, Rinehart & Winston, 1961.

Rudney, G. "A Quantitative Profile of the Independent Sector." Working Paper no. 40, Program on Non-Profit Organizations, Institution for Social and Policy Studies, Yale University, 1981.

Rudney, G. "The Scope and Dimensions of Nonprofit Activity." In W. W. Powell (ed.), *The Nonprofit Sector: A Research Handbook.* New Haven, Conn.: Yale University Press, 1987.

Rudney, G., and Weitzman, M. "Significance of Employment and Earnings in the Philanthropic Sector, 1972-1982." Working Paper no. 77, Program on Non-Profit Organizations, Institution for Social and Policy Studies, Yale University, 1983.

Rudolf, F. *The American College and University: A History.* New York: Knopf, 1962.

Ruggles, R., and Ruggles, N. "Integrated Economic Accounts of the United States, 1947-1978." Working Paper no. 841, Institution for Social and Policy Studies, Yale University, Nov. 1980.

Salamon, L. M. "The Results Are Coming In." *Foundation News,* July–Aug. 1984, pp. 16–23.

Salamon, L. M. "Of Market Failure, Voluntary Failure, and Third-Party Government: Toward a Theory of Government-Nonprofit Relations in the Modern Welfare State." *Journal of Voluntary Action Research,* 1987, *16* (1-2), 29–49.

Salamon, L. M., Musselwhite, J. C., and DeVita, C. J. "Partners in Public Service: Government and the Nonprofit Sector in the Welfare State." In *Philanthropy, Voluntary Action, and the Public Good.* 1986 Spring Research Forum Working Papers. Washington, D.C.: Independent Sector, 1986.

San Francisco Arts Commission. *The Impact of the Non-Profit Arts on the Economy of San Francisco.* San Francisco: San Francisco Chamber of Commerce, 1987.

Schuster, J. M. D. "Tax Incentives as Arts Policy in Western Europe." In P. J. DiMaggio (ed.), *Nonprofit Enterprise in the Arts: Studies in Mission and Constraint.* New York: Oxford University Press, 1986.

Seay, J. D., and Vladeck, B. C. *In Sickness and in Health: The Mission of Voluntary Health Care Institutions.* New York: McGraw-Hill, 1988.

Sills, D. L. "Voluntary Associations: Sociological Aspects." In D. L. Sills (ed.), *International Encyclopedia of the Social Sciences.* Vol. 16. New York: Macmillan, 1968.

Simon, J. G. "The Tax Treatment of Nonprofit Organizations: A Review of Federal and State Policies." In W. W. Powell (ed.), *The Nonprofit Sector: A Research Handbook.* New Haven, Conn.: Yale University Press, 1987.

Skloot, E. "Enterprise and Commerce in Nonprofit Organizations." In W. W. Powell (ed.), *The Nonprofit Sector: A Research Handbook.* New Haven, Conn.: Yale University Press, 1987.

Smith, D. H. "A National Endowment for Volunteerism: Concept Paper." In R. D. Herman (ed.), *Politics, Public Policy and the*

Voluntary Sector. Kansas City, Mo.: Association of Voluntary Action Scholars, 1987.

Smith, D. H. "The Impact of the Nonprofit Voluntary Sector on Society." In T. D. Connors (ed.), *The Nonprofit Organization Handbook.* (2nd ed.) New York: McGraw-Hill, 1988.

Smith, T. L. *Revivalism and Social Reform in Mid-19th Century America.* New York: Abingdon Press, 1957.

Starr, P. *The Social Transformation of American Medicine.* New York: Basic Books, 1982.

Steinberg, R. "Nonprofit Organizations and the Market." In W. W. Powell (ed.), *The Nonprofit Sector: A Research Handbook.* New Haven, Conn.: Yale University Press, 1987.

Sumariwalla, R. D. "A Taxonomy of the Tax-Exempt." *Foundation News,* May–June 1987, pp. 66–67, 70.

Sutton, F. X. "The Ford Foundation: The Early Years." *Daedalus,* 1987, *116* (1), 41–91.

Swift, L. B. *New Alignments Between Public and Private Agencies in a Community Family Welfare and Relief Program.* New York: Family Service Association of America, 1934.

Teltsch, K. "Corporate Pressures Slowing Gifts to Charity." *New York Times,* July 8, 1987, pp. 1, 30.

Tocqueville, A. de. *Democracy in America.* Garden City, N.Y.: Doubleday Anchor, 1969. (Originally published 1835.)

Tönnies, F. *Community and Society.* East Lansing: Michigan State University Press, 1957. (Originally published 1887.)

Tyack, D. B. *The One Best System: A History of American Urban Education.* Cambridge, Mass.: Harvard University Press, 1974.

U.S. Bureau of the Census. *Statistical Abstract of the United States: 1988.* Washington, D.C.: U.S. Department of Commerce, 1987.

U.S. Small Business Administration. *Unfair Competition by Nonprofit Organizations with Small Business: An Issue for the 1980s.* Washington, D.C.: Office of the Chief Counsel for Advocacy, U.S. Small Business Administration, 1983.

Useem, M. "Corporate Philanthropy." In W. W. Powell (ed.), *The Nonprofit Sector: A Research Handbook.* New Haven, Conn.: Yale University Press, 1987.

Useem, M., and Kutner, S. I. "Corporate Contribution to Culture and the Arts: The Organization of Giving and the Influence of the Chief Executive Officer and of Other Firms on Company Contributions in Massachusetts." In P. J. DiMaggio (ed.), *Nonprofit Enterprise in the Arts: Studies in Mission and Constraint.* New York: Oxford University Press, 1986.

Vitullo-Martin, T., and Cooper, B. *Separation of Church and Child: The Constitution and Federal Aid to Religious Schools.* Indianapolis, Ind.: Hudson Institute, 1987.

Vladeck, B. C. *Unloving Care: The Nursing Home Tragedy.* New York: Basic Books, 1980.

Weber, Max. "Max Weber's Proposal for the Sociological Study of Voluntary Associations." *Journal of Voluntary Action Research,* 1972, *1* (1), 20–23. (Originally published 1910.)

Webster, D. S. "America's Highest Ranked Graduate Schools, 1925–1982." *Change,* May–June 1983, pp.14–24.

Weisbrod, B. A. "Toward a Theory of the Voluntary Non-Profit Sector in a Three-Sector Economy." In E. S. Phelps (ed.), *Altruism, Morality, and Economic Theory.* New York: Russell Sage Foundation, 1975.

Weisbrod, B. A. *The Voluntary Nonprofit Sector.* Lexington, Mass.: Heath, 1977.

Weisbrod, B. A. *The Nonprofit Economy.* Cambridge, Mass.: Harvard University Press, 1988.

Williams, M. F. "Private School Enrollment and Tuition Trends." In U.S. Department of Education, Center for Education Statistics, *The Condition of Education: 1986 Edition.* Washington, D.C.: U.S. Department of Education, 1986.

World Vision. *Beyond Survival: 1987 Annual Report.* Monrovia, Calif.: World Vision, 1988.

Wright, L. B. *The Cultural Life of the American Colonies, 1607–1763.* New York: Harper & Row, 1957.

Yankelovich, Skelly and White. *The Charitable Behavior of Americans: A National Survey.* Washington, D.C.: Independent Sector, 1986.

Ylvisaker, P. N. "Foundations and Nonprofit Organizations." In W. W. Powell (ed.), *The Nonprofit Sector: A Research Handbook.* New Haven, Conn.: Yale University Press, 1987.

Young, D. R. *If Not for Profit, for What? A Behavioral Theory of the Nonprofit Sector Based on Entrepreneurship.* Lexington, Mass.: Lexington Books (Heath), 1983.

☆ ★ ★ Index

A

Abolition, 16, 28, 34, 38, 113, 115, 116–117. *See also* Slavery
Abortion issue, 39, 110
Adams, J., 50
Adams, J. Q., 50
Addams, J., 2, 31
Adelphi University, 49, 51
Adult education, 61
Advocacy and legal services, 4, 16–17, 109–122, 177; foundations and, 112–113, 121, 147; government and, 12, 109, 113–114, 116, 120, 121, 175; history of U.S., 114–120
Aetna Foundation, 149
AFL-CIO, 136
Africa: international assistance in, 123, 125–126, 128, 130. *See also individual countries*
Agency for International Development (AID), 124–125, 127, 131, 132–133, 135
Agricultural organizations, 164
Agriculture, world, 124–125, 129, 130, 135
AIDS, 181
Alcohol: prohibition against, 16, 35, 115; temperance movements against, 35, 110, 115, 164
Alcoholics Anonymous, 164
Alinsky, S., 2

Alliance for Progress, 131
American Association of Fund-Raising Counsel (AAFRC), Trust for Philanthropy, 10–11
American Asylum for the Education of the Deaf and Dumb, Hartford, 101
American Cancer Society, 68
American Civil Liberties Union, 35
American Council of Voluntary Agencies for Foreign Service (AC-VAFS), 134
American Council for Voluntary International Action (InterAction), 134
American Enterprise Institute, 52, 53
American Friends Service Committee, 125, 130
American Indian Movement, 118
American Jewish Joint Distribution Committee, 123
American Medical Association, 73, 75
American Philosophical Society, 162
American Red Cross, 31, 100, 101, 125, 130, 149
American Symphony Orchestra League, 81
American Tobacco Institute, 165
American University of Beirut, 128
Americas Watch, 124

Amherst College, 49
Amnesty groups, 124, 166
Amnesty International, 124, 166
Andover Theological Seminary, 128
Anglicans, 26, 55, 115
Animals, prevention of cruelty to, 3
Anthony, S. B., 117, 119-120
Apple, 141
Arena Stage, Washington, D. C., 89
Arms control. *See* Nuclear arms
Arts and culture, 4, 17, 81-93, 167;
    corporations funding, 82-83, 85,
    92, 141; foundation funding for,
    82-83, 89-90, 138; government
    funding for, 12, 18, 84-85, 90, 91,
    92, 106, 175; "high"and "low,"
    88; religion and, 21, 86-87; U.S.
    history of, 25, 86-93
Arts councils: local, 82, 84, 90, 92;
    state, 84, 90, 92
Asbury, F., 32
Asia: immigrants from, 125, 164. *See
    also individual countries*
Asian Foundation, 135
Assets, 8; foundation, 5, 8, 34, 138-
    139, 140, 144, 146; hospital, 70;
    private school, 5, 46. *See also*
    Revenues
AT&T Foundation, 142
Atheists Anonymous, 5
Atlanta, nonprofit economy of, 7
Atlantic Richfield, 141
Augustus, J., 101
Austria, government funding to arts
    and culture in, 84

B

B. Dalton, 141
Bailyn, B., 53
Baptists, 26, 31, 32, 36; and advocacy,
    55; and education, 55; hospitals
    of, 72; international missions of,
    128
Barnard, F. A. P., 58
Barnard College, 59
Barnum, P. T., 88
Barton, C., 101
BBC, 125-126

Bechtel, 141
Beecher, L., 32
Benefits, of nonprofit participants,
    166-167
Bennett, M., 83
Bennington, 51
Berger, P. L., 14, 161, 167
Berkeley, University of California at,
    50, 58, 63
Berra, Y., 108
Berrigan, D., 36
Berrigan, P., 36
Better Business Bureau, 108
Big Brothers, 21
Big Sisters, 21
Blacks: advocacy and legal services
    for, 113, 118 (*see also* Abolition;
    Civil rights movement); arts and
    culture of, 89; education for, 43,
    46, 48, 50, 58, 60; foundation
    power of, 153; health care for, 73;
    religion and, 17, 21, 32-33, 37-38,
    109; and social services, 103. *See
    also* Slavery
Blaine, J., 115
Blind, social services for, 101
Blue Cross, 68, 75, 165
Blue Shield, 68, 75, 165
Blumenthal, M., 139
Bolling, L. R., 124, 133
Bonifacius—Essays to Do Good
    (Mather), 28
Borlaug, N., 125
Boston: arts and culture in, 87, 88;
    education history in, 53-54; hi-
    tech firms of, 19; Massachusetts
    General Hospital in, 18, 71;
    South End House in, 101
Boston Symphony Orchestra, 88
Boston University, 49, 61
Bowdoin College, 58
Boy Scouts, 5
Brazil, international assistance in,
    123
Bremner, R. H., 125
Britain. *See* English colonies; Great
    Britain
British Columbia, private education
    in, 45

Broadcast media, 82, 83, 91; religion and, 23, 38. *See also* Television
Broadway plays, 83
Brook Farm, Massachusetts, 32, 33
Brookings Institution, 52, 53
Brown University, 55, 57, 58
Bryan, W. J., 35
Bryn Mawr College, 59, 101
Buddhism, 30
Budgets, 1-2; arts and culture organizations, 84, 92; NIH, 75; research institute, 53; social service organization, 96. *See also* Expenditures; Revenues
Bundy, M., 147
Burchard, S., 115
Bureaucratic organization, 181-182
Burma, international assistance to, 128, 130
"Burnout," in advocacy efforts, 121-122
Bush Foundation, 149
Business: advocacy organizations and, 109, 113-114, 116; arts and culture associated with, 83-84; and client selection issues, 178, 179; donations by, 8, 19, 177 (*see also* Corporate funders); and education, 19, 51, 59-60, 141, 150-151; foundations' relation with, 146, 148-149; GNP percentage of, 9; government kept out of, 14; and health care, 67; mutual benefit organizations doing, 165-166; nonprofit operations in, 12-13, 83-84, 177-178; nonprofit services purchased by, 8, 19; nonprofits' relationship to (general), 19, 176-178; nonprofits' societal importance and, 15-16, 17, 177; and religion, 24-25; sale of goods and services to nonprofits by, 8, 19, 177.
Business leagues, 164
Busing, 44

C

California: educational financing in, 62; and hospitals, 69. *See also* Los Angeles; San Francisco
California Institute of Technology, 49
Calvinists, 26, 62, 99
Cambodia, international assistance in, 125
Canada, 25-26
Capitalism, 59, 102, 145, 177
CARE, 126, 127, 131, 132
Caribbean, international assistance to, 130
Carleton, 43
Carnegie, A., 59, 144, 150
Carnegie Commission on Higher Education, 59
Carnegie Corporation, 139, 144, 151; and advocacy, 112; and arts, 89; assets of, 146; education and research funding by, 147; and health care, 74; and international assistance, 123, 129-130
Carnegie Endowment for International Peace, 144
Carnegie Foundation for the Advancement of Teaching, 144
Carnegie Institute, Pittsburgh, 144
Carnegie Institution, 144
Carnegie-Mellon University, 58, 59, 144
Carter administration, 12, 97
Catholicism, 25-42 *passim;* and advocacy, 36, 119; and education, 43-49 *passim,* 57, 60, 61; and health care, 72; international assistance by, 123, 127, 128, 130, 131; and mutual benefit organizations, 166
Catholic Relief Services, 123, 127, 131
Catholic Worker Movement, 36
Cato Institute, 52
Cause organizations. *See* Advocacy and legal services
Cedars of Lebanon, Los Angeles, 73
Census Bureau, U.S., 4, 44, 45, 111
Census of Service Industries, 4, 95, 111, 156
Center for Advanced Study of the Behavioral Sciences, 147
Center for Education Statistics, 44, 46

Center for Independent Living, 107
Center for the Study of Democratic
  Institutions, 137
Central Opera Service, 81–82
Ceylon, missions in, 128
Chambers, C. A., 102–103
Champlain, S. de, 25
Charismatic healing, 40
Charismatic organization, 181–182
Charitable Irish Society, 162
Charitable trust, 143–144
Charity Organization Societies, 100,
  101, 103–104, 109
Chavez, C., 119
Checks-and-balances system, non-
  profit sector providing, 14, 113
Chevron, 141
Chicago: Hull House in, 31, 101;
  Museum of Science and Industry
  in, 85; social services funding in,
  19; See also University of Chicago
Child abuse, 16, 97–98
Child labor legislation, 16
China: arts in, 86; missions in, 128
Christianity, 17–42 passim, 143; and
  civil rights movement, 17, 21, 36,
  37–38, 109; fundamentalist, 35,
  38, 61–62; and health care, 72;
  social services supported by, 96.
  See also Catholicism; Protestants
Christian Science Church, 33, 41
Christian Science Monitor, 33
Churches. See Christianity
Church of Jesus Christ of the Latter
  Day Saints (Mormons), 33, 128
Church World Service, 123
Civil Rights Act, 113
Civil rights movement, 16, 113, 114,
  118–119; religion and, 17, 21, 36,
  37–38, 109
Civil War, 31, 34, 36, 39, 103
Clark, R. C., 69
Cleveland Foundation, 149
Client selection issue, 178–179
Coalition for the Homeless, 94
Coleman, J. S., 44, 48–49
"College mania," 58
Colleges and universities. See Higher
  education

Colonial America, 179; and advocacy and legal services, 114–115;
  arts and culture organizations in,
  86–87; education in, 53–55, 56,
  57; and international assistance,
  127–128; mutual benefit organizations of, 162, 166; religion in,
  24–29; and social services, 98–99,
  105
Columbia University, 49, 50, 57, 58;
  government funding and, 18;
  medical school at, 74; religious
  origin of, 55; social work education at, 101
Columbus, C., 20, 25
Commission on Industrial Relations, 145
Commission on Private Philanthropy and Public Needs, 170, 176
"Committees of correspondence,"
  162
Common Cause, 10, 112
Commonwealth Fund, 153
Community Chests, 101, 150
Community college system, 61
Community development, 12, 95
Conference Board, 171
Confréries, 160
Congregationalists, 31, 55, 115
Congress: and arts and culture fund-
  ing, 12, 175; and business activi-
  ties of nonprofits, 13; and foun-
  dation and corporate giving,
  145–146, 150, 151, 152; and
  health care, 75; religious profes-
  sionals in, 22; and social services,
  101
Congress of Racial Equality, 118
Conrad Hilton Foundation, 21
Conservatives: advocacy organiza-
  tions of, 119; religion and, 39
Constitution, U.S., 20, 171; First
  Amendment, 22, 29–30, 86; Nine-
  teenth Amendment to, 113, 117;
  Prohibition and, 35
Consumer protection, 16–17
Consumers, health care, 78
Continental Congress, and arts and
  culture, 87

Contributions. *See* Donations
Coordination in Development (CODEL), 134
Cornell University, 50, 58, 101
Corporate funders, 8, 10, 19, 137–138, 140-143, 151-155, 175, 177; and advocacy and legal services, 113, 121; and arts organizations, 82-83, 85, 92, 141; history of, 25, 149-151
Corporation for the Propagation of the Gospel in New England, 127
Cosby, B., 84
Cost-revenue ratio, nonprofit, 10
Costs: of education, 43, 46-47, 63; health care, 78-79. *See also* Expenditures; Fees; Funding, government
Council on Foundations, 23, 124, 152, 171, 176
Cox Committee, 145
"Cream-skimming," by hospitals, 69-70
C. S. Fund, 148
Cults, religious, 38-39
Culture. *See* Arts and culture
Cynicism, 36-37

D

Dallas Symphony Orchestra, 81
"Dame schools," 54
Dancing, 87
Darrow, C., 35
Dartmouth College, 27, 55-56
Dartmouth College v. *Woodward*, 55-56
Darwinism, 35
Day-care programs, 98, 108
Deaf, social services for, 101
DEC, 141
Declaration of Independence, 116
de Mille, A., 91
Democracy, 14, 44, 47, 64
Democracy in America (Tocqueville), 13-14
Democratic party, 5
"Democratic Societies," 162
Densa, 5

Department of Education, U.S., 44, 46
Department of Health and Human Services, U.S., 78
Depression, Great: and corporate giving, 150; education during, 60; and health care, 74-75; Mormons in, 33; and mutual benefit associations, 164; and social reform, 118; and social services, 104, 105, 172
Dewey, J., 64
Dix, D. L., 2, 101
Donations, 2, 8, 9, 10-11, 19; advocacy organizations receiving, 121; arts organizations receiving, 82-83, 89-90, 92; individuals giving, 2, 10; religious organizations giving, 23; religious organizations receiving, 20-21; social services receiving, 96; tax deductibility of, 4, 120, 140-141, 146, 150-151. *See also* Grantmaking
Dooley, T., 69, 128
Douglas, J., 16, 165, 168
DuBois, W. E. B., 37
Duke Endowment, 139
Durkheim, E., 177
Dutch East Indies Company, 24

E

East: education in, 58; foundation assets in, 138-139; health care in, 73; religion in, 32
Eastern spirituality, 39, 40
Eaton, T., 53
Economy: health care in, 77; nonprofit presence in (general), 7-9, 15-16; private education affecting, 47, 51-52; religion and, 21, 33. *See also* Assets; Budgets; Business; Costs; Depression; Great Income; Labor force; Taxes
Eddy, M. B., 33, 41
Education and research, 4, 17, 43–66, 91-92, 95, 167, 180; and advocacy, 109-110; business and, 19, 51, 59-60, 141, 150-151; enroll-

ment figures in private, 44-45,
49, 61, 62; foundations funding,
138, 147; government funding
for, 12, 18, 44-66 *passim*, 79, 80,
98, 106, 175; health care, 67, 68,
69, 73-74, 75-76; history of U.S.,
25, 27, 28, 53-63; informal, 54;
international assistance in, 124-
125; mutual benefit organizations providing, 162; on nonprofit sector, 170-171; public,
43-44, 46-48, 53-66 *passim*, 85,
106; religion and, 21, 27, 28, 36-
49 *passim*, 55, 57, 60, 61-62; in
social services, 101
Education vouchers, 63
Egypt, ancient, 143
Eisenhower era, 118
"Elizabethan Poor Law," 99, 105
Emancipation Proclamation, 113
Emerson, R. W., 100
Employees: advocacy organization,
121-122; arts organizations, 82;
corporation, 142; education and
research (private), 46, 50, 53;
government, 6; health care, 70;
nonprofit (general), 1-8 *passim*,
41; social services, 95, 96
Employers: health care provided by,
78. See also Business
Encyclopedia of Associations, 156-
157, 159
England: "Elizabethan Poor Law"
of, 99; medieval voluntary agen-
cies in, 179. See also English
colonies
English colonies, 25, 26-28, 53-55,
98-99, 105, 127-128
Environmentalism, 17, 21, 38, 113,
125, 148
Environmental Protection Agency,
113
Epilepsy Foundation, 68
Episcopalians, 31, 41, 62
Erhard, W., 37
Erickson, D., 62
est, 37
Ethiopia: international assistance

in, 125-126; political instability
in, 136
Ethnic organizations, 17, 147, 159,
163, 164; and advocacy, 109, 117-
118; arts and culture, 88-89; religion and, 21, 31; and social services, 100
Europe: government funding for
arts in, 84, 91; immigrants from,
164 (*see also* Immigrants/Immi-
gration); medieval guilds of, 160.
See also individual countries
European Recovery Program, 131-
132
Evaluation, of social services, 108
"Exempt organizations," 2-3, 22, 69
Expenditures, 7, 8; arts organizations, 82; foundation, 144; hospital, 70; international assistance,
123-124, 130-131; private school,
46; of religious organizations, 23;
social services, 95

F

Faddishness, in funding world, 154
Faith healing, 33, 34
Falwell, J., 38
Family planning, 16, 125, 132
Family workers, 9
Farmers' organizations, 159
Federalist Papers, 30
Federal Theater Project, 89
Fees, 9-10, 180; health care, 72; so-
cial service, 97. See also Costs
Festivals, 83
Fidelity Investments, 165
Field Foundation, 113
Filer, J., 170
Filer Commission, 23, 170, 176
Fillmore, M., 33
First Amendment, 22, 29-30, 86
Flexner, A., 74
Flexner, S., 74
Food for Peace, 127, 131, 132
Food production, world, 124-125,
129, 130, 135
Forbes, 84
Ford, E., 146

Ford, H., Sr., 146
Ford, H. II, 146
Ford Foundation, 139; and advocacy, 112; and arts, 89–90; assets of, 5; black president of, 153; and health care, 69; history of, 146–147, 149, 151; international assistance by, 123, 124–125, 130, 133, 135; and social services, 94
Fordham, 49, 60
Ford Motor Company, 146
For-profit world. *See* Business
Foundation Center, 171
Foundations, 12, 34, 137–155, 166–167, 174, 175; and advocacy and legal services, 112–113, 121, 147; "alternative," 148; arts and culture organizations funded by, 82–83, 89–90, 138; assets of, 5, 8, 34, 138–139, 140, 144, 146; community, 138, 140, 149; corporate, 138, 148–149; history of U.S., 25, 144–149; independent, 138, 140; international assistance funded by, 123, 124–125, 128–130, 130, 133, 135; operating, 138; religion and, 21, 138
France: *confréries* of, 160; government funding to arts and culture in, 84; Hugenots of, 26; and Revolutionary War, 29. *See also* French colonies
Franklin, B., 71, 99, 162
Fraternal benefit societies, 164
Freedom: of advocacy, 120; of private education, 64, 66
French colonies, 25–26, 127–128
Friedman, M., 63
Friends Almshouse of Philadelphia, 99
Friends Asylum for the Relief of Persons Deprived of the Use of Their Reason, 72
Fundamentalism, religious, 35, 38, 61–62
Fund for the Advancement of Education, 147
Funding, government, 11–12; of advocacy and legal services, 12, 113, 121; arts and culture, 12, 18, 84–85, 90, 91, 92, 106, 175; for education and research, 12, 18, 44–66 *passim*, 79, 80, 98, 106, 175; for health care, 12, 18, 64, 67, 75–76, 78–79, 80, 106, 175; international assistance, 123, 127, 131–133; and religion, 22; for social services, 6, 12, 18, 96–97, 98, 104–106, 172
Funding activities. *See* Donations; Grantmaking; International assistance
Funding sources. *See* Corporate funders; Foundations; Funding, government; Revenues
Fund for the Republic, 147

G

Gallandet, T., 101
Gallup polls, 7, 22, 23, 70
Gannett Foundation, 149
Gardner, J., 10, 119, 171
Garrison, W. L., 2, 34, 116, 119–120
Gates, F., 128–129
Geldof, B., 126
General Education Board (GEB), 74
General Motors, 148
"Genius awards," 10
Genska, Father Depaul, 94
Germany, arts and culture in, 84, 86
Getty, G., 53
Getty (J. Paul) Trust, 5, 90, 138
GI Bill, 60–61
Girard, S., 56
Girard Will decision, 56
GNP (Gross National Product), 8–9
"Gospel of Wealth" (Carnegie), 144
Government: advocacy organizations and, 12, 109, 113–114, 116, 120, 121, 175; in arts and culture, 12, 84–85, 90, 91–93, 175; checks and balances on, 14, 113; and client selection issues, 178, 179; and education, 44, 54–55, 57, 63–64, 91–92, 98, 175 (*see also* Funding, government); employees of, 6; and international assistance,

124-125, 127, 131-134, 135, 175;
nonprofits' relationship with
(general), 10, 17-19, 171-177;
nonprofits' societal importance
and, 15-16, 17, 177; and religion,
12, 20, 22, 24-25, 29-30, 98, 175;
revenue to nonprofits from, 9,
11-12, 18-19, 22 (*see also* Funding, government); and social services, 11-12, 94-108 *passim*, 172,
175; "third-party", 98, 173. *See
also* Congress
Graham, Bill, 126
Graham, Billy, 2, 36
Grantmaking, 4, 10, 137-155; in arts,
82-83; in international assistance, 123-135 *passim. See also*
Corporate funders; Foundations
Great Awakening, 40, 114-115
"Great Books" colleges, 51
Great Britain: international assis-
tance by, 135; and social services,
99, 107. *See also* England
Great Society programs, 11-12, 96-
97, 98, 104, 172, 180
Greece, ancient, 143
Greeley, A. M., 47
Green Revolution, 125, 129, 133, 147
Grimké, A., 117
Gross National Product (GNP), 8-9
Growth rate, nonprofit sector, 6-7,
12, 180
Guilds, medieval European, 160

H

Hale, Mother, 94
Hall, P. D., 56
Handel and Haydn Society, Boston,
87
Handicapped, social services for,
107
Handlin, O., 17, 102
Hansmann, H., 2
Hare Krishna, 39
Harper's, 83
Harris, B. C., 41
Harrisburg, State Lunatic Hospital
in, 72-73
Hartford, American Asylum for the
Education of the Deaf and Dumb
in, 101
Harvard, J., 54
Harvard College, 24, 27, 28, 54-55,
57
Harvard Musical Association, 87
Harvard University, 43, 50, 58; as-
sets of, 5, 146; and business, 19;
government funding for, 18;
medical school of, 74
Hawaii, missions in, 128
Hayes, R., 94
Hayes, R. B., 50
Haymarket Foundation, 113, 148
Healing: religion and, 33, 34, 40.
See also Health care
Health care, 3, 4, 17, 67-80, 108; ef-
ficiency in, 78-79; foundation
funding for, 73-74, 129, 138, 144-
145; government funding for, 12,
18, 64, 67, 75-76, 78-79, 80, 106,
175; history of U.S., 25, 70-76;
international assistance in, 69,
74, 124-125, 129; mental, 16, 28,
72-73, 101; religion and, 21, 33,
36, 40, 72-73; social services and,
95, 101; statistics, 70. *See also*
Hospitals
Health food, 34
Henry, P., 87
Henry Street Settlement, New York,
101
Heritage Foundation, 52
Herzlinger, R. E., 69, 77, 79-80, 167
Hewlett, W., 19
Hewlett foundation, 139, 149
Higher education, 49-52, 57-66 *pas-
sim*, 171, 175. *See also individual
colleges and universities*
High-tech firms, 19
Hill-Burton Act, 75
Hispanics, 43, 46, 48, 50, 118, 153
Hispanics in Philanthropy, 153
Historical societies, 17
History. *See* United States history
Hodgkinson, V. A., 12, 46, 94-95
Hoffer, T., 48
Hofstadter, R., 118

Hookworm, 74
Hoover, H., 150
Hopkins, Johns, 141
Hospitalism, 72
"Hospital orders," 72
Hospitals, 4, 36, 40, 67-77 *passim*, 167, 180; admission practices of, 69; statistics on, 70
House Select Committee to Investigate Tax-Exempt Foundations and Comparable Organizations, 145
House Subcommittee on Oversight of the House Ways and Means Committee, 13
Howe, S. G., 56, 101
Hudson Institute, 52
Huguenots, French, 26
Hull House, Chicago, 31, 101
Human potential movement, 37
Human services. *See* Social services
Hutchins, R. M., 137
Hutchinson, A., 41

I

IBM, 141
Illinois: University of, 58. *See also* Chicago
Immigrants/Immigration, 17, 159, 163, 173; and advocacy, 115, 117-118; and education, 56, 57, 60; refugee, 125, 164; and religion, 30-35 *passim;* and social services, 100, 101, 102-103, 105, 106-107
Income: of arts and culture performers, 84; national, 9; social security, 75; of students' families, 46, 47, 48, 65. *See also* Revenues
Independent Sector, 6-10 *passim*, 23, 114, 121, 171, 176
India, international assistance to, 128, 130, 135
Indiana, University of, 58
"Indian College," 27
Indonesia, international assistance to, 130
Industrialization, 105

"Information economy/society," 51-52, 107
Institute for Policy Studies, 52
Insurance, health care, 68, 75, 76, 78
Internal Revenue Code, 2-4, 120, 150, 165. *See also* Taxes
Internal Revenue Service (IRS), 3-6 *passim*, 46, 83-84, 111, 152, 156, 165. *See also* Internal Revenue Code
Internal Revenue Service Act, 150
International assistance, 4, 79, 123-136, 175; health care, 69, 74, 124-125, 129; history of U.S., 25, 127-131; religion and, 21, 36, 40, 123-134 *passim*
International Ladies Garment Workers Union, 4, 130
International Maize and Wheat Improvement Center (CIMMYT), 124-125
International Monetary Fund, 40
International Physicians for the Prevention of Nuclear War, 125
International Planned Parenthood Federation, 132
International Rescue Committee, 125
International Rice Research Institute, 124-125
"Invisible sector," 169
IQ, organizations formed around, 5
IRS. *See* Internal Revenue Service
Irvine Foundation, 139
Islam/Mosques, 20, 37
Israel, 36, 62, 131; ancient, 143

J

Jackson, J., 38
Jazz, 89
Jefferson, T., 22, 87, 162
Jencks, C., 63
Jenkins, J. C., 109, 119
Jews, 20, 23, 27-41 *passim*, 62, 72, 73, 131
Jobs. *See* Employees; Labor force
Johns Hopkins University, 43, 50, 52, 58, 59, 74

Johnson, P., 126–127
Johnson administration, 104, 105, 147. *See also* Great Society programs
Johnston, M., 94
John XXIII, Pope, 36
Johnson (Robert Wood) Foundation, 68, 74, 139
Jonestown, 38
Journal of the American Medical Association, 33
Judaism. *See* Jews
Juilliard School, 49, 51
Junto, 162

K

Kaiser Family Foundation, 74
Karl, B. D., 147
Katz, S. N., 147
Keillor, G., 83
Kellogg, J., 34
Kellogg, W., 34
Kellogg Company, 34
Kellogg (W. K.) Foundation, 34, 139; and health care, 68, 69, 74, 130; and international assistance, 123, 125, 130
Kennedy, J. F., 36, 37, 50, 131; adminstration of, 147
Kennedy, R., 146
Keppel, F., 89
Kettering Foundation, 130, 149
Kilgore, S., 48
King, M. L., Jr., 2, 36, 37, 38, 118, 119–120
Kissinger, H., 139
Klein, H., 90
Knights of Columbus, 166
Kramer, R. M., 95, 98
Krasker, W. S., 69, 77, 79–80, 167
Kraushaar, O. F., 54
Kresge Foundation, 149

L

Laboratory of Hygiene, 75
Labor force: child, 16; female percentage of, 41; nonprofit percentage of, 6; social services and, 107. *See also* Employees; Labor unions
Labor unions, 4, 130, 136, 159–165 *passim*
Latin America: immigrants from, 125, 164; international assistance to, 130
Leadership: of nonprofits, 17; private education, 50–51; religious, 41–42
Leakey (L. S. B.) Foundation, 53
Lebanon, American University of Beirut in, 128
Lee, Mother Ann, 32, 41
Legal assistance, 17, 95, 112, 175. *See also* Advocacy and legal services; Public-interest law groups
Lerner, 161
Levi Strauss Foundation, 149
Levy, R., 142
Lewis, S., 163–164
Liberals, religion and, 39
Liberator, 34, 116
Lilly Endowment, 21, 130, 139
Literary societies, 3
"Live Aid," 126
Lobbying: by advocacy organizations, 110, 120–121; by mutual benefit organizations, 166
Local Initiatives Support Corporation (LISC), 94
Los Angeles: Cedars of Lebanon in, 73; foundations of, 139
Lowry, W. M., 90
Lucky Stores, 141
Lutheranism, 30, 35, 62, 72, 130
Lutheran World Relief, 123
Lyman, R., 1, 63
Lynd, H. M., 164
Lynd, R. S., 164

M

Mabee Foundation, 139
MacArthur Foundation, 10, 123, 139, 152, 153
McCarthy, J., 152
McKnight Foundation, 139

McNamara, R., 139
Magnalia Christi Americana (Mather), 28
Male domination, of religion, 41-42
Mann, H., 44, 47, 56, 57, 64
March of Dimes, 68
Marin Community Foundation, 153
"Market discipline," in health care, 77, 79-80
Marmor, T. R., 70
Marquette, 49
Marriage, religion and, 42
Marshall Plan, 131-132
Marty, M., 128
Masons, 166
Massachusetts: Brook Farm community in, 32, 33; education in, 28, 53-54 (*see also individual institutions*); religion in, 24, 28, 29. *See also* Boston
Massachusetts Bay Company, 24, 127
Massachusetts General Court, 28, 54-55
Massachusetts General Hospital, 18, 71
Massachusetts Institute of Technology (MIT), 19, 43, 50, 58, 59
Mather, C., 28
Media, 82, 83-84, 91; and advocacy, 117; and international assistance, 125-126; religion and, 23, 38, 117; *See also* Television
"Mediana," 166
Medicaid, 12, 75-76
Medical care. *See* Health care
Medical establishment: Christian Science Church and, 33. *See also* Health care; Hospitals; Medical schools; Physicians
Medical schools, 67, 68, 69, 73-74
Medicare, 12, 64, 75-76, 175
Mellon, A., 59
Mellon (A. W.) Foundation, 123, 139
Mencken, H. L., 163-164
Mensa, 5
Mental health care, 16, 28, 72-73, 101
Merton, T., 35

Mesopotamia, ancient, 143
Methodists, 31, 32, 35, 72, 114-115, 128
Metropolitan Museum of Art, New York, 12-13, 18
Metropolitan Opera, New York, 88, 92
Michigan, University of, 58
Middle East, international assistance to, 130
Midwest: education in, 58, 59; foundation assets in, 138-139; health care in, 73; religion in, 32; social services in, 103
Mikes of America, 5
Military aid, international, 127
Military-industrial complex, 120. *See also* Nuclear arms
Miller, W., 33-34
"Millerites," 33-34
Minneapolis: social services funding in, 19; Tyrone Guthrie Theater in, 89
Minnesota: University of, 58. *See also* Minneapolis
Minorities: foundation power of, 153; mutual benefit organizations of, 159 (*see also* Ethnic organizations); in private schools, 43, 46, 47. *See also* Race
Missionaries, 20, 25-26; international, 127-128; medical, 69
MIT, 19, 43, 50, 58, 59
"Monkey trial," 35
Moon, Sun Myung, 39
"Moonies," 39
Moral Majority, 38
Mormons, 33, 128
Morrell, L., 66
Mosques/Islam, 20, 37
Mother Jones, 83-84
Mott, (Charles Stewart) Foundation, 149
Mott, L., 117
Mott, M., 148
Mount Holyoke Seminary, 58-59
Mount Sinai, New York, 73
Mount Zion, San Francisco, 73
Moyers, B., 83

Ms., 83
Mudd, R., 83
Museum of Fine Arts, Boston, 88
Museum of Natural Science, New York, 85
Museums, 17, 82, 85, 88
Museum of Science and Industry, Chicago, 85
Music, 81-82, 83, 87, 88, 89
Musical theater, 81-82, 83
Mutual benefit organizations, 3, 12, 156-168; history of U.S., 162-164; "public benefit" organizations distinguished from, 3, 16, 156, 159-160; religion and, 21, 31, 33; and social services, 100, 102-103, 106-107; and tax deductibility, 4. *See also* Ethnic organizations

N

Nader, R., 110, 112, 119, 121
Nation, 83
National arts policy, 91-93
National Association for the Advancement of Colored People (NAACP), 112
National Center for Charitable Statistics, 4
National Center for Educational Statistics, 44, 46, 49
National Charities Information Bureau, 108
National Council of Churches, 36, 119
National education policy, 91-92
National Endowment for the Arts (NEA), 12, 84, 90, 91, 93, 175
National Endowment for the Humanities, 12, 91
National Geographic, 53
National income, nonprofit percentage of, 9
National Institutes of Health (NIH), 67, 75, 91
National Merit Scholarship program, 147
National Opinion Research Center, 53

National Prison Congress, 102
National Public Radio, 83
National Review, 83
National Science Foundation, 91
Native Americans, 25, 26, 27, 32-33, 37, 118
NBC, 125-126
Netherlands, government funding to arts and culture in, 84
Neuhaus, R. J., 14, 161, 167
New Deal, 177
New England: colonial, 26-28, 98-99; social services in, 103. *See also* English colonies; *individual states*
New England Asylum for the Blind, 101
New England Conservatory of Music, 49
New Harmony, Indiana, 32
New Orleans, 26
New World Foundation, 113
New York: advocacy organizations in, 115; arts and culture in, 83, 85, 87, 88, 92; Mount Sinai in, 73; Rockefeller Foundation chartered by, 145; social services in, 18-19, 101, 103-104, 109
New York Hospital, 71
New York Philharmonic Society, 87
New York Public Theater, 83
New York Temperance Society, 115
New York University, 49, 61
New York Yankees, 108
Nielsen, W. A., 113, 143, 152, 176
Nightingale, F., 72
"Nightly News," 125-126
NIH. *See* National Institutes of Health
Nineteenth Amendment, 113, 117
Nisbet, R., 18, 174
Nixon administration, 63, 104
Nobel Peace Prize, 125
"Nondistribution constraint," 2
Nonprofit Sector (Yale Program on Non-Profit Organizations), 167
North, schools in, 44
Northeast, foundation assets in, 138-139

Notre Dame, University of, 60
Noyes, John Humphrey, 32
Nuclear arms, 110-111; movement
  to control, 17, 36, 39, 110-111,
  112, 125, 130, 147, 181
Nursing homes, 36, 40

O

Oberlin College, 49, 58
O'Connell, B., 114, 121
Ohio, higher education in, 58
Ohio University, 58
"Old-field schools," 54
Olympics team, U.S., 141
Oneida, New York, 32-33
O'Neill, E., 89
Opera companies, 81-82, 88
Orchestras, 81
Orphanages, 101
Owen, R., 32
Oxfam America, 125, 132

P

Pacifism, 28
Packard, D., 19
Paintings, 83
Pakistan, international assistance
  to, 130
Panama Canal, 40
Papp, J., 83
Parsons, T., 177
Patiño, D., 153
Patman, W., 145-146, 152
"Patron control," 16
Peabody, G., 60
Peabody Education Fund, 60
Peabody (George) Fund, 144
Peace Corps, 127, 131
Peace movement, 119-120, 125; and
  civil rights movement, 38; foun-
  dations funding, 130, 147, 148;
  and nuclear arms control, 17, 36,
  39, 110-111, 112, 125, 130, 181;
  religion and, 21, 36; and Vietnam
  War, 17, 36, 38
Peale, N. V., 36
Peking Union Medical College, 129

Pembroke State University, 59
Pennsylvania: arts and culture in, 87;
  hospitals in, 71, 72-73; Quakers
  in, 28; social services funding in,
  19
Pennsylvania Hospital, Philadel-
  phia, 71, 72
Pentecostalism, 40, 41
Perot, H. R., 81
Pew Memorial Trusts, 139, 153
Philadelphia, Pennsylvania Hospi-
  tal in, 71, 72
Philadelphia Library Company, 162
Philippines, international assis-
  tance in, 123
Physicians, 68, 73, 75, 167
Pickens, T. B., 141
Pickle, J. J., 13
Pierce, F., 101
Pietists, German, 26
Pillsbury, 141, 148
Pillsbury, G., 148
Pittsburgh, social services funding
  in, 19
Pius IX, Pope, 101
Ploughshares Foundation, 113, 122
Poland, and AFL-CIO grant, 136
Political parties, 5, 109, 115, 160, 161
Political science theories, of impor-
  tance of nonprofit sector, 16-17
Politics: and arts, 86, 91; founda-
  tions and, 146; and international
  assistance, 127, 131-133, 135-136;
  mutual benefit organizations
  and, 166; religion and, 21-22, 38,
  39-42; and social services, 106.
  See also Government; Political
  parties
Polygamy, 33
Poor Laws, 99, 100, 105
Population control, 16. See also
  Family planning
Population Council, 132
Poverty: alcoholism bringing, 115;
  international, 135, 136; social
  services and, 99. See also Relief
Prep schools, 43, 57
Presbyterians, 31, 32, 55, 72, 114-
  115, 128

Princeton University, 50, 55, 57, 58, 150–151
Print media, 82, 83–84; and advocacy, 117; religion and, 23, 38, 117
Prisoners, social services for, 101
Private Agencies Collaborating Together (PACT), 134
Private Agencies in International Development (PAID), 134
Private voluntary organizations (PVOs), 132–136
Program on Non-Profit Organizations, 167, 170
Progressive Era, 102, 117–118
Prohibition, 16, 35, 115
Property value, religion and, 21
Protestants, 26–41 *passim*, 117; and advocacy, 114–115; and arts and culture, 86–87; and education, 28, 43, 55, 61–62; and health care, 72–73; international missions of, 128
Provincetown Players, 89
Public-interest law groups, 111, 147
Publishing: arts and culture, 82, 83–84; religious, 23. *See also* Print media
Pulitzer Prize, 83
Purchase-of-service contracts, 64
Puritans, 26–27, 28, 41, 55, 86–87
Purpose, of nonprofits, 2

Q

Quakers, 26, 28, 31; and arts and culture, 86–87; international assistance by, 130; and mental health care, 28, 72–73; mutual benefit organizations of, 162; and slavery issue, 28, 34; and social services, 115
Quality: health care, 68; of social services, 108
Quality-of-life studies, 85

R

Race: of private students, 43, 46, 48. *See also* Blacks; Ethnic organizations; Hispanics; Whites

Radcliffe College, 59, 66
Radio broadcasting, 82, 83, 91
Railroad companies, donations by, 149, 151
Rand Corporation, 52
Reagan, R.: administration of, 12–13, 174, 175–176; and arts and culture, 12, 84, 91, 175; and education and research, 12, 63, 175; and health care, 12, 175; and international assistance, 132, 175; and religion, 22, 38; and social services, 6, 12, 94, 97, 104–105, 107, 172, 175
Recordings, musical, 83
Recreation clubs, 164
Red Cross, American, 31, 100, 101, 125, 130, 149
Redford, R., 84
Reed, 43
Refugee relief, international, 125
Relief: international, 124, 125–127, 130–131, 134, 135; war, 130–131. *See also* International assistance
Religion, 17, 20–42, 159, 180; and advocacy, 17, 21, 36, 37–38, 109, 114–115, 116, 118, 121; and arts and culture, 21, 86–87; assets of organizations, 8; and education, 21, 27, 28, 36–49 *passim*, 55, 57, 60, 61–62; foundation funding for, 21, 138; government and, 12, 20, 22, 24–25, 29–30, 98, 175; and health care, 21, 33, 36, 40, 72–73; history of U.S., 24–39; and international assistance, 21, 36, 40, 123–134 *passim*; and social services, 21, 36, 95, 99–100; tax exemption for, 5. *See also* Christianity; Jews
Religious toleration, 28–30
Rensselaer Polytechnic Institute, 59
Republican party, 5, 115
"Republican Societies," 162
Research institutes, nonprofit, 52–53
Research. *See* Education and research
Revenue Act (1935), 146

Revenues, 3, 5, 9-13, 18-19, 137-155, 180; advocacy and legal services, 112-113, 121, 122; of arts and culture organizations, 82-83, 85, 89-90, 91, 92; education and research (private), 49-50, 53-55, 62-63; health care, 67, 68, 69, 70, 71, 74, 76, 77; international assistance, 123, 124-125, 127, 128-131, 132-133; social service, 6, 12, 18-19, 79, 94, 96-97, 98. *See also* Donations; Fees; Funding, government; Insurance, health care
Revolutionary War, 29, 39, 128, 162
Rhode Island, colonial, 26-27, 98-99
Richard King Mellon Foundation, 139
Riis, J., 102
Rockefeller, J. D., 1, 59, 73-74, 128-129, 142-148 *passim*, 169
Rockefeller, "Junior," 148
Rockefeller Brothers Fund, 112, 130, 135, 148
Rockefeller Family Fund, 148
Rockefeller Foundation, 139; and arts, 90; assets of, 146; and health care, 69, 74; history of, 144, 145, 148, 151; and international assistance, 123, 124-125, 130, 133
Rockefeller Institute for Medical Research, 73-74, 129, 144-145
Rockefeller Sanitary Commission, 74
Rockefeller University, 58, 73-74, 145
Rome, ancient, 143
Roosevelt, F. D., 50, 104-105, 177
Roosevelt, T., 50
Rosenwald, J., 60
Rossi, P. H., 47, 162, 166
Rudney, G., 7, 8, 10, 177
Rudolf, F., 56
Ruggles, N., 8
Ruggles, R., 8
Russell Sage Foundation, 138, 144, 151
Rutgers, 57

S

Sage, M. O. S., 144
St. Andrew's Society of Charleston, South Carolina, 99
St. John's, 51
St. Paul, social services funding in, 19
Salamon, L. M., 12, 16, 170, 172-173
Salvation Army, 21
Sandwich Islands, missions in, 128
San Francisco: arts and culture organizations in, 85, 88, 153; Mount Zion in, 73; nonprofit economy of, 7; social services in, 104
Sanger, M., 2
Sarah Lawrence College, 51
Satanic cults, 38-39
Schlesinger, M., 70
Schools: alternative, 43; arts and culture funded by, 85; elementary, 4, 12, 44-49, 52, 57-66 *passim*, 98, 175; medical, 67, 68, 69, 73-74; prep, 43, 57; public, 43-44, 46-48, 53-66 *passim*, 85, 106; secondary, 4, 12, 44-49, 52, 57-66 *passim*, 98, 175. *See also* Education and research; Higher education
Schorr, D., 83
Schweitzer, A., 69, 128
Science, foundation funding for, 138
Scientific research institutes, 52-53
Scots Charitable Society, 99, 162
Sculpture, 83
Sears Roebuck, 60
Segregation, schools and, 44, 47-49
Self-help organizations, 164
Semanticization, of nonprofit sector, 169-170
Senior citizens' lobby, 78-79
Separation of church and state, 29
"Service clubs," 166
Seton, Mother Elizabeth, 41
Settlement houses, 100, 101
Seventh Day Adventists, 33-34, 41, 62, 73, 128
Sex, religion and, 42

Shakers, 32, 33, 41
Sierra Club, 111, 112, 120, 121
"Silicon Valley," 19
Sills, D. L., 161
Simon, J., 170
Simon, N., 81
Slater (John F.) Fund, 144
Slavery, 25, 37–38; abolition movement, 16, 28, 34, 38, 113, 115, 116–117; Civil War over, 31, 34, 36, 39, 103
Sloan (A. P.) Foundation, 74, 139
Sloan-Kettering Institute for Cancer Research, 74
Small Business Administration, U.S., 13
Smith, Adam, 63
Smith, Al, 22
Smith, D. H., 14, 176
Smith, J., 33
Smith (A. P.) Manufacturing Company, 150–151
Smith College, 49, 59
Smithey, R. W., 70
Smithsonian Institution, 85
Sociability, 17
Social change activities, 16–17, 95, 113. See also Advocacy and legal services; individual movements
Social clubs, 164, 165–166
Socialism, 10
"Social risk capital," 16
Social Security Act, 75, 97, 104
Social services, 4, 17, 94–108, 109; funding for, 6, 12, 18–19, 79, 94–98 passim, 104–106, 138, 141, 172, 175; history of U.S., 25, 98–105; religion and, 21, 36, 95, 99–100
Societal importance, of nonprofit sector, 13–17, 177
Society of the Cincinnati, 162, 166
Society for Promoting Christian Knowledge, 127
Society for the Propagation of the Gospel in Foreign Parts, 127
Sociological theories, of importance of nonprofit sector, 14–15
Solidarity, 136

Somalia, international assistance in, 125
Sons of Liberty, 162
Sophie Newcomb, 59
South: advocacy in, 113; foundation assets in, 139; religion in, 32; schools in, 44; social services in, 103
South End House, Boston, 101
Southern Christian Leadership Conference, 118
Soviet Union: and AFL-CIO grant, 136; international assistance by, 135
Spalding, E., 32, 41
Spanish colonies, 25, 127–128
Sports competition, organizations promoting, 3, 85
Stanford, L., 59, 142
Stanford University, 19, 43, 50, 59, 63
Stanton, E. C., 2, 117
Stark, F., 69
State Department, U.S., 127
State Lunatic Hospital, Harrisburg, 72–73
Statue of Liberty celebration, 141
Stern Family Fund, 113
Stock market crash (October 1987), 11, 176
Stokes, C., 146
Stone, L., 117
Stowe, C., 56
Stowe, H. B., 32, 56, 116–117
Students: federal assistance to, 12; private school, 44–47, 49, 61. See also Schools
Sub-Sahara, international assistance in, 123, 130
Suffrage, women's, 16, 28, 34, 38, 113, 117
Sundance Institute, 84
Supreme Court: New Jersey, 150–151; U.S., 22, 55–56, 61, 150, 151; Utah, 69
Swarthmore College, 43
Sweden, government funding to arts and culture in, 84
Syms, B., 53

Synagogues, 20, 23, 39. *See also* Jews

T

Taconic Foundation, 113
Tammany Hall, 117
Taxes: advocacy organizations and, 120-121; donations deductible from, 4, 120, 140-141, 146, 150-151; education and, 47, 62-63, 66; exemptions from, 2-6 *passim*, 22, 69, 76-77, 120, 146, 165; health care institutions and, 69, 76-77. *See also* Internal Revenue Service
Tax Reform Act (1969), 146, 174
Tax Reform Act (1986), 11, 176
Teachers Insurance and Annuity Association and the College Retirement Equities Fund (TIAA-CREF), 59, 165
Television: and international relief, 126; public, 83, 90, 91; religious, 23; United Way advertising on, 171
Temperance movements, 16, 35, 110, 115, 164
Tennessee, and hospitals, 69
Terman, F., 19
Thatcher government, 107
Theaters, 82, 83, 87, 88, 90
"Think tanks," 52-53
"Third-party government," 98, 173
Thomas, F., 153
Thoreau, H. D., 100, 169
TIAA-CREF, 59, 165
Time, 112
Tisch, L., 139
Tocqueville, A. de, 5, 13-14, 19, 157, 160-161, 163, 171, 172, 174; and religion, 20; and social services, 100; and temperance societies, 115
Tönnies, F., 161
Tony Award, 83
Toynbee Hall, 101
Transcendentalism, 32, 33
Trilateral Commission, 166
Trinity, 59

Trusts, charitable, 143-144
Tuition costs, higher education, 63
Tyrone Guthrie Theater, Minneapolis, 89

U

UCLA, 58, 81
Uncle Tom's Cabin, 34, 56, 116-117
Unification Church, 39
Union Fire Company, 162
Unions, labor, 4, 130, 136, 159-165 *passim*
Unitarians, 130
United Farm Workers, 38, 118
United Funds, 150
United Nations: international assistance by, 135; on poverty, 136
United States government. *See* Government
United States history: of advocacy and legal services, 114-120; of arts and culture, 25, 86-93; of education and research, 25, 27, 28, 53-63; of foundation and corporate philanthropy/grantmaking, 25, 143-151; of health care, 25, 70-76; in international assistance, 25, 127-131; of mutual benefit organizations, 162-164; of religion, 24-39; of social services, 25, 98-105. *See also* Colonial America; Immigrants/Immigration
United Way, 21, 96, 97, 108, 142, 150, 171, 176
Universities. *See* Higher education
University of California, Berkeley, 50, 58, 63
University of Chicago, 49, 50, 53, 59, 74, 101, 145
University of Illinois, 58
University of Indiana, 58
University of Michigan, 58
University of Minnesota, 58
University of Pennsylvania, 57
University of Southern California, 49, 61
University of Washington, 58
University of Wisconsin, 58

Unpaid workers: in national income, 9. *See also* Volunteers
Upper classes, and social services, 100–101
Urban Institute, 7, 18–19, 52, 96, 104, 112, 147
Urbanization, 100, 105, 116, 160, 162–163
Ursuline Sisters, 26, 99
Utah, Mormons in, 33
Utah State Supreme Court, 69
Utopian communities, 32–33, 38

V

Values, in private schools, 47
Vane, H., 28
Vanguard Foundation, 113
Varian Associates, 19
Vassar, M., 60
Vassar College, 59, 60, 101
Vatican Council, Second, 36
Vermont, and hospitals, 69
Victoria, Queen, 101
Vietnam War, 17, 36, 38, 131
Virginia, education in, 53, 54
Virginia Company, 24, 27, 127
"Voluntary failure," 16
Volunteers, 2, 6, 7, 9; advocacy organization, 111; arts organizations, 82; in health care, 70; in religious organizations, 20; social services, 95–96
Voter registration: black, 113. *See also* Suffrage, women's
Vouchers, education, 63

W

Walsh Commission, 145
War Relief Commission, 130
War Relief Services, 131
War veterans associations, 164
Washington, D.C.: Arena Stage in, 89; mutual benefit organizations in, 166; Smithsonian Institution in, 85
Washington, G., 162
Washington, University of, 58

Watergate, 36–37
"We Are the World," 126
Weber, M., 14, 161, 177, 181
Webster, D., 55–56
Weingart Center, 94
Weisbrod, B. A., 176, 177–178
Weitzman, M. S., 46, 94–95
Weld, T., 117
Welfare. *See* Social services
"Welfare societies," 160
Wellesley, 49, 59
West: education in, 58, 59; foundation assets in, 139; health care in, 73; religion in, 32; social services in, 103
Westinghouse, 141
Weyerhauser, 141
Wheelock, E., 27
White, E. G., 33–34, 41
"White flight," 44
Whitehead, A. N., 182
White House conferences, 119
"White men's club" issue, 153
Whites, 46, 48, 103
Whitman, M., 32
Whitman, N., 32, 41
William and Mary College of, 55, 57
William Penn Foundation, 139
Williams College, 43, 128
Wilson, A., 83
Wilson Fellowships, 147
Winthrop, J., 28
Wisconsin, University of, 58
Witchcraft, 38–39
Women: education for, 28, 58–59; employed in private education, 46, 50; foundation power of, 153; leadership in nonprofits by, 17, 41–42; and religious leadership, 41–42; suffrage for, 16, 28, 34, 38, 113, 117. *See also* Women's movement
Women and Foundations/Corporate Philanthropy, 153
Women's movement, 17, 38, 41, 114, 117, 181. *See also* Suffrage, women's
Works Progress Administration (WPA) programs, 89

World Vision, 123–124, 132
World War I, 34–35, 118, 129, 130, 149
World War II, 35, 40, 62, 118, 130–131, 150, 164
Wyoming, and women's suffrage, 117

Y

Yale Repertory Theater, 83
Yale University, 49, 50; government funding for, 18; medical school of, 74; Program on Non-Profit Organizations of, 167, 170; religious origin of, 55
Yellow fever, 129
Ylvisaker, P. N., 143
Young, B., 33
Young, D. R., 16
Young Men's Christian Association (YMCA), 21, 31, 100, 101, 149
Young Women's Christian Association (YWCA), 101